Music for the
Superman

ALSO BY DAVID HUCKVALE
AND FROM MCFARLAND

*A Dark and Stormy Oeuvre: Crime, Magic and Power
in the Novels of Edward Bulwer-Lytton* (2016)

Poe Evermore: The Legacy in Film, Music and Television (2014)

Hammer Films' Psychological Thrillers, 1950–1972 (2014)

*The Occult Arts of Music: An Esoteric Survey
from Pythagoras to Pop Culture* (2013)

*Visconti and the German Dream: Romanticism,
Wagner and the Nazi Catastrophe in Film* (2012)

*Ancient Egypt in the Popular Imagination:
Building a Fantasy in Film, Literature, Music and Art* (2012)

*Touchstones of Gothic Horror:
A Film Genealogy of Eleven Motifs and Images* (2010)

Hammer Film Scores and the Musical Avant-Garde (2008)

*James Bernard, Composer to Count Dracula:
A Critical Biography* (2006; softcover, 2012)

Music for the Superman
Nietzsche and the Great Composers

DAVID HUCKVALE

McFarland & Company, Inc., Publishers
Jefferson, North Carolina

LIBRARY OF CONGRESS CATALOGUING-IN-PUBLICATION DATA

Names: Huckvale, David.
Title: Music for the superman : Nietzsche and the great composers /
    David Huckvale.
Description: Jefferson, North Carolina : McFarland & Company,
    2017 | Includes bibliographical references and index.
Identifiers: LCCN 2016047360 | ISBN 9781476663401 (softcover :
    acid free paper) ∞
Subjects: LCSH: Music and literature. | Nietzsche, Friedrich Wilhelm,
    1844–1900—Criticism and interpretation.
Classification: LCC ML3849 .H79 2017 | DDC 780.92/2—dc23
LC record available at https://lccn.loc.gov/2016047360

ISBN (print) 978-1-4766-6340-1
ISBN (ebook) 978-1-4766-2711-3

BRITISH LIBRARY CATALOGUING DATA ARE AVAILABLE

© 2017 David Huckvale. All rights reserved

No part of this book may be reproduced or transmitted in any form or by any means, electronic or mechanical, including photocopying or recording, or by any information storage and retrieval system, without permission in writing from the publisher.

Cover art: Portrait of Friedrich Nietzsche by Edvard Munch, oil on canvas, 79" × 63", 1906

Printed in the United States of America

*McFarland & Company, Inc., Publishers
    Box 611, Jefferson, North Carolina 28640
        www.mcfarlandpub.com*

To Ursula and Peter Branfield

"Vielleicht hat es nie einen Philosophen gegeben, der in dem Grade in Grunde so sehr Musiker war, wie ich es bin" ("Perhaps there has never been a philosopher who to such an extent was so profoundly a musician as I am")
—Nietzsche's letter to Herrmann Levi, October 20, 1887

A Philosopher for Everyone and No One: Friedrich Nietzsche (1844–1900). Photograph by Gustav-Adolf Schutze, Naumburg, 1882 (Wikimedia Commons).

Table of Contents

Overture   1

1. Leider, Nietzsches Lieder   11
2. Tribschen Idyll   22
3. Beethoven   41
4. The Case of Wagner   51
5. The Antidote   66
6. Richard Strauss   76
7. Gustav Mahler   93
8. Alexander Scriabin   104
9. Frederick Delius   119
10. Benjamin Britten   128
11. Béla Bartók   138
12. Karol Szymanowski   147
13. Alphons Diepenbrock   156
14. Ferruccio Busoni   164
15. Thomas Mann   172

Finale: Nietzsche and Popular Music   187
Chapter Notes   199
Bibliography   213
Index   217

Overture

It was music—specifically the music of Richard Wagner (1813–1883)—that led me to the writings of Friedrich Nietzsche (1844–1900). Rather in the manner of a blindfolded initiate being led into a Masonic temple, I did not know where I was going or what the ritual meant, but I willingly gave myself up to the process. Without Wagner I might never have bothered to get to know Nietzsche, who subsequently illuminated my understanding of Wagner. Both immeasurably enriched my life and helped me negotiate it, illuminating, in the process, the historical reasons for the way we live now. Later, I realized that Nietzsche's first response to Wagner was similarly overwhelming and as deeply significant as my own had been.

Nietzsche had discovered Wagner by playing Hans von Bülow's transcription of his music on the piano: "From the moment there was a piano score of Tristan—my compliments, Herr von Bülow!—I was a Wagnerian."[1]

For me, Wagner came in several equally blinding flashes: first, and most powerfully, on the soundtrack of Werner Herzog's 1979 remake of F. W. Murnau's 1922 vampire film, *Nosferatu*. Herzog's juxtaposition of Romantic, brooding nature with the prelude to *Das Rheingold* really was a transcendent experience, so much so that I returned to the cinema to check the end titles for details (this was before DVDs or indeed the advent of VHS in my own life), but they flashed by too quickly for me to grasp which particular Wagnerian bleeding chunk Herzog was using. Undeterred, I rushed to a record store and found an LP, with a photo of Neuschwanstein Castle on the cover (not that I knew anything of King Ludwig's fantasy castle at that time, either). Back home with my purchase, I lay on the floor (I always listened to records lying down in those days) and experienced for the first time Stokowski conducting further celebrated excerpts, one of which was the "Entrance of the Gods into Valhalla" from

Wagner and Vampires: Bruno Ganz as Jonathan Harker enters Count Dracula's domain, accompanied by the Prelude to Wagner's *Das Rheingold* in *Nosferatu: Phantom der Nacht* (dir. Werner Herzog, 1979).

Das Rheingold. This grand finale to the first *Ring* opera contains the "Rhine" motif, but not in its extended, oceanic E-flat rumination at the opening of that work, which the Finnish semiotician Eero Tarasti eloquently described as the musical expression of an "archaic stratum of the human mind, wherein a certain wind instrument suggests the creation of the world by blowing the first tone declaring the emergence of the cosmos."[2] Further research was therefore necessary. The following year, when I was a drama student, I was taken to a dress-rehearsal of *Götterdämmerung* at Covent Garden. The occasion had been organized by my voice tutor, who also happened to be the sister of the great conductor Sir Colin Davis. I had no idea what was going on during this rehearsal, but, unlike other students in my group who all trendily complained about the "oppression of the proscenium arch" and the "over-blown" nature of opera as a genre in general, I was fascinated, and began to piece together what Wagner's art was all about. The college library contained a copy of Andrew Porter's translation of the text of *The Ring* (a hardback edition, no less, in an attractive slip case). I was hooked, and thanks to then-generous government grants for students, it wasn't long before I invested in a box set of Karajan's *Ring* cycle on vinyl. Nervous after spending so much money I staggered back to my little flat at the back of a house owned by a rather uncommunicative couple and began to listen in earnest; and it was here that I was first overwhelmed by Brünnhilde's immolation and Wagner's masterly musical depiction of the end of the world. (Somehow, the Covent Garden rehearsal had failed to make the same impact.) My compliments, Herr von Karajan!

My journey towards Nietzsche had also begun, but I was to pass down many a cul-de-sac and follow many a diversion *en route*. Grasping what Nietzsche stood for took a great deal of time and effort; working out why he turned against Wagner took even longer, for before I knew more about Wagner I couldn't quite understand why anyone should turn against his music, which was so sublime, so powerful, so luxurious and so emotive that it no longer seemed like music at all but rather a quite different form of expression, making all other music pale into insignificance by comparison. Of course, I was not the first to suffer such a delusion.

Eventually, I bought a copy of *Thus Spoke Zarathustra*, and reading it was like swimming too far from the shore. I understood very little of it, but was pulled out by Nietzsche's current of words and images until I was in danger of drowning. Music once again came to my rescue. It was those composers who had themselves been inspired by Nietzsche who guided me back to safety and towards understanding. The process proved to be endlessly fascinating and rewarding, and helped explain what I had hitherto responded to in a purely instinctive manner. I also began to understand how what seemed so glorious and transcendent had unfortunately but by no means inevitably culminated in the catastrophe of a war that had ended only 16 years before I was born.

Of course, there were many preconceptions about Nietzsche to overcome. One vivid memory I have is of catching a train to London with my father, who asked what I was reading. When I showed him the cover of *Zarathustra* with its portrait of Nietzsche wearing that famous mustache, I could tell that he thought I might be wasting my time. Nietzsche's reputation, in England at least, is still problematic. In his short story "Jeeves Takes Charge" (1916), P. G. Wodehouse has the famous butler advise his employer against reading Nietzsche whom Jeeves regards as "fundamentally unsound."[3] That later, equally representative bastion of Britishness A. N. Wilson similarly censures Nietzsche's philosophy in general as "disturbing"[4] (which is surely precisely what Nietzsche intended), and refers to the Death of God as "being *shrieked about*" by Nietzsche (my italics), as opposed to the much more muted response to the subject by David Hume (presumably a much more respectable philosopher), for whom the subject "is only considered worth mentioning in parentheses."[5]

Many people still think of Nietzsche as a proto-Nazi (which he wasn't), that his ideas were as crazy as the insanity he eventually suffered (again, untrue), and that his books are anyway quite impenetrable (but of all philosophers, Nietzsche's prose is the most lucid and musical). I soon discovered that his influence on music was almost as significant as his influence on literature and politics. Here was a philosopher who also regarded himself as a musician, who wrote "musical" prose, who had known Wagner, turned against his hero and then inspired a host of composers who set his writings and ideas to music, often in the Wagnerian style he himself had rejected in favor of Bizet's *Carmen*. I hope this book will help explain why all that happened.

But first, it might be instructive to consider some of the reasons why music was so crucial to the late-Romantic German culture Nietzsche inspired, and a good starting point is the difference in attitudes to music in Britain at the time. It was the German critic Oscar Adolf Hermann Schmitz (1873–1931) who accused England of being "das Land ohne Musik" ("the land without music"). It was in fact the title of a book he had written, with the significant subtitle "Englische Gesellschaftsprobleme" ("Problems of English Society"), which was first published in 1904. In it, Schmitz addresses a variety of issues from a blatantly prejudicial perspective in a futile attempt to explain why the British are so apparently unmusical. The chapter headings include "Selfishness," "Jews in Whitechapel," "Church and Class in London," "The Puzzle of Superiority," "Puritanical Eroticism," "Suffragettes," "Language," "Manners," "Servants," "Theatre," "Politics," "Democracy," etc. The claim of the book's title was patently untrue, as throughout the nineteenth century there had been a great deal of music in England, both homegrown and imported; so what does the phrase mean? Patently not a quantitive observation, it is far more of a qualitative one, which came at a time when Parry, Elgar, Vaughan Williams, Holst and Stanford were only just beginning the so-called English Musical Renaissance. Eduard Hanslick, the conservative Viennese music critic (and scourge of Wagner), acknowledged the success of Gilbert and Sullivan's operetta *The Mikado*,[6] but nonetheless had this to say about the conducting style of Sir Arthur Sullivan (1842–1900), comparing it to that of the somewhat less celebrated Sir William Sterndale Bennett, who had nonetheless been admired for a while by Robert Schumann:

> If Sterndale Bennett was a slack and unenergetic conductor, Sir Arthur Sullivan, his successor, is altogether a drowsy fellow. That large close-cropped head on a firm neck, that dark face with its black eyes, give one an impression of a passionate man whose anger might explode suddenly like a cannon. Instead of this we have unequalled phlegm. The G minor Symphony of Mozart is performed. Sullivan conducts without lifting his eyes from the full score—just as though he saw it for the first time. The heavenly piece is played badly, without feeling or elegance. It ends, and the public applaud enthusias-

tically and continuously, but Sullivan does not think of turning round to the audience. He remains unmoved in his arm chair, and awaits the second piece.[7]

There was, therefore, a perceived lack of *passion*, intensity and commitment about the English musical scene when viewed from Germany. So ubiquitous had Schmitz's term become by 1914 that on the outbreak of World War I, that Italian-composer-in-Germany Ferruccio Busoni observed "how fortunate it is that the English have no music of their own to speak of, for they would have had it thrown in their faces" by patriotic Germans.[8] Generally speaking, Britain, with its vast choral spectaculars at the Crystal Palace, which stripped Handel of his umlaut and tried to claim him as its own, its adoption of Mendelssohn as the unofficial court composer to the House of Saxe-Coburg-Gotha (as it was before war with Germany made it advisable to change it to "Windsor"), its worthy tradition of brass bands, its vibrant music-hall culture, and its adoration of German classics notwithstanding, was still regarded, by the land of "Dichter und Denker" (Poets and Thinkers), as a land without significant music of its own. England's last "great" composer, universally judged able to hold his head high amid his European colleagues, was generally believed to have been Henry Purcell (1659–1695), and, as Peter J. Pirie, a later historian of the British Musical Renaissance suggests (echoing Schmitz), "from his death until the first works by Elgar almost exactly two hundred years later we were virtually silent.... The sum total of our musical achievement in the Victorian era was meagre, reactionary and undistinguished."[9]

Value judgments are always contentious, but whatever qualitative difference there might be, it is apparent that music meant something different to Germans, whose country was not even a political unity until 1871. Having developed out of principalities, each with its prince who wished to outdo his neighbors in the splendor of his court, music had developed in a very different way to that of Britain, where commercial forces had replaced courtly patronage, profoundly effecting the formulation of culture. As Pirie observes, "England was a shop; a brisk, philistine emporium with a stinking factory in the back premises."[10] The idea of music being of spiritual, still less of national importance, was largely missing in such a mercantile society. Germany, politically backward, with no real power, had for generations diverted its energies into the cultivation of philosophy and music. Indeed, the two were identified by the philosopher Gottfried Wilhelm Leibniz as two sides of the same coin. As Arthur Schopenhauer significantly quoted in his *World as Will and Representation*, Leibniz wrote: "Musica est exercitium metaphysices occultum nescientis se philosophari animi" ("Music is an unconscious exercise in metaphysics in which the mind does not know it is philosophizing").[11]

As we shall see, Schopenhauer (1788–1860) greatly influenced Wagner (not that Wagner agreed with all of his hero's musical opinions—far from it), and thus the connection between music and philosophy was popularized and made to seem inseparable. The connection had a longer history than that, though, and was not, of course, an exclusively German preoccupation. The ancient Greeks had much to say about the philosophical implications of music, but it was German Romanticism in the nineteenth century that gave that relationship a special resonance, with far-reaching social, cultural and political implications. Romanticism was not concerned with the abstract. It searched for meaning in everything, and it harnessed music to a conceptual carriage it was perhaps ill-suited to pull. Franz Liszt (1811–1886) was well aware of the problem, but nonetheless desirous of the journey. "Heaven forbid," he argued, "that anyone, in holding forth on the utility, validity and advantage of the program, should forswear the old faith and assert that the heavenly art does not exist for its own sake," but he went on to insist that "through song there have always been *combinations* of music with literary or quasi-literary works; the present time seeks a *union* of the two which promises to become a more intimate one than any that have offered themselves thus far."[12]

Music is, in fact, the most "meaningless" of all the arts, being incapable of conveying any non-musical idea independently. As the anthropologist Claude Lévi-Strauss decreed, "Music is a language without meaning: this being so, it is understandable that the listener, who is first and foremost a subject with the gift of speech, should feel himself irresistibly compelled to make up for the absent sense, just as someone who has lost a limb imagines that he still possess it through the sensations present in the stump."[13]

Given the correct prompting—or program—correlations, it is true, can be made between concepts and chords, meaning and melody, natural phenomena and orchestral effects, but these are all, by the very nature of music, approximations, symbols, codes and subject to cultural conventions. Semiotics is therefore a useful tool when negotiating "meaning" in music. Speaking of music's relationship to myth, particularly in the hands of nineteenth-century Romantic composers such as Liszt and Wagner, Tarasti observes:

> Music also possesses a formal world, history and rules of its own, but in the hands of myth it acquires a new function and its original properties are put in "brackets," because its only task now is to support the mythical meaning and content. Does not this explain

the structural paucity and a certain syntactical scarcity of musical discourse during those periods when music was closely allied with myth?

The musical defects in Wagner's works have been pointed out frequently but without seeing them in relation to the underlying mythical system.[14]

He adds that "a given musical culture provides a composer with substance for composition; in other words scales (established by a tuning system), rhythms, dynamics, harmonic progressions etc. which are given a form by a composer in his composition."

> Concerning the listener, culture operates in the opposite direction establishing a form for his experiences, and it is due to this form that the meaning discovered in a musical work by a listener is the "logical expression" of his internal feelings and not merely an emotional stimulant.... These forms are in the nature of universal patterns, "archetypes" which arise from the subconscious of the listener and thus constitute a part of the stock of symbols common to every music listener of the period.[15]

But for earlier philosophers, music was more than a "mere" sign system. For Schopenhauer, who so influenced Nietzsche himself, music was the expression of something that was otherwise inaccessible to us:

> The inexpressible depth of all music, by virtue of which it floats past us as a paradise quite familiar and yet eternally remote, and is so easy to understand and yet so inexplicable, is due to the fact that it reproduces all the emotions of our innermost being, but entirely without reality and remote from its pain. In the same way, the seriousness essential to it and wholly excluding the ludicrous from its direct and peculiar province is to be explained from the fact that its object is not the representation, in regard to which deception and ridiculousness alone are possible, but that this object is directly the will; and this is essentially the most serious of all things, as being that on which all depends.[16]

Thus, E. T. A. Hoffmann (1776–1822), an older contemporary of Schopenhauer, elaborated on Mozart's overture to *Don Giovanni* as an embodiment of specific emotions and ideas rather than a "mere" equivalent to them:

> During the *andante*, my spirit was seized with premonitions of horror. I shuddered in awe of the infernal *regno del pianto*. The seventh bar of the *allegro*, with its jubilant fanfare, became the voice of crime itself, exulting. Out of the dark night I saw demons stretch their fiery claws and loom menacingly over the lives of carefree mortals dancing merrily on the thin lid of a bottomless pit. The conflict between human nature and the unknown, the terrible powers that confront man on every side and lie in wait for his ruin, took on a visionary intensity with the music.[17]

Similarly, for Hector Berlioz (1803–1869), the French equivalent of Liszt and Wagner, the storm in Beethoven's *Pastoral* Symphony is not a "mere" symbolic representation of that natural phenomenon, it is "no longer an orchestra that one hears, it is no longer music, but rather the tumultuous voice of the heavenly torrents blended with the uproar of the earthly ones, with the furious claps of thunder, with the crashing of uprooted trees, with the gusts of an exterminating wind, with the frightened cries of men and the lowing of the herds. This is terrifying it makes one shudder, the illusion is complete. The emotion that Rossini [in the storm of the Overture to *William Tell*] arouses in the same situation falls far short of attaining the same degree of.... But let us continue."[18]

Ironically, it is this very verisimilitude in Beethoven that Schopenhauer attacks in his own critique of music. Such profoundly imitative music "does not express the inner nature of the will itself, but merely imitates its phenomenon inadequately."[19] By contrast, "no one has kept so free from this mistake as Rossini, hence his music speaks its *own* language so distinctly and purely that it requires no words at all, and therefore produces its full effect even when rendered by instruments alone."[20]

Though not surprising, it is deeply ironic that Schopenhauer should have reacted so vehemently against Wagner's poem of the *Ring* cycle, for Schopenhauer's view of music was actually quite seriously at odds with Wagner's highly imitative and word-integrated one, though they did both agree on the idea that music expresses the Will—the noumen beyond the mere phenomena. This idea that music expresses what is inexpressible in the other arts, that it accesses a world of ur-emotion, also inspired Jean Paul Richter, the Romantic novelist whom Robert Schumann claimed had taught him more about composition than any musician could.[21] Jean Paul (1763–1825) described the effect of music as "a celestial echo of his dream, answering to a being whom one did not see and did not hear."[22] Schumann (1810–1856) seems to be echoing these words in his famous essay on Brahms of 1853: "Later, if he will wave with his magic wand to where massed forces, in the chorus and orchestra, lend their strength, there lie before us still more wondrous glimpses of the spirit world."[23] Liszt too, no friend of Brahms' music, which was regarded at the time as the very opposite of his own programatic approach, used similar terminology: "Is not music the mysterious language of a faraway spirit world whose wondrous accents, echoing within us, awaken us to a higher, more intensive life? All the passions battle with one another, their armor shimmering and sparkling, perishing in an inexpressible yearning which fills our breasts."[24]

Despite being hailed as the "English Mozart" by an audience that pelted him with flowers while standing on their chairs after the première of his oratorio *The Golden Legend* in 1886, one would not exactly describe the music of Sir Arthur Sullivan in Liszt's terms. One did not play in British brass bands to fill one's armor-plated breast with inexpressible yearning; attending a monster Handel choral festival was stirring, certainly, though not really intended to be the expression of a "faraway spirit world." But for Germany, music *was* an expression of this nouminal plane. It was not "mere" entertainment or distraction, it was worship and revelation. As Wagner wrote in his short story "A Pilgrimage to Beethoven," "No Mohammedan more devotedly longed to journey to the grave of his Prophet, than I to go to the house where Beethoven lived."[25] Wagner also put into the mouth of his fictional character in "An End in Paris" the credo "I believe in God, Mozart and Beethoven."[26] No British composer, until the advent of John Lennon (1940–1980), had ever inspired that kind of fanaticism.

The inflated idealism that Germany claimed for music reached its heights just before the First World War. In his introduction to the luxurious Breitkopf und Härtel vocal score edition of Wagner's *Götterdämmerung* in 1914, Carl Waack wrote:

> All the principal themes referring to Siegfried's life ... group themselves like giant buttresses about the majestic progress of this sublime music, which solemnly transcends the terrors of death in its luminous splendour. After the last transformation, Brünnhilde's great scene forms the conclusion of the entire trilogy.... After a final recurrence of the Siegfried Motive the strains of the Motive of Love's Redemption resolve themselves into waving passages, fade away to the sound of harps, and lose themselves in ethereal heights.[27]

It was no doubt the case with many of the German volunteers who enthusiastically enlisted during the war hysteria of August 1914 that this musical emotion was translated into a patriotic desire to reach similarly "ethereal heights" on the field of battle. Even Thomas Mann was guilty of such misguided delusions. In *Reflections of a Nonpolitical Man*, written during the conflict, he contrasts "the spirit of the *Lohengrin* prelude" with the superficialities of so-called "international elegance,"[28] in other words those forces of materialism that Germany was apparently fighting to defeat. He discusses the widely-felt conviction of many German intellectuals at the time of the "need" for the war ("'need' was Richard Wagner's favorite word")—a need which was a "spiritual fact, the basic fact of this war," which was, apparently, the need of "the highest creative passion."[29] That "spiritual necessity" identified by Modris Eksteins was "a quest for authenticity, for truth, for self-fulfillment."[30] Mann also confesses to having been caught up in "the exaltation of 1914," which in no small measure was the consequence of his exaltation in Wagner. The power of German music seemed to give validity to his belief in Germany's "right to rule."[31]

For Nietzsche, music was "the judge over the whole visible world of the present." And he put into Wagner's mouth the plea to "help me to discover that culture whose existence my music, as the rediscovered language of genuine feeling, prophesies; reflect," he continued, "that the soul of music now wants to create for itself a body, and that it seeks its path through all of you to visibility in movement, deeds, structure and morality!"[32] The complex story of why Nietzsche changed his tune I leave for later pages, but transferring his allegiance from nouminal musical philosophy to music as an expression of Dionysian joy, he summed up in a comment about the "Habanera" of Bizet's *Carmen*, the opera on which he pinned his new, anti-Wagnerian hopes: "This is Eros as the ancients felt him—seductive, playful, malicious, demonic, invincible. To perform this you need a real witch: I know of no song quite like it—and it must be sung in the Italian way, *not* the German!"[33]

1

Leider, Nietzsches Lieder

The title of this chapter translates as "Unfortunately, Nietzsche's songs." Here I am perhaps guilty of committing the same crime as Lord Henry Wooton in Oscar Wilde's *The Picture of Dorian Gray*, who is accused of sacrificing anybody for the sake of an epigram,[1] but many people have indeed found Nietzsche's own attempts at composition tiresome—even execrable. This, however, seems unreasonable, for what strikes me most forcefully about Nietzsche's songs is how very *pleasant* and traditionally reassuring they are—often melancholy, true, but no less appealing for that. There is nothing in his songs of the ironic wit we find in his prose. Neither is there a desire to philosophize with a hammer, which is how he subtitled his iconoclastic work *Twilight of the Idols* (1889); nor do they have much in common with the style of his one-time idol Richard Wagner, whose music he had yet to discover, for Nietzsche began to compose songs when he was still a schoolboy at the famous Schulpforte, Germany's equivalent of England's Rugby or Eton. He continued to compose as a student at Bonn University, setting texts by some of Germany's leading poets, along with several by foreign authors including Alexander Pushkin and the Hungarian Sándor Petőfi (whose death in the Hungarian War of Independence was commemorated by Liszt in the sixth piece of his *Historical Hungarian Portraits* of 1885). Nietzsche also set verses by the French-born Adalbert von Chamisso, who had also inspired Schumann's song-cycle *Frauenliebe und -leben*, and it was probably Schumann's cycle that introduced Schumann to the poet's work, for Schumann was the young Nietzsche's musical hero years before he discovered Wagner.

From Schulpforta in 1865, he wrote his friend Freiherr Karl von Gersdorff, full of anticipation for the Rheinland Music Festival at Cologne, which was to include Handel's *Israel in Egypt*, Haydn's *The Seasons* and (surely more important to him at the time) Schumann's *Scenes from Goethe's Faust*. "I am taking part in it," he proudly proclaimed.[2] As with

Wagner, Nietzsche later turned against Schumann. "The Germans," he wrote in *Ecco Homo*, "are *incapable* of any conception of greatness: proof Schumann. Expressly from wrath against this sugary Saxon, I composed a counter-overture to Manfred [Schumann has composed his own overture to Byron's play in 1848]."[3]

Songs fitted well with Nietzsche's aphoristic approach to creativity in general. Concise and self-contained, they were the perfect musical form for his particular talents. He even set some of his own poems. One of them, "Junge Fischerin," is particularly attractive, though distinctly melancholy, with its echo of Heinrich Heine's famous and much set-to-music phrase from "Die Loreley," "Ich weiß nicht, was soll es bedeuten,/ Daß ich so traurig bin" ("I do not know the meaning of why I am so sad"). Nietzsche's line is very similar: "O niemand weiß von allen,/ daß ich so traurig bin" ("Oh, no one knows how sad I am"). He subtly reflects the sea imagery of his poem, suggesting the lapping of waves with oscillating figures in the piano, while sustained chords evoke the mist within which Death might well lurk.

One of the most unconventional aspects of some of the other songs is that they come to an end on unresolved cadences. This applies to his settings of Klaus Groth's "Mein Platz vor der Tür" ("My Place outside the Door"), August Hoffmann von Fallersleben's "Wie sich Rebenranken schwingen" ("As the Vine Branches Sway," a text also set by Brahms in his Op. 3 set of songs from 1853), and Petöfi's "Ständchen" ("Serenade"). Such unresolved cadences not only echo Schumann's use of the effect in *Dichterliebe*'s "Im Wunderschönen Monat Mai," but also foreshadowed the comparably unresolved dominant seventh that brings the Act I Prelude of Wagner's *Parsifal* to its questioning conclusion. Wagner employed this harmonic device to suggest, among many other things, the title of his 1879 antisemitic essay, "Shall We Hope?," which was written in tandem with the composition of that final music drama, the racial message of which he summed up in the line: "That I myself have to abandoned hope, I have proved by completing the music for my 'Parsifal' within the past few days."[4] Nietzsche, of course, had no such intentions, but the emotional effect of the unresolved cadences is similar, leaving the listener in a state of emotional suspended animation, as it were. Such a mood appropriately matches the poet's regret at the passing of time in the Groth setting ("die Welt da draußen mir,/ es war darin nicht halb so schön/ als damals an der Tür" ["the world outside—it was not half as fair as the world at my door was then"]), the lovesick imagery of absent love in von Fallersleben's text, in which the poet thinks of his beloved's "trautes liebes Bild" ("dear and homely image"), and Petőfi's lines "Denn meine Liebe ist's, die singt,/ ist meine Seele, die verklingt." ("It's my love that is singing, my soul is dying away!")

Other songs strongly betray the influence of Schubert—particularly the water imagery of Schubert's song-cycle *Die schöne Müllerin*. In Nietzsche's setting of Groth's "Da geht ein Bach" ("There Flows a Brook"), the poem itself uses the mill-wheel and maid-of-the-mill imagery that is central to the Wilhelm Müller texts set by Schubert:

> Das Rad, das dreht, die Mühle geht,
> und drinnen tönt Gesang,
> komm' ich, so guckt ein Kopf heraus,
> läßt mich nicht warten lang.
>
> (The mill wheel turns, the mill grinds, and songs sound from within. I come, a head looks out, and does not make me wait long.)

Nietzsche obliges Groth's imagery by providing watery arpeggios in the piano accompaniment. Schubert's style also hovers over Petőfi's "Standchen," which seems to be echoing the Schubert setting of Walter Scott's "Ave Maria," with its harp-like arpeggio accompaniment. And once more, Schubert's music for "Ungedult" ("Impatience") from *Die schöne Müllerin* informs Nietzsche's response to Chamisso's "Gern und Gerner" ("Gladly and Gladlier"). Both composers suggest the impetuosity of young love with agitated triplet figuration, which is expressed in the Chamisso text by the lines "und gerner vom roten, vom süßen Mund/ erwärmende Flammen saugen" ("and soak up the fiery warmth of your sweet, red lips").

Perhaps less successful is his setting of von Fallersleben's "Wie sich Rebenranken schwingen," mainly due to the rather wide tessitura demanded of the singer; but Fallersleben is an interesting choice, as it was he who wrote the text of what became the German national anthem, with its now much misunderstood line, "Deutschland, Deutschland über alles." Such words were not originally intended as an incitement to war and conquest but rather an appeal for national unification—i.e., "a united German above all other considerations," but they soon acquired more threatening connotations, and given Nietzsche's later despair of his fellow countrymen in the wake of that longed-for unification after the Franco-Prussian war, the choice of Fallersleben is, in retrospect, somewhat ironic. Nietzsche even disparagingly quoted this notorious line in *Ecce Homo*, his unconventional autobiography: "'German' is an argument, '*Deutschland, Deutschland über alles*' a principle, the Germans represent the 'moral world-order' in history.... The 'German spirit' is *my* bad air: I find it hard to breathe in the proximity of this uncleanliness.... I expressed my *mistrust* of the German character already at the age of twenty-six (third untimely essay)—the Germans are impossible for me."[5]

It is thus appropriate that Nietzsche also chose texts by poets from other nations. However, his setting of Theodor Opitz' translation of Pushkin's "Beschwörung" ("Invocation") is, musically speaking, firmly in the German Romantic tradition, foreshadowing, in fact, the style of Hugo Wolf (1860–1903). Nietzsche again looked back to Schumann when it came to setting Lou von Salomé's text "Gebet an das Leben" ("Prayer to Life"). This invocation to love and living, despite the pain and suffering both bring, echoes Schumann's setting of Friedrich Rückert's "Widmung." Nietzsche also made his own Rückert setting—arguably his most successful song, "Aus der Jugendzeit" ("From My Youth")—and I will be returning to this in the last chapter when considering how far John Lennon might be said to have been a Nietzschean composer.

In 1863, Nietzsche also tried his hand at musical recitation, that once fashionable form in which a rhythmically spoken text is accompanied by the kind of incidental music that subsequently developed into film music. Nietzsche chose Joseph von Eichendorff's poem "Das zerbrochene Ringlein" ("The Broken Ring")—a tragic, four-stanza text, again featuring mill-wheel imagery and a love-sick tale that is similar to that of *Die schöne Müllerin*: The mill is empty, for the poet's sweetheart who used to live there has moved away. She promised to be faithful and gave her lover a ring as a token of her devotion, but she broke her word and the ring broke in two. No doubt Nietzsche would have been familiar with Schumann's two experiments in this form: "Schön' Hedwig" (1849), setting lines by Christian Friedrich Hebbel, and "Die Flüchtlinge" (1852–1853), a translation of Shelley's poem "The Fugitives." Liszt also wrote five musical recitations, three in German, and two others in Russian and Hungarian. Nietzsche may well have known the German ones, as they all appeared between 1858 and 1860. Liszt's setting of Nikolaus Lenau's Gothic horror poem, "Der traurige Mönch," is famous because of its unprecedented use of the whole-tone scale, which hurls the musical lance Liszt aimed to throw as far as possible into the boundless realm of the future, and looks forward, in the process, to the harmonic idiom of Debussy. Nietzsche was not so experimental as that, though his dreamy, improvisatory piano accompaniment does reach out from its Schumannesque model, and, combined with the spoken declamation, might be said to have laid a very deep foundation stone of the Sprechgesang style later to be employed by Schoenberg in his expressionist phase.

Nietzsche was proud of his compositions, and even had eight of them bound in lilac-colored morocco with a silhouette of himself as a frontispiece, as a gift for his sister. He also included instructions on how to perform them. Two should be sung "as tenderly, as simply, as ingeniously as possible"; one "seriously, mournfully, and with determination until the middle verse, which forms a contrast with what comes before and after." Others "must be performed with drive, pertness and grace" or "with unrestrained passion."[6] All in all, Nietzsche's songs are a commendable and accomplished body of work, and it is a pity that subsequent criticism of his larger pieces put an end to his compositional career. It is true, however, that larger musical structures proved more problematic for Nietzsche's amateur abilities. By the time he wrote the majority of these larger works he had begun the friendship with Wagner, which would later turn to such an acrimonious falling out. Nietzsche's father had died when Friedrich was only five years old, and Wagner became very much a father figure for him in the early years of their relationship. Wagner's music also influenced the composition of Nietzsche's two large-scale piano works. The *Manfred Meditation*, with its *Tristanesque* questioning theme, Lisztian tremolos and improvisatory formlessness, had been preceded by another piece called *Nachklang einer Sylvesternacht* (*Echo of New Year's Eve*), also composed when he was still at school in 1864. Originally conceived as a violin piece, it was reworked as a piano duet, and he later transcribed it for piano and violin, which is perhaps its most successful incarnation. He presented a copy of the piano duet version as a birthday gift to Wagner's wife, Cosima, who perceptively wondered if it had originally been conceived for orchestra?[7] Indeed, with its "Processional Song" and "Peasant Dance" it rather obviously echoes the Dance of the Apprentices in the third act of Wagner's *Die Meistersinger*. It is also infused with other Wagnerian reminiscences, mostly drawn from *Die Meistersinger*, though punctuated with a repetitive triplet figure straight out of the *Siegfried Idyll*.

The *Nachklang* also includes an imitation of bells, which count out the midnight hour at the end, and this looks back to the final bars of Schumann's Op. 2 piano cycle *Papillons*, in the finale of which, as the marking above the stave explains, "the noise of the Carnival-night dies away. The church clock strikes six." Schumann duly obliges with six A-naturals as the waltz rhythm fades away into the distance; but Nietzsche's peal of midnight bells also looks forward to his famous poem in *Thus Spoke Zarathustra*, "O Mensch, gib acht," each line of which is announced by numbers that count the chiming hours. Midnight was a sacred hour to Nietzsche, symbolic of solitude, of the overthrow of old values and the beginning of a new outlook, which, like "the eternal hourglass of existence is turned over again and again, and you with it, speck of dust!"⁸

Nietzsche had high hopes for his compositions, and in a letter to Georg Brandes, he confessed, "Life for me without music would be a blunder."⁹ This statement, slightly changed would later find its way into *Twilight of the Idols*, as we shall see. Unfortunately, professional musicians held a rather different opinion of Nietzsche's musical abilities. Most outspoken of all was Cosima's ex-husband, Hans von Bülow, whose response to Nietzsche's subsequent *Manfred Meditation* for piano, must rank as the world's worst review:

> The one question I asked myself was—shall I hold my tongue, or send a civil and trivial note in reply—or shall I open my heart quite freely? The latter course required courage almost to the extent of daring and to adopt it I had first to assume that I could rely on your firm belief in the respect I feel for you as a genial and creative champion of science—and secondly to take refuge in two privileges I possess and to which I only refer with the greatest reluctance—one of them indeed melancholy enough—the fact that I am a score of years or so your senior, and the other that I am a professional musician. In the latter capacity I am accustomed like the commercial man who "in matters of business drops friendship" to practise the precept; in *materia musicæ* [musical matters] politeness ceases.
>
> But to turn to the matter in hand. Your Manfred Meditation is the most extreme example of fantastic extravagance and the most unedifying and most anti-musical composition I have met for some time. Again and again I had to ask myself whether the whole thing was not a joke and whether it had not perhaps been your intention to write a parody of the so-called Music of the Future. Was it not on purpose that without exception you put every rule of harmony to scorn from the higher syntax to the most ordinary conventions of correct composition?¹⁰

Hans von Bülow (1830–1894). Photograph by Emil Beiber, Berlin, 1897 (Wikimedia Commons).

Claiming that Nietzsche had tortured Euterpe, the muse of music, with his "musical convulsions,"[11] he recommended a performance of *Lohengrin to* cure him of further attempts at musical composition. Having said that, Liszt sadly shook his head when Cosima related to him her ex-husband's opinion, which the much more kindly Liszt regarded as having been too extreme.[12] Gustav Mahler later leapt to Nietzsche's posthumous defense as well, observing in an interview that "Nietzsche's talent as a composer was far greater than is generally assumed."[13] Bülow's verdict was nonetheless very depressing. "I have been brought very low," Nietzsche confessed. "I am now no more a musician than is domestically necessary to me as a philosopher.... Just consider that until now, from my *earliest* youth, I have lived under the most absurd illusion and had a *very great deal* of joy from music!"[14] Henceforth, all that innate musicality was channeled into his prose.

Just as Thomas Mann would later call Schopenhauer's *World as Will and Representation* a symphony in four movements,[15] so did Mahler call *Zarathustra* "absolutely 'symphonic' in its construction."[16] Originally, *Zarathustra* was confined to three movements, though Nietzsche later added a fourth section, which some commentators felt to be unnecessary. (Liszt's addition of a choral finale to his three movement *Faust* Symphony received similar criticism.) Mahler's use of Nietzsche's writings in his own compositions is something to which we will return later, but it is important at this stage to balance Bülow's devastating response with a more sympathetic opinion. What is certainly not in doubt is Nietzsche's commitment to music, which he considered the ultimate expression of the human spirit.

Nietzsche's compositions also include lightweight but charming piano pieces in the manner of the Album Leaves, so popular at the time, along with a "Hymn to Friendship" also for solo piano, and a choral *Hymnus an das Leben;* but they remain curiosities and would have been forgotten had not his genius as a philosopher cast its light upon them; but if Nietzsche's compositional talent was modest, his ability to use prose in a musical manner was outstanding. He was well aware of this talent himself, claiming that with *Zarathustra* he had brought the German language "to the acme of perfection."[17] Equal if not superior to Schopenhauer as a prose stylist in German, Nietzsche was the first truly great modern writer *about* music, and he opened the way for all those other musical novels that followed: *The Triumph of Death* by Gabriele D'Annunzio (1863–1938); the Wagnerian romance *Evelyn Innes* by George Moore (1852–1933); the epic Bildungsroman *Jean Christophe* by Romain Rolland (1866–1944); *Doctor Faustus* by Thomas Mann (1875–1955), to which we will be returning later;

and *Axel*, the epistolary novel about a young musician's admiration for the music of Sibelius by Bo Carpelan (1926–2011), to name but five.

D'Annunzio's prose rhapsody on *Tristan und Isolde* at the end of *The Triumph of Death* (1894) owes much to Nietzsche's ambivalent effusions about Wagner's "poison." Nietzsche's comments about this music drama in *The Case of Wagner* not only identify the decadent elements in *Tristan*, but, with its reference to Leonardo da Vinci and his use of emotive words such as "sweet," "shuddery," "dangerous" and "voluptuousness," also provides the context for D'Annunzio's self-consciously "decadent" description of it.

Nietzsche:

> I still today seek a work of a dangerous fascination, of a sweet and shuddery infinity equal to that of Tristan—I seek in all the arts in vain. All the strangenesses of Leonardo da Vinci lose their magic at the first note of Tristan. This work is altogether Wagner's *non plus ultra;* he recuperated from it with the Meistersinger and the Ring. To become healthier—that is *retrogression* in the case of a nature such as Wagner.... I take it for a piece of good fortune of the first rank to have lived at the right time, and to have lived precisely among Germans, so as to be *ripe* for this work: my psychologist's inquisitiveness goes that far. The world is poor for him who has never been sick enough for this "voluptuousness of hell."[18]

D'Annunzio:

> In the shadow and the silence of the secluded spot, through the shadow and the ecstatic silence of every breathless soul there, a sigh floated up from the invisible orchestra, a moan rose and fell, and from a subdued voice came the first mournful appeal of solitary desire, the first indistinct forebodings of future anguish. Sigh and moan and voice all rose and swelled up from a vague plaint to the sharpness of an imperious cry, with all the pride of dreams, the anguish of superhuman aspirations, the terrible and relentless power of possession. With a devouring fury, like a fire blazing up out of some nameless abyss, desire spread wide and quivered and flamed higher and higher, fed by the pure essence of a double life. All things fell a prey to the intoxication of that melodious flame.[19]

D'Annunzio also tapped into the Romantic correlation between music and death in this novel. Its hero, Giorgio, becomes increasingly suicidal, both oppressed by and obsessed with the woman he loves. Like Tristan and Isolde, the passion of Giorgio and Ippolita can only be fully consummated in death; but Giorgio is also morbidly fascinated by his suicidal uncle, who was also a fine violinist. Appropriately, for Giorgio, "music initiated him into the mystery of Death,"[20] for both music and death lead us to the nouminal reality beyond the superficial phenomena of life—that "Welt-Atems wehendem All" of which Isolde sings at the end of Wagner's opera, and into which she descends "unbewusst" in "höchste Lust!" ("The World's Spirit's infinite all—descending, unconscious—highest bliss").

Similarly jeweled and musical prose inspired by Wagner, infuses D'Annunzio's later novel *Il fuoco* (*The Flame* [1900]), in which Wagner himself is described as a godlike embodiment of natural forces:

> Instantly the image of the barbarian composer came to mind, the lines of his face became visible, his blue eyes beneath his great forehead glittered, his lips closed tightly in sensuality, pride and contempt over his strong chin. His tiny body, bent with age and glory, straightened, became as huge as his works, assumed the shape of a god. His blood flowed like mountain torrents, his breathing sighed like the wind in a forest. Then suddenly all the youthfulness of Siegfried entered him, ran through him, shone out of him like dawn behind a cloud.[21]

George Moore echoed Nietzsche's reference to da Vinci in *Evelyn Innes*, his 1898 novel about the seduction of a Wagnerian soprano by the wealthy Sir Owen Asher: "To him 'Parsifal' was a fresco, a decoration painted by a man whose true genius it was to reveal the most intimate secrets of the soul, to tell the enigmatic soul of longing as Leonardo da Vinci had done. But he had been led from the true path of his genius into a false one of a rivalry with Veronese."[22] Rolland's Jean Christophe also takes a Nietzschean scalpel to German music: "that false idealism is the secret sore even of the greatest—of Wagner."

> As he read his works Christophe ground his teeth. *Lohengrin* seemed to him a blatant lie. He loathed the huxtering chivalry, the hypocritical mummery, the hero without fear and without a heart, the incarnation of cold and selfish virtue admiring itself and most patently self-satisfied. He knew it too well, he had seen it in reality, the type of German Pharisee, foppish, impeccable, and hard, bowing down before its own image, the divinity to which it has no scruple about sacrificing others. *The Flying Dutchman* overwhelmed him with its massive sentimentality and its gloomy boredom. The loves of the barbarous decadents of the *Tetralogy* were of a sickening staleness. Siegmund carrying off his sister sang a tenor drawing-room song. Siegfried and Brünnhilde, like respectable German married people, in the *Götterdämmerung* laid bare before each other especially for the benefit of the audience, their pompous and voluble conjugal passion. Every sort of lie had arranged to meet in that work: false idealism, false Christianity, false Gothicism, false legend, false gods, false humans. Never did more monstrous convention appear than in that theater which was to upset all the conventions.[23]

Though published much later, in 1986, Carpelan's novel, *Axel*, is still firmly in this tradition. One of Axel's diary entries from 1895 observes: "Wagner—if only there were not all this pernicious, fat-bellied symbolizing."[24] And Nietzsche's literary response to Wagner's music also paved the way towards the modernist "stream of consciousness" technique of Édouard Dujardin, James Joyce and Virginia Woolf. All these writers used literary leitmotifs and all grew out of the Wagnerian monologue. Dujardin (1861–1947), editor of the *Revue Wagnérienne* and author of the first, highly influential stream of consciousness novel, *Les lauriers sont coupés* in 1887, openly acknowledged the connection in his essay on "Interior Monologue": "Just as a page of a Wagner score is most often a succession of undeveloped motifs each of which expresses an impulse of the soul, interior monologue is a succession of short sentences each of which also expresses an impulse of the soul, being alike in that they are not linked together according to a rational order but according to a purely emotional order, irrespective of all intellectual arrangement."[25] Nietzsche's approach to ideas through the juxtaposition and accumulation of loosely connected aphorisms has much in common with stream of consciousness technique. Instead of a sustained linear argument, Nietzsche, inspired as much if not more by Wagnerian models than by the example of that other great aphoristic writer La Rochefoucauld, arranges clusters of "miniaturist" ideas, which function in a similar manner to the organically developing webwork of leitmotifs that Wagner combines with each other to illuminate the psychological implications of his text.

But Nietzsche's own musical prose owed something to others as well. In a letter to the wife of the famous philologist Friedrich Wilhelm Rischl, in 1868, Nietzsche discusses a book about music by the German composer Louis Ehlert (1825–1884), which he had been reading at the time: "At bottom it is music though it happens to be written not in notes but in words."[26] When it came to describing his own books, he often used the same analogy. "The whole of Zarathustra might perhaps be reckoned as music,"[27] he explained, pointing out that he completed the closing section exactly at the moment when Wagner died in Venice. *Zarathustra* consequently marked the final purging of his musical tastes. Wagner's death symbolized the birth of his new musically "Mediterranean" outlook. The period of *Zarathustra*'s conception also coincided with Nietzsche's *Hymn to Life* for choir and orchestra, which he hoped would "one day be sung to my memory."[28] The title was echoed by Frederick Delius when he set of passages from *Zarathustra* in his own *Mass of Life*. There is, of course, no comparison between the two works musically speaking (Nietzsche asked his friend Heinrich Köselitz [aka Peter Gast] to help with the orchestration of the *Hymn to Life*, assistance Delius certainly did not require), but Nietzsche really believed in the musical merit of his *Hymn*, which he hoped would "*seduce* people to my philosophy."[29] In a letter to Brandes, he asked: "I wonder if you are musical. A choral work of mine, with orchestra, is just being published, called 'A Hymn to Life.' It is designed to go down to posterity as my 'musical remains.'"[30]

The following year, in May, he wrote to Brandes again: "We philosophers appreciate nothing so much as to be mistaken for artists. Moreover,

I am told by leading and competent judges that the hymn is in every way good for representation, and its performance would be certain of success. The praise which pleases me most is that it is pronounced 'pure in phrasing.' [Felix] Mottl, the distinguished Carlsruhe conductor (you know he conducted the Bayreuth festivals) has suggested giving a performance of it."[31]

The text, however, was not written by Nietzsche himself but by his girlfriend Lou von Salomé, who was in wholehearted agreement with Nietzsche's program. So enamored of the work was he that he quoted from the text in *Ecce Homo*: "Pain does *not* count as an objection to life: 'Have you no more happiness to give me, well then! *still do you have your pain...*' Perhaps my music is also great at this point."[32] It is a kind of paraphrase for Nietzsche's own maxim in *Twilight of the Idols*, that "what does not kill me makes me stronger."[33] Musically, it is fair to say that this seven-minute rumination would not even qualify to feature among the lists of innumerable nineteenth-century "horroratorios" by now obscure British composers such as the splendidly named E. T. Chipp, Pattison Haynes, E. Ouseley Gilbert, Percy Pitt, E. Cuthbert Nunn and Charles Swinnerton Heap (who is perhaps now best remembered, if at all, as the elderly, and thus somewhat ineffectual choral conductor for the first performance of Elgar's *The Dream of Gerontius*). These were published prolifically in England by Novello and Co alongside standard classics by Brahms and Schumann, and there are indeed echoes of Brahms and Schumann in Nietzsche's Hymn, but, alas, that is all they are. Only Nietzsche's philosophical reputation has preserved the composition from obscurity, as there is nothing in this essentially conventional music to match the world-shattering visions of the Übermensch.

2

Tribschen Idyll

Mist was drifting over the Vierwaldstättersee one May morning in the late 1980s, and Lucerne was rather chilly. Walking towards Tribschen, once Richard Wagner's residence-in-exile, I passed through a quiet but fairly built-up modern residential area of the town. In my naivety I had thought my surroundings might have been a little less prosaic; after all, Tribschen was where Wagner's *Die Meistersinger*, *Siegfried* and the *Siegfried Idyll* had been composed; it had been visited on several occasions by his illustrious patron King Ludwig II of Bavaria, and Nietzsche had been a regular house-guest there. Time, however, had moved on and it was difficult to imagine either of these men, let alone Wagner, strolling through this modern Swiss suburbia, with its parked cars, fluorescent signs and street lamps. I even began to wonder if I had wandered to quite the wrong place; but suddenly there it stood—Haus Tribschen, now half Richard Wagner Museum, half Municipal Musical Instrument Collection. It was just as I had seen it in all the Wagner books I had read over the years: an elegant sugar-cube of a building perched on a grassy mound, flanked by two tall trees and enclosed by a neatly clipped hedge. Its three floors punctuated at regular intervals by green window shutters support oval casements in the dormers on each side of the sloping roof; and the overall effect is of the kind of building a child might draw—the idea we all share of an archetypal "home," summoned from the collective unconscious. No wonder Wagner felt so happy here; no wonder Nietzsche should have remembered it as an "Isle of the Blessed,"[1] with its grassy slope leading down to the shore of the tranquil lake.

By the time Wagner took up residence here, he had been miraculously rescued from poverty (and possibly suicide as well) by the beneficence and generosity of King Ludwig, who installed him in this comfortable dwelling at his own expense. Too hot to handle in Munich, thanks to Wagner's scandalous lifestyle and inflammatory political views, Switzerland was considered a more viable location. The king occasionally visited his beloved friend in private, fleeting visits, but this only inflamed the scandalous reputation of the composer. A few years before my own visit to Tribschen, Tony Palmer's 1983 film about Wagner's life, starring Richard Burton in the title role, had included a scene with a pleasure steamer on the lake (nicely named the "Schiller"), with nosey tourists staring out at Wagner's lakeside home (some with binoculars), while Wagner is shown indoors forging the overture to *Die Meistersinger* on the piano. The tour guide saucily explains: "And there is Tribschen, where the famous German composer, Herr Richard Wagner is living with his friend the Baronin von Bülow and her children." (Cosima and Wagner were unmarried at the time.) Palmer cleverly had Ronald Pickup's Nietzsche, as one of the passengers, countering a philistine reaction to Wagner's reputation from a fellow traveller with the line, "Herr Wagner is quite simply the greatest living artist Germany—indeed the world—possesses." The philistine insists that Wagner's music is "so loud he cannot be heard. His music—it blows your head off, so no one can hear it; and he wears clothes that women wear; for which, and other things, Ludwig sent Herr Loud-and-Silky-Wagner packing too with all his friends—packing—all of them. Let the Swiss have them!"

So, I was now not only about to enter Wagner's past but also a movie location. So much had happened since the 1870s, but all seemed unchanged, at least from the outside. Two short flights of steps flanked each side of the front door. The wind rustled in the trees. Birds chirruped in the morning mist. A boat could be heard on the lake. To my dismay, however, everywhere looked shut up: no light glimmered from the windows that were not shuttered, and there was no sign of other visitors.

When Friedrich Nietzsche first visited this place on May 17, 1869, he too hesitated, unsure if he had the courage to knock at the door. Twice he walked away before overcoming his shyness. In the event he was invited to lunch. "A quiet and pleasant visit," Cosima recorded in her diary, impressed that the young professor of philology "even quotes from [Wagner's essay] *Opera and Drama* in his lectures."[2] Even though Haus Tribschen is now a museum, open to all, I too felt somewhat apprehensive, mainly because I did not want to discover that it was indeed closed for the day and that my pilgrimage, for which I had traveled so far, would have to be aborted. I walked up the steps, and to my relief the door handle turned and the door swung back just as it had when welcoming Wagner and his entourage: Nietzsche and King Ludwig, not to mention Richard Burton, Ronald Pickup and László Gálffi who played the king in Palmer's film.

The author on the staircase at Tribschen, Lucerne, in 1989 (photograph by Iris Huckvale).

I appeared to be the first visitor. Wagner's *Siegfried Idyll* drifted from a hidden loudspeaker and a pleasant lady behind the ticket desk smiled politely at my no doubt absurdly Wagnerian German; and there was the famous staircase where the *Siegfried Idyll*, Wagner's "Symphonic Birthday Greeting," composed especially for Cosima, had been first performed by a rather cramped chamber orchestra on Christmas Day 1870. Cosima naturally recorded the occasion in her diary:

> About this day, my children, I can tell you nothing—nothing about my feelings, nothing about my mood, nothing, nothing. I shall just tell you, drily and plainly, what happened. When I woke up I heard a sound, it grew ever louder, I could no longer imagine myself in a dream, music was sounding, and what music! After it had died away, R. [i.e.,

Richard] came in to me with the five children and put into my hands the score of his "Symphonic Birthday Greeting." *The Tribschen Idyll*—thus the work is called.³

This, at least, was what the *Siegfried Idyll* had originally been called. Unlike the re-enactment of this celebrated moment in Visconti's film *Ludwig* (1972), in which Trevor Howard's Wagner conducts his assembled musicians on the grandest of sweeping staircases, the real Tribschen stairs are a very modest affair, which would not have been out of place in the modern houses I had passed on my way to Haus Tribschen. Nietzsche had also been present on this uniquely symphonic staircase. Originally an ardent champion of Wagner's aims and ideals to transform society by means of music drama, he had become a regular guest at Tribschen, and so great an impact did the *Tribschen Idyll* have upon him that he presented Cosima his own composition, *Nachklang einer Silvesternacht* (*Memory of a New Year's Eve*), for her next birthday, as I mentioned in the previous chapter. In a letter written to his friend Erwin Rohde just before that Christmas visit in 1870, Nietzsche had enthused about Wagner's Bayreuth project (then only an idea) and Wagner's ideas about music in general: "A book of Wagner's about Beethoven that had just been published you will find full of suggestions about what I desire for the future. Read it; it is a revelation of the spirit in which *we—we!*—shall live in the future."⁴ Wagner's aim was indeed not "only" artistic but also social—the regeneration of society itself by means of Wagnerian music, as the "Beethoven" essay makes clear:

> As for our Civilisation, especially insofar as it influences the artistic man, we certainly may assume that nothing but the spirit of our Music, that music which Beethoven set free from bondage to the Mode, can dower it with a soul again. And the task of giving to the new, more soulful civilization that haply may arise here from, be reserved for the German Spirit alone, that spirit which we ourselves shall never rightly understand till we cast aside each serious tendency ascribed thereto.⁵

But Nietzsche's enthusiasm for Wagner's mission soon went into reverse. Even so, towards the end of his life in *Ecce Homo*, Nietzsche insisted that despite all his pulverizing attacks on a man on whose philosophical program he had by then turned his back, nothing in his life had been a precious to him as his "intimate association" with Richard Wagner: "I offer all my other human relationships cheap; but at no price would I relinquish from my life the Tribschen days, those days of mutual confidences, of cheerfulness, of sublime incidents—of *profound* moments.... I do not know what others may have experienced with Wagner: over *our* sky no cloud ever passed."⁶ For all his later criticisms of Wagner and his music, he still loved both. It was perhaps because he loved them both so much that his attacks reached such levels of almost hysterical denunciation.

In truth, what Nietzsche was really dealing with was Wagner's massive betrayal of trust. Wagner drained everyone like a vampire. Indeed, Nietzsche once dreamt that Wagner was just that, and "sucked out his life's blood."[7] (Even more appropriate, then, that Wagner should have been such an admirer of Heinrich Marschner's opera *Der Vampyr* and that his own music should turn up in Herzog's *Nosferatu*.) Drained to the dregs of their money, patience and loyalty, his associates, friends, colleagues—even wives and mistresses—were all sacrificed on the altar of the Great Wagner. Some (Cosima was one) managed to stay the course; indeed she drooled with positively canine loyalty over her adored husband. Others were sustained by their devotion to the grandeur and genius of the Wagnerian cause, but many fell by the wayside. The last straw in Nietzsche's case was the notorious letter Wagner wrote Nietzsche's doctor Otto Eiser, in October 1877, suggesting that his friend's troubling headaches were the result of excessive masturbation. Wagner warned the doctor that Nietzsche's condition seemed precariously like those of "a poet who died in Leipzig many years ago, [who] became totally blind when he was N.'s age, while the other, equally talented, friend, who now ekes out a pitiful existence in Italy, with his nerves completely shattered, began to suffer the most painful eye disease at exactly the same age as N. One thing that struck me as being of great importance was the news that I recently received to the effect that the doctor whom N. had consulted in Naples some time ago advised him first and foremost—to get married."[8] (Eiser, it ought to be pointed out, was a committed Wagnerian himself.) When Nietzsche learned of the contents of this letter, he could take the humiliation and betrayal of trust no longer.

However, the problems of his relationship with Wagner took root in the early years of their friendship at Tribschen. Later in his life, in 1888, Nietzsche wrote a letter to Karl Knortz, a professor in Indiana, U.S.A., who championed the Nietzschean cause to American readers: "For some years, which belong to the most precious of my life, I was bound to Wagner and Frau Cosima Wagner by feelings of the deepest confidence and most cordial friendship. If at the present day I belong to the opponents of the Wagnerian movement, it is obvious that no personal motives have induced me to assume this position."[9] But this is surely disingenuous. True, Nietzsche was principally attacking the pessimistic and Romantic "decadence" of Wagner's music dramas and their accompanying philosophy, but without the sense of personal betrayal, Nietzsche's disappointment over those aspects of Wagner's art would never have reached so inflated a level. Nietzsche was personally wounded by, not merely in philosophical disagreement with the man he had once loved so much and in whom he saw a cultural savior not only for Germany but also for Europe as a whole.

Nietzsche originally regarded Wagner's music dramas as the renaissance of Greek tragedy. In his first book, *The Birth of Tragedy from the Spirit of Music* (1872), he equated the life-enhancing effect of ancient Greek drama with the music-dramas of Richard Wagner, thus incurring the displeasure of his professional peers who were appalled by the comparison, the style in which he made it and the book as a whole, filled as it is with speculation and eulogy for a composer whose reputation and works were by no means respectable at that time. So bold and unorthodox a statement effectually ruined Nietzsche's academic career. His peers ridiculed and attacked him; his students abandoned his lectures, and it didn't even sell very well either. Cosima concisely summed up the situation in her diary by observing that he had been "excommunicated on account of his book."[10] But Nietzsche really felt that Wagner's art could—and would—transform what he (and Wagner) considered to be the "corrupted" culture of late nineteenth-century Europe.

In those early years, Nietzsche regarded music as a "Dionysian" art, which, unlike the "Apollonian" arts of sculpture or painting, was not, as Schopenhauer puts it, merely "a copy of the Ideas, but *a copy of the will itself.*"[11] Such concepts in fact originated in the writings of Immanuel Kant (1724–1804), whose "Thing in Itself" refers to the the ever-unknowable *essence* rather than the mere *appearance* of the world, which we assume, erroneously, to be the whole story. Ironically, Kant had little time for music, dismissing it

Title page of Nietzsche's first book, *The Birth of Tragedy.*

in his *Critique of Judgement* as playing "merely with sensations" and therefore occupying "the lowest place among the fine arts." It was also a superficial nuisance:

> For owning chiefly to the character of its instruments, it scatters its influence abroad to an uncalled-for extent (through the neighbourhood), and thus, as it were, becomes obtrusive and deprives others, outside the musical circle, of their freedom. This is a thing that the arts that address themselves to the eye do not do, for if one is not disposed to give admittance to their impressions, one has only to look the other way. The case is almost on a par with the practice of regaling oneself with a perfume that exhales its odours far and wide. The man who pulls his perfumed handkerchief from his pocket treats all around to it whether they like it or not, and compels them, if they want to breathe at all, to be parties to the enjoyment."[12]

This is a far cry from Schopenhauer's view of music. He saw music as the art form that most closely expresses the "Thing in Itself," or, in his own terminology, the "Will" beyond our "Representation" or "Idea" of the world. Wagner agreed, while side-stepping many of Schopenhauer's qualifications with regard to opera, such as his belief that "if music music tries to stick too closely to the words, and to mould itself according to the events, it is endeavoring to speak a language not its own."[13]

For Schopenhauer, music is also a metaphor for existence itself, in which man is pulled between the polar opposites of desire and satisfaction: "happiness and well-being consist only in the transition from desire to satisfaction and from this to a fresh desire, such transition going forward rapidly, for the non-appearance of satisfaction is suffering; the empty longing for a new desire is langour, boredom." In music a similar process is at work. Hence, "rapid melodies without great deviations are cheerful. Slow melodies that strike painful discords and wind back to the keynote only through many bars, are sad, on the analogy of the will, namely languor, could have no other expression than the sustained keynote, the effect of which would soon be intolerable; very monotonous and meaningless melodies approximate to this."[14]

Initially, Nietzsche believed that in Wagner's music dramas he had found the highest and most overwhelming demonstration of music as an expression of the "Will." Wagner's art also aimed to revive the spirit of Greek tragedy for the modern world, for, as Nietzsche explained, *"tragic myth* is to be understood only as a symbolization of Dionysian wisdom through Apollonian artifices."

The myth leads the world of phenomena to its limits where it denies itself and seeks to flee back into the womb of the true and only reality, where it then seems to commence its metaphysical swan song, like Isolde:

2. Tribschen Idyll

> *In the rapture ocean's*
> *billowing roll,*
> *in the fragrance waves;*
> *ringing sound,*
> *in the world breath's*
> *wafting whole—*
> *to drown, to sink—*
> *unconscious—highest joy!*[15]

For Nietzsche at this stage, Wagner represented the culmination of the German musical tradition, and it was Wagner's music to which he believed the German people would "be indebted for the *rebirth of German myth*."[16]

Nietzsche also believed that the ancient Greeks had found a way of affirming life while simultaneously facing up to its undeniable horrors; and they had achieved this by means of the Dionysian dramatic festivals which, with their fusion of music and myth, had created Greek tragedy itself:

> Dionysian art, too, wishes to convince us of the eternal joy of existence: only we are to seek this joy not in phenomena, but behind them. We are to recognize that all that comes into being must be ready for a sorrowful end; we are forced to look into the terrors of the individual existence—yet we are not to become rigid with fear: a metaphysical comfort tears us momentarily from the bustle of the changing figures. We are really for a brief moment primordial being itself, feeling its raging desire for existence and joy in existence; the struggle, the pain, the destruction of phenomena, now appear necessary to us, in view of the excess of countless forms of existence which force and push one another into life, in view of the exuberant fertility of the universal will. We are pierced by the maddening sting of these pains just when we have become, as it were, one with the infinite primordial joy in existence, and when we anticipate, in Dionysian ecstasy, the indestructibility and eternity of this joy. In spite of fear and pity, we are the happy living beings, not as individuals, but as the *one* living being, with whose creative joy we are united.[17]

Nietzsche now transferred his view of the life-enhancing, society-renewing phenomenon of Greek tragedy to Wagner's art. The power of Wagner's music, he believed, would reveal the reality of the world beyond its merely phenomenal appearance, while the mythical drama it imbued with life would awaken the collective unconscious of the German people, raising existence to an esthetic state of permanent creative ecstasy. (Alas, the Nazi's hijacked this laudable ideal, exploiting it to legitimize their counterfeit culture of kitsch in the twentieth century; and it was this cultural context that made the Third Reich such a peculiarly German phenomena. Britain had no such cultural context, perhaps explaining the abject failure of Sir Oswald Mosley and his infamous blackshirts.) Nietzsche later condensed his esthetic ideal in his essay on "Richard Wagner in Bayreuth" at the end of his *Untimely Meditations*, as the desire to "found the state upon music."[18] Wagner, the "Dithyrambic dramatist," would give the visible world a voice and the audible world a form: "We feel certain that in Wagner all that is visible in the world wants to become more profound and more intense by becoming audible, that it seeks here its lost soul; and that all that is audible in the world likewise wants to emerge into the light and also become a phenomenon for the eye; that it wants as it are to acquire corporality."[19] Of course, Nietzsche, being both a friend of Wagner and a fanatical supporter of his art at this time, was biased: "Measured against Wagner's, all earlier music seems stiff or timid, as though it were ashamed to be seen from all sides,"[20] he pontificated; but it was precisely this musical power that he believed would create such transformative effects. Nietzsche believed that modern man was in a wretched condition of debased feeling and materialistic superficiality, and that Wagnerian music drama would actually have the power to save him. In the character of Siegfried, the hero of Wagner's *Ring* cycle, Nietzsche thought he had found a prototype for what he would later call the Übermensch, which is usually and somewhat misleadingly translated as "Superman." Nietzsche was clear about what he meant by this term. As he never wearied of pointing out, "mankind is something that should be overcome."[21] Existing religious and social systems, he believed, restricted the development of human happiness. Nietzsche taught the way of the Superman to redeem humanity from what he termed "slave" morality—the rule of the weak who are unable to face the terror of existence and therefore construct illusory ideals that both deny and repress the truth in order to cope. In contrast, the modern Superman will be philosophically courageous enough to be able to face the abyss of life's essential meaninglessness and, like the ancient Greeks before him, integrate the horror of that meaninglessness into life-enhancing affirmation through *art*. By facing up to the truth about existence, and encouraged by the insights of art, the Superman will be able to say "Yes" to life, accepting both its negative and positive aspects, without the need for the comforting illusions of morality and religion.

This profound idea became the basis of Nietzsche's theory of Eternal Recurrence, which argues that if you have ever said "Yes" to a single joy in life, you have also to accept all the sorrows of life that accompany it. The Superman is strong enough to accept both the joy and sorrows, the pleasures and pains of life to such an extent that he would be willing to live them again and again throughout eternity. This is total affirmation of life, and, in Nietzsche's terms, the complete antithesis of Christianity, which collapses under the pains and sorrows of life while promoting the consolation of a "better world" in paradise. In stark contrast, Wagner's Siegfried is a child of nature, uncorrupted by the deadening values of modern civilization, in touch with his instincts, living each minute of his life vitally, true to his nature and consequently so much more alive than the other characters in the *Ring* cycle, whose natural impulses have been caught and perverted in the web of conventional social contracts. It was these qualities that Nietzsche most admired about Wagner's hero.

Amid all these high-flown ideals, however, the somewhat more mundane issue of Wagner's personality was simultaneously at work on Nietzsche's much more refined sensibilities. Wagner, he later realized, was the most impolite genius in the world,[22] whereas Nietzsche himself was extremely polite and very well-mannered. He was also, very probably, homosexual and an adoring fan of Wagner's art, and Wagner immediately sensed in these three characteristics of his new friend some very exploitable weak points, which he could play off against each other to his own advantage. If the relationship had been purely an intellectual, esthetic and world-redeeming one, things may have continued happily for much longer, but Nietzsche soon realized that there was a price to pay for communing intimately in the domestic arena of this particularly monstrous genius.

On his third visit to Tribschen, Nietzsche was plunged into the very heart of its domestic arrangements. Cosima was heavily pregnant and about to give birth to Wagner's son, Siegfried. There was some doubt about the advisability of a houseguest at this critical moment, but Wagner decided to adhere to the day's arrangements and things went ahead as planned. Later that night, however, Cosima's birth pangs were almost as loud as a gathering of Wagner's Valkyrie maidens. Even so, Nietzsche somehow managed to sleep through all this commotion in a neighboring bedroom. (Being such a valuable friend, he had his own quarters, especially reserved for him.) Neither did Nietzsche experience the celebrated meteorological effects that accompanied the momentous birth itself—the rich glow of the sun on the orange wallpaper, which was reflected in a blue jewel box, along with the sound of the early-morning bells ringing in Lucerne. Wagner was in tears of joy and distributed gifts to the servants, but only after all of this did Nietzsche join Wagner for lunch.

This event, so memorably commemorated in the exquisite *Siegfried Idyll* the following year, took place on June 6, 1869. Cosima had given birth to a genial, bisexual Gemini, whose destiny it was to marry an English orphan called Winifred Williams, who bore him four children and later became an adoring and infatuated fan of the future Führer, Adolf

Hitler; but Siegfried had always preferred the company of homosexuals. His marriage was therefore more of an expediency than a love-match. Siegfried had already been implicated in the scandal of the Harden-Eulenberg affair of 1907–1909 (which was originally triggered by the heart failure of one Dietrich von Hülsen-Haeseler, a minister in Kaiser Wilhelm's court, while wearing a ballet tutu). Cosima wished to silence rumors and prevent further embarrassments. Siegfried only barely outlived his mother, collapsing from a heart-attack induced by the shock of her death in 1930. Despite having written 18 rather ineffectual operas of his own, he was hardly the world-transfiguring hero his father had envisaged.

Two years after Siegfried's idyllic birth, Cosima's diary reveals evidence that Nietzsche was already beginning to find Wagner's personality a burden. She describes Nietzsche in August of that year as "certainly the most gifted of our young friends, but a not quite natural reserve makes his behavior in many respects most displeasing. It is as if he were trying to resist the overwhelming effect of Wagner's personality."[23] Patently, Nietzsche's disillusionment with Wagner the man began quite early in their relationship.

The following year, Nietzsche was back at Tribschen, playing his *Manfred Meditation* to both Richard and Cosima—"very beautifully,"[24] according to her; but as we have seen, this piece had incurred the wrath of von Bülow, who had called it "the rape of the muse by an incompetent dilettante."[25] Wagner was polite enough not to comment, but obviously agreed with the man whose wife he had stolen. By 1873, the Wagners had become rather put-out by Nietzsche's improvising: "We are a little vexed by our friend's music-making pastimes," Cosima reported on April 11.[26] But Wagner, who confessed that he played the piano "like a rat plays a flute,"[27] was always put out by pianists. His father-in-law, the inimitable Liszt, was the worst offender. Every time they met, Liszt always displayed a transcendental technique that no one could match—Wagner least of all. Though Wagner laughed at Nietzsche's attempts at composition, he may well have been jealous of his interpretive skills. Nietzsche's friend von Gersdorff wrote, "I do not think Beethoven could have improvised more impressively than Nietzsche, especially when the sky was thundery."[28] Cosima was certainly impressed by the young professor's performances of the preludes to *Tristan und Isolde* and *Die Meistersinger*. Nietzsche's enthusiasm for and passion at the keyboard even caused Cosima to enter into one of her habitual trance states—a state of mind that no doubt hovered over the proceedings when Nietzsche and the Wagners tried their hands at table-turning.[29]

Could it be that the misogynist and probably homosexual Nietzsche fell in love with Cosima? During his later madness, he wrote her a letter confessing, "Ariadne, I love you."[30] Or did she become an idealized mother figure for him? Nietzsche never lost his respect for her, even when his tirades against Wagner had risen to the level of pathological obsession. He certainly played the piano to her when Wagner was away from Tribschen in April 1872. "Prof. N. plays for me,"[31] was all that Cosima recorded of the occasion; but the following day she reports: "Prof. Nietzsche gone. Great weariness!" The brevity of the remarks suggests an undercurrent of some kind. Indeed, Cosima later reflected that "few people have as much feeling for our sufferings and joy as he."[32] One should, perhaps, expect this from the future prophet of the Superman, who affirms both suffering and joy to the point of willing their eternal recurrence.

Nietzsche's feelings for Wagner were far more complicated. Wagner once insisted to Nietzsche that musicians "are wild beasts, not educated creatures, very close in fact to actors."[33] This no doubt stuck a chord, for in his much later attack on Wagner in *The Case of Wagner*, Nietzsche threw Wagner's analysis back in his face with a three-fold demand.

> *That the theater should not lord it over the arts.*
> *That the actor should not seduce those who are authentic.*
> *That music should not become an art of lying.*[34]

Nietzsche rightly recognized that Wagner was above all, and in everything, a man of the theater first and a musician, philosopher and world-redeemer second; but Wagner was also an opinionated table-talker who took on every subject under the sun. He argued with Nietzsche's vegetarianism, which he considered, as Cosima recorded in her diary, "nonsense, arrogance as well, and when the Prof. says it is morally important not to eat animals, etc., R. replies that our whole existence is a compromise, which we can only expiate by producing some good. One cannot to that just by drinking milk—better, then, to become an ascetic. To do good in our climate we need good nourishment, and so on. Since the Prof. admits that Richard is right, yet nevertheless sticks to his abstinence, R. becomes very angry."[35]

"R." also became increasingly angry with Nietzsche on his subsequent Tribschen visits. Cosima noted that Wagner found Nietzsche's writing "immature," repetitious and "brought out too quickly" without a "real plan." He added, "I don't know anybody to whom I could give it to read, because nobody could follow it."[36] And things boiled over when Nietzsche presented Wagner with a copy of Brahms' *Triumphlied*—Brahms, whose music Wagner despised and rejected: "Handel, Mendelssohn, and Schumann wrapped in leather" was "R's" "very angry" verdict of that particular piece; and countless vexations and disagreements between Nietzsche and Wagner are tersely noted by Cosima at the end of their friend's visit with the statement: "Prof. N. departed, having caused R. many difficult hours."[37]

Nietzsche certainly found himself at odds with Wagner philosophically as time went on, as Joachim Köhler for one observes in his book about their relationship, Nietzsche also grew to realize that the price he had to pay for entering the enchanted magic garden of Tribschen, presided over by this musical Klingsor was "the sacrifice of his own personality."[38] This he was understandably unwilling to do. In the early days, things had indeed been too good to be true. The euphoria of those days is recorded in a letter to his mother from 1869:

> Never have I been happier than during the last few days. The warm, hearty and increasing intimacy with Wagner and Frau von Bülow [at this stage, Cosima was still not actually married to Wagner, merely separated from her former husband], the complete agreement between us all on the questions that chiefly interest us, Wagner absolutely in the prime of his genius and marvelous creations only just come into being, glorious Tribschen arranged on such a regal and ingenious scale—many things conspire to exhilarate me and strengthen me in my calling.[39]

Amid his lonely, alienated and sickly existence, Tribschen was very much Nietzsche's refuge and apparent salvation. Writing to Erwin Rohde, Nietzsche insisted that "it is absolutely necessary that you too should be initiated into this magic."[40] Two years later he continued, "I have concluded an alliance with Wagner. You cannot think how near we stand to each other and how closely related our schemes are."[41] So carried away was Nietzsche by his enthusiasm for Wagner's world-redeeming project that he began to entertain plans for his own "Greek Academy" and, rather more prosaically, considered playing the national lottery to raise funds for it.[42]

Wagner, meanwhile, was working hard on *Siegfried*, the third of his *Ring* cycle dramas, which he had abandoned 13 years earlier when *Tristan* and *Meistersinger* had taken precedence. Siegfried—the opera, the Idyll and the baby boy—dominated life at Tribschen, so it was perhaps to be expected that this hero made such an impression on Nietzsche, chiming with his own ideas about affirmation, courage and freedom from convention and traditional morality. Siegfried's very conception breaks the oldest taboo of all, for his parents, Siegmund and Sieglinde, are brother and sister. This child of incest then grows up to be an impetuous youth who has never experienced fear. Wagner, like Nietzsche, felt that fear, particularly the fear of death, was "the source of all lovelessness."[43] His argument is that the fear of death prevents us from enjoying life; but perhaps even more revealingly, he points out that we are also frightened of being free. Siegfried, however, fears neither death nor freedom. Wagner, always more of an anarchist than a socialist or authoritarian, and more of an artist than a politician, insisted that the pursuit of freedom should be our primary concern:

> But what is "freedom"? is it—as our politicians believe—"licence?"—of course not. Freedom is: *integrity*. He who is true to himself, i.e. who acts in accord with his own being, and in perfect harmony with his own nature, is *free*, strictly speaking, outward constraint is powerless unless is succeeds in destroying the integrity of its victim, inducing him to dissemble and to persuade himself and others that he is a different person from the one he really is. That is true servitude."[44]

That paragraph is taken from Wagner's long and important letter to his fellow-revolutionary, August Röckel, who was languishing in prison after Wagner had made his escape from the failed Dresden revolution of 1849. It is also the kernel of Nietzsche's subsequent philosophical system. All that Nietzsche had to do was expand upon it, and he did so, at first, by discussing Greek Tragedy; but Wagner had anticipated him here too, when he claimed that his music dramas were rooted in the spirit and aims of the ancient Greeks. Nietzsche, however, added his own dichotomy. Like Wagner, Nietzsche believed that the ancient Greeks had achieved a Siegfried-like affirmation of life in their dramatic festivals in honor of Dionysus, the god of intoxication, music, instinct, freedom and sexual ecstasy. By combining these Dionysian qualities with those associated with the god Apollo (restraint, poetry, form and beauty), the Greeks had been able to accept life's reality and celebrate it for what it is, rather than what a weak idealist thinks it ought to be—to celebrate its joys and horrors *without fear.* Nietzsche's Superman is the opposite of an idealist; he is a realist. Faced with reality, an idealist grows depressed, unable to accept his disillusionment; but the realist remains cheerful because he has fully absorbed the terrifying reality of life, faced up to it and created something beautiful out of it. It was therefore the pagan culture of ancient Greece rather than the monotheistic culture of mournful Christianity to which Nietzsche looked for salvation—and the name he gave to his new anti–Christian outlook was "Dionysian"—but now refined and redefined.

By "Dionysian" Nietzsche, like Wagner before him when he was discussing "freedom," did not mean we should all become drunken libertines, but rather act as responsible individuals who unite the Apollonian and Dionysian elements within ourselves. Thomas Mann, so profoundly influenced by both Nietzsche and Wagner as he was, understood this more than most, and in his novella "Death in Venice" (1912) we see very much a Nietzschean allegory along these lines, in which the hero Gustav von Aschenbach, unable to integrate the erotic impact of the young boy, Tadzio, on his life, is destroyed by the god Dionysus, whom he has not fully acknowledged in his pursuit of Apollonian virtues. He has spent so long searching for Apollonian beauty of form in his prose writings, that he has ignored the emotional demands on Dionysus. Mann was bisexual, and there is a strong sense of sexual liberation behind the ideas of both writers. Indeed, some writers such as Köhler have suggested that the main emotional drive behind the whole of Nietzsche's oeuvre derived from his own repressed sexuality—a case, par excellence, of a moral system destroying the freedom and integrity of a personality. The 75th aphorism of Nietzsche's book *Beyond Good and Evil* is of deep significance here: "The degree and kind of a man's sexuality reaches up into the topmost summit of his spirit."[45] Why else would Nietzsche have written this aphorism—and used such loaded words as "the degree and *kind* of a man's sexuality"—if this were not a reference to his own nature? At the very least, such a phrase suggests that there is more than one "kind" of male sexuality. Christian morality, which at that time denied the very basis of Nietzsche's entire personality, was therefore a personal, not only philosophical opponent. No one can aspire to happiness without first acknowledging who they are, and Nietzsche had the misfortune to live in a period and culture that absolutely denied the basis of his own psychosexual reality. It was not merely homosexuality, but *all* sexuality with which conventional nineteenth-century morality took issue, and which Wagner had exposed in his explicitly erotic music: the Liebestod of *Tristan;* the graphic symbolism of the sword in the love-scene between Siegmund and Sieglinde, the disturbed emotional exploitation of Kundry with Parsifal. A hatred of the body was one of the primary foundations of Christianity (which, as Nietzsche pointed out had little in common with the teachings of Jesus himself). In stark contrast, the Superman is foremost a philosopher of the body: As there is no metaphysical soul for a Superman, the temple in which Nietzsche worshipped was his own body. Siegfried, with whom he identified, owns nothing else, apart from his sword, but the trouble was that Nietzsche's own body was far from being that of a strong, healthy hero, even though his sword (which was in fact a pen) was razor sharp.

For Nietzsche, mankind was an animal ensnared by a civilization that was of dubious benefit: it repressed what was animalistic and instinctual by means of morality and law. In nature, however, there are no laws—

only necessities,[46] and it was on the precipice of this devastating observation that the whole problem of integrating the Superman into a social system lies, for what is the nature of human reality? If the ideals of religion are proved to be illusions, what are the real motivating forces behind the actions of men and how can they be reconciled with the demands of living together? Nietzsche's answer was his theory of the Will to Power.

> What is good?—All that heightens the feeling of power, the will to power, power itself in man.
> What is bad?—All that proceeds from weakness.
> What is happiness?—The feeling that power *increases*—that a resistance is overcome.[47]

There are, of course, various levels to this Will to Power. Its crudest manifestation is physical violence; but the most powerful man is he who has mastered himself and has no interest in dominating others. Crudely powerful individuals such as Cesare Borgia, for example, are not Nietzsche's role model at all, but are at least preferable to weak men, who are a danger not only to themselves but everyone else as well. He would rather have a Cesare Borgia than a Parsifal.[48]

> I have found strength where one does not look for it: in simple, mild, and pleasant people, without the least desire to rule—and, conversely, the desire to rule has often appeared to me as a sign of inward weakness: they fear their own slave soul and shroud it in a royal cloak (in the end, they still become the slaves of their followers, their fame, etc.). The powerful natures *dominate*, it is a necessity, they need not lift one finger. Even if, during their life time, they bury themselves in a garden house.[49]

The crucial aspect to all of this is that salvation lies in the sublimation.

In the personality and achievements of Richard Wagner, Nietzsche received an object lesson in the Will to Power. He was there to witness the miraculous creation of Bayreuth and the first Bayreuth Festival in 1876. In the early years of their friendship, Nietzsche thought of Bayreuth as the fulfillment of his hopes. All that changed when he came to regard Wagner not as a Superman but merely a Romantic, a Christian pessimist, a decadent. And on top of all that there were all the problems of Wagner's overwhelming ego, antisemitism, rudeness and exploitation to cope with. For Wagner, the pessimistic philosophy of Schopenhauer was an end in itself. For Nietzsche, however, Schopenhauer was merely a springboard for optimism. Nietzsche fully accepted Schopenhauer's convictions that there is no God and no metaphysical salvation for mankind, but he argued vehemently against Schopenhauer's conclusion that life was so awful it should be denied. As we shall see, Nietzsche felt that the original optimistic message of the *Ring* cycle had been hijacked by Schopenhauerian pessimism.[50]

If the Superman was to live, Nietzsche needed to escape from Bayreuth. After all, Siegfried is actually a failure, destroyed by the poison of a civilization that is symbolized by the magic potion given to him by Hagan, the villain of *Götterdämmerung*. Hagan kills him, and Brünnhilde, acknowledging the futility and evil of the world, sets that world on fire. Nietzsche's Superman, on the contrary, would always remain a cheerful philosopher of freedom, whose message is one of hope rather than despair, of freedom rather than oppression. His mission is to succeed, not fail. The Superman was to be a champion of reality, a hero whose mission is to fulfill his own destiny by becoming truly who he is, regardless of what society might try to make him. Such freedom can be very frightening to those who cling to the false securities of conventions and outmoded moral structures, and Nietzsche knew it: "I know my fate. One day there will be associated with my name the recollection of something frightful—of a crisis like no other before on earth, of the profoundest collision of conscience, of a decision evoked *against* everything that until then had been believed in, demanded, sanctified. I am not a man I am dynamite."[51]

Wagner was the first genius Nietzsche had ever encountered, and the strength of feeling Wagner inspired, followed by the betrayal not only of ideas Nietzsche felt he had shared with him but also those very personal ties which so wounded him, transformed Wagner into an archetypal symbol of all that Nietzsche opposed. He consequently found himself trapped between loathing and love, admiration and accusation. In Palmer's film, the screenwriter Charles Wood gives Nietzsche a final tirade against his former idol, in what is perhaps the finest speech of the entire seven-hour film:

> All these people, Wagner. All these Germans who flock to Bayreuth: clubs, societies, decked in ribbons blowing trumpets, slashing at each other with sabers, spouting their antisemitic rubbish. You! You have the nerve to write that Christ was not a Jew, do you not? Do you care? To imagine you could herd all the Jews into a theater of your choosing and then burn it to the ground! As if that would solve the world problem, whatever you think the world problem is—not to mention a cellar full of silk in boxes, a house fit for a king, paid for by a king, children who treat you like a god, your tomb built already waiting to receive your body. That picture: "The Holy Family" [Wagner's children painted in Biblical costumes by Paul Joukowsky]. Claptrap! Mumbo-jumbo and claptrap! Not you: your music will still rise above the posturing, but this is all play-acting. You're a small-time theater-manager who by some strange trick of fate has been given the biggest, brightest most glittering over-decorated barn to call a theater of a scene and it's all to you. Opera's all. There's nothing else of value to you. The whole of Germany must flock to you. In your estimation they have fought their war simply so that you might tug on a curtain and shout: "See the face of Art as according to Wagner."
>
> I've things to do. I've hopes and aims beyond Bayreuth. You've come into your own.

> Ah, you know what it is the people want, your so-called German people. You know what this age brought about by war and the yearnings for power is in the market for. You throw it all together: music, war, death, ecstasy, torment, bangs and crashes, floods and conflagrations, exquisite neuroses, obsessions, sensual and profane hand-in-hand with vulgar, coarse twitchings of sexual fantasy; and potent, *real* grandeur. Dangerous, elevating and plunging and convincing stirrings in such a soup will feed criminals as well as genius. You're dangerous! You're a dangerous man, Wagner. You talk of gods, but you know there is no god but Wagner, yet you have the power to convince fools they might become gods.

After his break with Wagner, Nietzsche simultaneously eulogized his friendship and lashed out at the man who had inspired it: "So long had I been seeking for the man who stood on a higher plane than I did, and who really comprised me. I believed I had found this man in Wagner. It was a mistake. And now it would not even be right to compare myself with him—I belong to another order of beings."[52] Even so, he still lamented in 1880:

> Nothing can compensate me, for instance, for the fact that for the last few years I have lost Wagner's friendly interest in my fate. How often do I not dream of him, and always in the spirit of our former intimate companionship! No words of anger have ever passed between us, not even in my dreams—on the contrary, only words of encouragement and good cheer, and with no one have I ever laughed so much as with him. All this is now a thing of the past—and what does it avail that in many respects I am right and he is wrong? As if our lost friendship could be forgotten on that account![53]

To his sister Elisabeth, he confessed that his Tribschen idyll was "the happiest I have had in my whole life. But the omnipotent violence of our tasks drove us asunder and now we can never more be united; we have grown too strange to each other."[54] To Peter Gast, he confessed on the occasion of Wagner's death, that "it was hard for six years to have to be the opponent of the man one had most reverenced on earth ...; as to the genuine Wagner, I shall yet attempt to become in a great measure his *heir*."[55] And by that he meant the prophet of freedom he would have recognized as a kindred spirit in the letter Wagner had written to Röckel. He even went so far in a further letter to Gast to state that he and Wagner "loved each other and hoped everything *for each other*—it was truly a profound *love*."[56]

Of course, Wagner, in his own way, was equally hurt, though rather less reverential of the memory of what had been. "I have had fine friends," he complained to Cosima.[57] "That bad person has taken everything from me, even the weapons with which he now attacks me. How sad that he should be so perverse—so clever, yet, at the same time so shallow."[58] He grumbled about how miserably Nietzsche had failed him[59]—significantly employing the regal "us." When the Bayreuth court pianist, Josef Rubinstein, raised the subject of Nietzsche one evening, Cosima noted that "R.

becomes very upset, he cannot get over the perversity of such a character."[60] Indeed, Nietzsche became Wagner's litmus test of the world's general acidity: "One can see how bad the modern world is, says R., from the fact that promising people like Nietzsche so swiftly go the bad in it."[61] Wagner labeled Nietzsche "childish and malicious,"[62] and insisted that his former friend "possessed no real intelligence but could be magnetized."[63] Wagner refused to read Nietzsche's *Human, All Too Human* (1878), in which Nietzsche boldly stated his new ideas, attacking Wagner in the process. "R. feels he would be doing the author a favor ... if he did not read it. It seems to me to contain much inner rage and sullenness." It was "strangely perverse"[64] and "dismal."[65] Cosima also confided to herself that "I lack the ability to keep bad experiences constantly in mind; with Nietzsche, for instance, I think only of his friendly aspects."[66] But things were never to be the same again. The friendship was over.

3

Beethoven

As we have seen, Beethoven was eulogized by both Wagner and Nietzsche, each of whom interpreted Beethoven's legacy in their own image. Nietzsche, while under Wagner's spell, was influenced, though not always convinced by his friend's idea of the earlier composer, whom Wagner regarded as a prophet of his own art; for Wagner saw himself as the union of Beethoven and Shakespeare, and Beethoven's Ninth Symphony as the gateway through which Wagnerian music drama had made its triumphant entrance into the world.

Wagner regarded Beethoven's choral finale as the inevitable re-union of music and poetry, which foreshadowed his own Gesamtkunstwerk; but even as early as 1871, Nietzsche was privately doubtful of this claim, which he called a "monstrous aesthetic superstition," suggesting that the choral finale had not "unlocked the gates of a new art in which music is able to represent even the image and the concept." He went on to compare Beethoven's music of "dithyrambic jubilation" to an ocean of flames drowning out the pale moonlight of Schiller's poem. Schiller's text even seems "irritating, disturbing, not to say crude and offensive: except that we do not hear it, because the ever fuller development of the choral singing and the orchestral masses keeps that sense of incongruity away from us."[1] Indeed, there has always been some doubt as to Beethoven's conviction that the choral finale was entirely appropriate, somewhat dampening Wagner's over-heated claims. Accordingly, Alexander Thayer remarked in his celebrated late nineteenth-century biography of the composer: "That Beethoven may have had scruples touching the appropriateness of the choral finale, is comprehensible enough in view of the fact that the original plan of the symphony contemplated an instrumental close and that Beethoven labored so hard to establish arbitrarily an organic union between the Ode and the first three movements; but it is not likely that he gave long thought to the project of writing a new finale."[2]

Later, in 1874, Nietzsche addressed the problem again, arguing that Wagner's "error was to assume that "a means of expression, *the music*, is turned into the purpose, and the purpose of the expression into the means.... Without the drama he regards the music on its own as an absurdity: it raises the question 'what is all the racket for?' That was why he regarded the 9th Symphony as Beethoven's real feat, because by adding the words he had given the music its purpose, to be the means of expression."[3]

But, as with so many influences in his life and art, Wagner's celebrated centenary essay on Beethoven in 1870 interpreted Beethoven's music very much along Wagnerian lines. To emphasize the point, Wagner even sprinkled allusions to his own opera poems in the text, which his useful, though stylistically rather challenging English translator W. Ashton Ellis, helpfully points out.[4] We have already seen how highly Nietzsche regarded the Beethoven essay, despite his private misgivings about aspects of it, and it is therefore not at all surprising that it influenced his first book *The Birth of Tragedy*. Indeed, the subtitle of that work was indebted to Wagner as well. But both its subtitle and its basic idea are foreshadowed in Wagner's words:

> Everywhere we see the inner law, only conceivable as sprung from the spirit of Music, prescribe the outer law that regulates the world of sight: the genuine ancient Doric State which Plato tried to rescue for philosophy, nay, the order of war, the fight itself, the laws of Music led as surely as the dance.—But that paradise was lost: the fount of motion of a world ran dry. Like a ball once thrown, the world span round the curve of its trajectory, but no longer was it driven by a moving soul; and so its very motion must grow faint at last, until the world-soul had been waked again.[5]

Nietzsche took these ideas (and the words "from the spirit of Music") and made them his own, arguing that "the choral parts with which tragedy is interlaced are, as it were, the womb that gave birth to the stage."[6] With the corruption of art (for which Nietzsche at this time blames French culture, as did Wagner), he calls for *"the rebirth of German myth"*[7] and the corresponding rebirth of Dionysian musical insight by Wagnerian means:

> —My friends, you who believe in Dionysian music, you also know what tragedy means to us. There we have tragic myth reborn from music—and in this myth we can hope for everything and forget what is most painful. What is most painful for all of us, however, is the prolonged degradation in which the German genius has lived, estranged from house and home, in the service of vicious dwarfs. You understand my words—as you will also, in conclusion, understand my hopes.[8]

The implication is clear, especially in the context of his dedication of the work to Wagner and the many Wagnerian references throughout the text: It is Wagner who will redeem art and society through music drama. Alas,

Nietzsche came to the realization that this was not to be, that Wagner's music was not dithyrambic but merely Romantic and, even worse, decadent, and that society required something more efficacious to cure it of its ills.

But before Wagner, came Beethoven, and one might be tempted to suggest that Beethoven originally regarded Napoleon as a kind of freedom-forging Übermensch, before proving to have feet of clay when he crowned himself Emperor and Beethoven famously obliterated Napoleon's name from the title page of his *Eroica* Symphony; and in Wagner's image of Beethoven, Nietzsche may have found another prototype for his own Superman: "The well-nigh unearthly poignance of his eye saw nothing in the outer world but plaguing perturbations of his inner world, and to hold them at arm's length made out his almost only rapport with that world. Thus paroxysm (Krampf) becomes the expression of his visage: the paroxysm of defiance holds his nose, the mouth at strain, a strain that never can relax to smiles, but only to gargantuan laughter."[9]

Such laughter resonated with Nietzsche, for, far from the scowling image of the Nietzsche legend, Nietzsche pursued laughter, joy and "weightlessness." Wagner goes on to discuss Beethoven's C-sharp minor Quartet in terms of "inner joy" and "rhythmic dance,"[10] terms that also resonated. Indeed, Wagner's final statement about the emotional effect of this Quartet suggests the idea of Nietzsche's theory of Eternal Recurrence: "'Tis the dance of the whole world itself: wild joy, the wail of pain, love's transport, utmost bliss, grief, frenzy, riot, suffering; the lightning flickers, thunders growl: and above it the stupendous fiddler who bans and bends it all, who leads it haughtily from whirlwind to whirlpool, to the brink of the abyss;—he smiles to himself, for to him this sorcery is the merest play."[11] Nietzsche virtually paraphrases this passage in *The Birth of Tragedy* when arguing that when we are absorbed in the Dionysian art of music "we are really for a brief moment primordial being itself, feeling its raging desire for existence and joy in existence; the struggle, the pain, the destruction of phenomena, now appear necessary to us, in view of the excess of countless forms of existence which force and push one another into life, in view of the exuberant fertility of the universal will. We are pierced by the maddening sting of these pains just when we have become, as it were, one with the infinite primordial joy in existence, and when we anticipate in Dionysian ecstasy, the indestructibilty and eternity of this joy."[12]

Wagner's thoughts on Beethoven's *Pastoral* Symphony, couched in the mystical terminology close to his heart, also anticipate Nietzsche's cult of joy: "All grief of Being breaks before this vast enjoyment of the play therewith; the world-creator Brahma is laughing at himself."[13] Indeed, Beethoven, himself well-versed in Hindu literature, also refers to "Brahma: his spirit is enwrapped in himself. He, the mighty one, is present in every part of space—his omniscience is in spirit by himself and the conception of his comprehends every other one."[14] It is true that Beethoven himself supplied programmatic subtitles to each of his symphonic movements, and Wagner happily took these on board while insisting that the experience of the music reveals "the essence of things" rather than their mere phenomena, permitting one to "understand the woods, the brook, the fields, the clear blue sky, the merry throng, the raging of the storm, the happiness of the rhythmic rest."[15] Nietzsche, even in the same year that Wagner's essay first appeared, also privately insisted that if Beethoven "describes a symphony as 'pastoral' and a movement as a 'scene by the brook' or as 'merry gathering of country folk,' these are nothing but allegorical representations bourne out of the music, which can teach us nothing whatsoever about the Dionysian content of the music and which in fact have no exclusive value in relation to other images."[16] He reiterated these ideas in public in *The Birth of Tragedy* two years later, adding that "music itself in its absolute sovereignty does not *need* the image and the concept, but merely *endures* them as accompaniments." Music, for Nietzsche, "symbolizes a sphere which is beyond and prior to all phenomena. Rather, all phenomena, compared with it are merely symbols: hence *language*, as organ and symbol of phenomena, can never by any means disclose the innermost heart of music."[17] This seems to go against the whole of Wagner's ideas of Gesamtkunstwerk, but Wagner had already come to believe in the supremacy of music, and indeed would describe his music-dramas as "ersichtlich gewordene Thaten der Musik"—or "acts of music made visible." (Ashton Ellis translates this as "*deeds of music brought to sight.*"[18]) The major difference between Wagner and Nietzsche here is Nietzsche's insistence that there is no need for them to become visible in the first place. One wonders what Nietzsche would have made of Wagner's plans to devote himself to purely orchestral works after *Parsifal* had come to fruition.

Last, but by no means least, Beethoven's setting of Schiller's "Ode to Joy" at the end of his Ninth Symphony was bound to appeal to Nietzsche, the philosopher of joy, who describes it in *The Birth of Tragedy* as "Dionysian" music. "The noblest clay, the most costly marble, man, is here kneaded and cut, and to the sound of the chisel strokes of the Dionysian world-artist rings out the cry of the Eleusinian mysteries: 'Do you prostrate yourselves, millions? Do you sense your Maker, world?'"[19]

The essence of Nietzsche's ideas about tragedy occur in section 7 of *The Birth of Tragedy*. The experience of the tragic chorus (the essence of music itself) reveals the "terrible destructiveness of so-called world history as well as the cruelty of nature," but Art saves us from despair. As Nietzsche's translator Walter Kauffmann puts it, "One can be as honest and free of optimistic illusions as Schopenhauer was, and still celebrate life as fundamentally powerful and pleasurable as the Greeks did."[20] In Beethoven's own personal tragedy of deafness, Nietzsche found a personification of the purpose of Greek Tragedy, for Beethoven himself was similarly saved from despair by his own art. As Wagner put it, genius is "freed from all outside it, at home forever with and in itself."[21] Nietzsche encapsulated all this in his aphorism, "Without music, life would be a mistake."[22]

In his *Untimely Meditations*, Nietzsche makes some absurdly Wagnerian claims about the nature of Beethoven's music. Beethoven was apparently "the first to let music speak a new language, the hitherto forbidden language of passion"[23] and before Wagner, "music was as a whole narrowly bounded."[24] In the first of these four essays he attacks the writer David Strauss for not whole-heartedly admiring Beethoven, shooting down in Wagnerian flames Strauss' suggestion that Haydn's music is "honest soup" as compared with Beethoven's "confectionary"[25]—in themselves equally absurd categorizations, admittedly, but bound to raise the ire of a Wagnerian acolyte, which Nietzsche still was, though increasingly less so, when he wrote his essays. It wasn't long, however, before he woke up and began to think independently.

After his break with Wagner, Nietzsche gained a more realistic perspective on Beethoven. The spiraling vortex of sublimity which had hitherto raised Beethoven into a deity is removed and the *effect* of Beethoven's music is separated from Wagner's esthetic agenda. While still acknowledging Beethoven's power and genius, Nietzsche strips the music of metaphysical import. In section 153 of *Human, All Too Human*, he now feels that *"art weighs down the thinker's heart,"* observing that "the highest effects of art easily produce a reverberation of a long-silenced, or even broken metaphysical string. At a certain place in Beethoven's Ninth Symphony, for example, he might feel that he is floating above the earth in a starry dome, with the dream of *immortality* in his heart."[26] Here, incidentally, is a classic example of how quoting Nietzsche out of context (beginning with "At a certain place...") completely transforms his meaning. Nietzsche also confronts the creative process as one of labor rather than Wagnerian "divine inspiration," by observing that Beethoven's notebooks reveal how his melodies were "gradually assembled" and had "disparate beginnings." Wagner was equally laborious but would never have admitted that "all great men were great workers, untiring not only in invention but also in rejecting, sifting, reforming, arranging."[27] Such a candid confession would have seriously threatened his carefully cultivated Promethean— even god-like image.

Having previously disparaged music composed before Beethoven as lacking passion, Nietzsche now hails Mozart for his "tender enthusiasm, his child-like delight in *chinoiserie* and ornament, his politeness of the heart, his longing for the graceful, the enamoured, the dancing, the tearful, his faith in the south."[28] Above all, he praises Mozart for being a good European, of which Beethoven was the last musical example. "Whatever German music came afterwards belongs to romanticism." Schumann, whom he once rated so highly is now "a merely *German* event in music, no longer a European event, as Beethoven was, as to an even greater extent Mozart had been."[29] Indeed, Nietzsche's opinions evolved so rapidly that by the time of *The Gay Science* he was comparing Beethoven unfavorably with Goethe as "semi-barbarism beside culture, as the people beside nobility, as the good-natured human being next to the good and more than merely 'good' human being, as the visionary beside the artist."[30] In the end, he comes to regard Goethe as "the last German before whom I feel reverence."[31]

This leaves the composer so often claimed as Beethoven's legitimate successor, Johannes Brahms, hanging in mid-air. All his life, Brahms self-consciously walked in the footsteps of the great Viennese master, and his first symphony was baptized by von Bülow as "Beethoven's Tenth." As we have seen, Nietzsche attacked Wagner with a copy of Brahms' *Triumphlied*, but what did he really think of Brahms' music and position in musical history? His most sustained statement on the subject can be found in the second postscript of *The Case of Wagner* where he defined Brahms as an example of "the melancholy of impotence," and asked "what does Johannes Brahms matter now?" arguing that Brahms' main function was to have been an antagonist to Wagner. (Brahms had infamously been involved in the unsuccessful petition against "The New German School" of Liszt and Wagner as advancing "new and unheard-of theories, to the detriment of the intrinsic nature of music."[32]) Nietzsche admitted that "an antagonist was *needed*," but added: "That does not make for *necessary* music, that makes, above all, for too much music."[33] He described Brahms as "a master of imitation," adding, "People like to call Brahms the *heir* of Beethoven: I know no more cautious euphemism."[34] Brahms' conservative approach to music, honoring the old forms of sonata, concerto and symphony, constantly looking behind himself to make sure he fitted into Beethoven's shadow, suggested the actions of a man who not only deceived himself but also denied the necessary progression of history. What made Beethoven great—his innovation in form and evolutionary approach to harmony, not to mention his radical urge towards freedom and joy, was apparently completely lacking in the music of his self-conscious imitator: Hence the melancholy. In a sense Nietzsche's opinion of Brahms is also a definition of kitsch—the attempt to re-animate what is already dead. Kitsch, no matter how appealing it may be (and it often is) is always the rictus grin of death. There is something desperately sad about it: Neuschwanstein, Tchaikovsky's *Mozartiana*, Tenth, Strauss' *Arabella* (the kitsch nature of which the composer recognized only too well, as we shall discover in the chapter 5), Liberace, Nazi art. Some of these are delightful, some less so, but all look back in denial. Nietzsche was able to launch a two-pronged attack on conservative Brahms and progressive (or at least decadent) Wagner because he regarded no other composer as capable of writing "better" music than Wagner; it was merely more "indifferent" music. In the question of German taste everything was corrupt. A totally fresh approach was needed.

Earlier in his philosophical development, however, Nietzsche, like Wagner, believed that Beethoven's "Ode to Joy" had redemptive Dionysian qualities:

> Freely earth proffers her gifts, and peacefully the breasts of prey of the rocks and desert approach. The chariot of Dionysus is covered with flowers and garlands; panthers and tigers walk under its yoke. Transform Beethoven's "Hymn to Joy" into a painting; let your imagination conceive the multitudes bowing to the dust, awestruck—then you will approach the Dionysian. Now the slave is a free man; now all the rigid, hostile barriers that necessity, caprice, or "impudent convention" have fixed between man and man are broken. Now, with the gospel of universal harmony, each one feels himself not only united, reconciled, and fused with his neighbor, but as one with him, as if the veil of *māyā* had been torn aside and we were now merely fluttering in tatters before the mysterious primordial unity.[35]

This quotation goes on to discuss how, in song and dance, mankind "expresses himself as a member of a higher community; he has forgotten how to walk and speak and is on the way toward flying into the air, dancing."[36] Not only is this one of Nietzsche's first statements about the importance of dancing in his philosophy, it also anticipates Scriabin's actual attempts at trying to fly by flapping his arms, and the less ridiculous imagery of flight in his music—expressive as it is of weightlessness of the soul, elation, ecstasy. Nietzsche's instinct to dance during the "Ode to

Joy" therefore casts its light on Scriabin's esthetic, to which we will be returning in chapter 8.

Nietzsche also included an image of Prometheus on the title page of his *Birth of Tragedy* as well as mentioning this famous mythological figure in his dedication of the book to Wagner, which acknowledged that he began to think about the ideas contained within it around the same time that Wagner's Beethoven essay first appeared in 1870. Later in the book, he explains that Prometheus was torn to pieces by vultures because of his "titanic love for man."[37] Prometheus, like his brother Atlas, wished to carry humanity on a broad back, higher and higher, farther and farther—and this is what Dionysus and Prometheus have in common: the desire to further the development of mankind—and, in Nietzsche's view at least, ultimately to create the Superman, mankind being a bridge not a goal. Such a constellation was bound to appeal to the Prometheus-loving Scriabin,

Prometheus of Sound: Max Klinger's Beethoven Statue in its original position at the 1902 Vienna Secession Beethoven Exhibition. Taken from "Klinger's Beethoven und die Moderne Raum-Kunst" by Joseph August Lux in *Deutsche Kunst und Dekoration: illustr. Monatshefte für moderne Malerei, Plastik, Architektur, Wohnungskunst u. künstlerisches Frauen-Arbeiten* (Darmstadt: Alexander Koch, 1902), p. 489 (http://digi.ub.uni-heidelberg.de/diglit/dkd1902/0191?sid=793344a9dded1f519077659a8db759dd).

whose last symphonic work takes Nietzsche's ideas about Prometheus to a mystical level, and combined with Nietzsche's rather Wagnerian ideas about Beethoven at this period. It also reaches out to Max Klinger's statue of Beethoven as a Promethean figure, complete with punishing eagle (the alternative to the vulture in some versions of the legend), enthroned and deified in polychrome marble. It was for the unveiling of this statue at the Vienna Secession's Beethoven exhibition in 1902 that Mahler indeed conducted extracts from Beethoven's Ninth Symphony, re-scored for wind and brass alone.

As visitors made their way to the statue they passed Gustav Klimt's famous Beethoven frieze with its central image of a naked couple kissing, directly reflecting Schiller's line, "O ye millions I embrace you. Here is a kiss of the whole world!" Klimt had had many lovers and therefore knew all about kissing. One of his former

Bust of Beethoven. Sculptor unknown (author's collection).

lovers had been none other than the future Alma Mahler. Mahler and Alma were married in 1902. He was 42 at the time and she was just 23. Alma also fell in love with the architect of the Vienna Secession building, Joseph Maria Olbrich. This was the temple at which the secession worshipped their cult of spring and artistic innovation, duly inscribed with the motto "Ver Sacrum" (Sacred Spring).

Not everyone understood Klimt's frieze, however. On the narrow wall of the frieze, which Klimt entitled "The Hostile Powers," a kind of secessionist King Kong is surrounded by his Gorgon daughters, along with personifications of Sickness, Mania, Death, Debauchery, Unchastity, Excess and Corroding Grief. Together, these so-called Hostile Powers form an allusion to a program note written by Richard Wagner for a performance of Beethoven's Ninth Symphony, which he conducted in 1846. In this note, Wagner attempted to explanation the meaning of the symphony, suggesting that it represented "a titanic struggle of the soul, athirst for Joy, against the veto of that hostile power which rears itself 'twixt us and earthly happiness."[38] (This is presumably the passage that Nietzsche was thinking of when he wrote of "hostile barriers" in *The Birth of Tragedy*.) In response to Wagner's description of "our restless quest of happiness and noble Joy,"[39] Klimt accordingly entitled the first long wall of his frieze as "The Yearning for Happiness Finds Fulfillment in Poetry," adding, "It is the arts which lead us into the kingdom of the Ideal, where alone we can find pure joy, pure happiness and pure love." All this, it has to be said, is rather more Wagnerian than Beethovenian, and the almost horror film imagery of the frieze certainly seems to reflect Wagner's belief that without art and love, life would be an unendurable nightmare. Klimt ultimately changed the title of "A Kiss for the Whole World" (the third panel) to "My Kingdom Is Not of This World," which derives from lines intended for Jesus in Wagner's poetic draft for his abandoned *Jesus of Nazareth* project: "My kingdom is not of this world: I strive against no man, since I fight for all."[40] Klimt's frieze is therefore as much a response to Wagner's ideas as it is about Schiller and Beethoven.

In the panel "The Yearning for Happiness Finds Fulfillment in Poetry" humanity is represented by three figures who are beseeching a knight in golden armor, armed with a sword, to come to their aid. Klimt dubbed this golden knight "The Well-Armed Strong One," and explained that the figures standing behind him represent Compassion and Ambition, who are urging the knight to go forth on his artistic quest. One might expect to find the features of Beethoven here, but the face in fact looks much more like that of Mahler—surely a deliberate likeness. Without Alma, Mahler might never have got to know any of the secessionist painters or taken any interest in their work. He had once stated that musicians have little interest in the plastic arts, but he had his eyes opened by the Secession, and it was all really thanks to Alma and her circle of artistic acquaintances. Arch-Wagnerian that he was, Mahler would have enthusiastically gone along with this interpretation of the "Ode to Joy," but he might also have brought to it the Nietzschean/Dionysian elements that Nietzsche himself derived from Wagner's essay.

4

The Case of Wagner

The overwhelming power of Wagner's music was one of the reasons why Nietzsche felt so ambivalent about it. So powerful a phenomenon, so all-encompassing in its effect, which indeed seemed to explain the world (giving, the visible world a voice and the audible world a form), seemed, like any drug, potentially addictive and even destructive. Many famous composers had felt the same. Debussy (1862–1918), for one, wrestled with the power of "old Klingsor," as he liked to call Wagner. Nietzsche called Wagner "a Cagliostro of music,"[1] who had made it so difficult for anyone who followed in his path to say anything original—at least in the idiom of late German Romanticism, which was why Arnold Schoenberg (1874–1951), arch-Wagnerian that he was, invented his new serial system of composition. To his mind, Wagner had exhausted the expressive possibilities of conventional tonality, and anything Schoenberg attempted in this style would merely be a less successful imitation. Critics of the time somewhat ironically agreed, suggesting that Schoenberg's earlier post-Wagnerian *Verklärte Nacht* (1899) "sounds as if an orchestra playing Wagner's *Tristan and Isolde* had become confused and mixed up."[2] As Robin Holloway pointed out in his book on Debussy and Wagner, the French Wagnerian composer Emmanuel Chabrier (1841–1894) agreed: "When a genius as powerful, as dominating as Richard Wagner appears in the world, he gives off so much splendour that after him there follows a kind of darkness … hence general uncertainty, gropings, attempts in all directions to try to escape from the crushing glory which seems to obstruct every road."[3]

Wagner's music significantly motivated Debussy's experiments with whole-tone scales, oriental timbres, and ethereal orchestral textures, in an attempt to find his own voice; but through it all, he remained in thrall to Wagner's muse. From his early choral work, *La damoiselle élue* (1888) to his choreographic masterpiece *Jeux* in 1913), Wagner's *Parsifal*, which

Debussy magnificently described as "one of the loveliest monuments of sound ever raised to to the serene glory of music,"[4] is always there. Elements of *Parsifal* float in the earlier work. The waltz rhythms of the *Parsifal* flower-maidens pervade the latter, and when Richard Strauss first heard Debussy's only completed opera *Pelléas et Mélisande* (1902) he observed "it's just *Parsifal*."[5] It is as if Debussy had poured all of Wagner's perfumes into a different atomizers and diffused them throughout his own scores. The same problem occurs, as we shall see, in the music of Frederick Delius (1862–1934), who was simultaneously overwhelmed by Nietzsche's philosophy. Rimsky-Korsakov (1844–1908) and Sibelius (1865–1957) tried to distance themselves from Wagner, but similarly could not help but be influenced by his music. Rimsky's opera *The Legend of the Invisible City of Kitezh* (1905) and Sibelius' "Swan of Tuonela" (1895) respectively echo the *Parsifal* bells and the melancholy cor anglais of *Tristan*'s third act.

Der Meister: Richard Wagner (1813–1883). Photograph by Pierre Petit, Paris, 1861 (Wikimedia Commons).

It is impossible to over-estimate Wagner's impact on late nineteenth-century and early twentieth-century music; but Nietzsche's influence on composers has been just as intense if less all-pervasive, and that influence stems not only from the philosopher's profoundly musical personality but also from his obsession with Wagner's music. Nietzsche's writings are peppered with references and allusions to Wagner, along with some of the world's most eloquent descriptions of the nature and effect of the music itself; but if Nietzsche liked to think of himself as the most musical of all philosophers, he was not the first to use music as a tool of philosophy. Schopenhauer, whom Nietzsche both revered and attacked as he revered and attacked Wagner, was also musical. He played the flute, rather than the piano, and had much to say about the nature of music, which in turn profoundly influenced Wagner. As I briefly mentioned earlier, music served Schopenhauer well as a metaphor of the human condition:

> Melody is always a deviation from the keynote through a thousand crotchety wanderings up to the most painful discord. After this, it at last finds the keynote again, which expresses the satisfaction and composure of the will, but with which nothing more can then be done, and the continuation of which would be only a wearisome and meaningless monotony corresponding to boredom.
> All that these remarks are intending to make clear, [… is] the impossibility of attaining lasting satisfaction and the negative nature of all happiness.[6]

But Schopenhauer's main impact on Wagner was his belief that music was the most important of the arts. This, as we have seen, was because he believed music to be the only art form that is capable of expressing the Will that lies beyond the mere representation of the world—the noumen beyond the phenomenon. For Schopenhauer, music "is by no means like the other arts namely a copy of the Ideas, but a *copy of the will itself*, the objectivity of which are the Ideas. For this reason the effect of music is so very much more powerful and penetrating that is that of the other arts, for these others speak only of the shadow, but music of the essence."[7] For this reason, Wagner's approach to his music-drama changed quite significantly after he had read Schopenhauer's magnum opus. Wagner's earlier theories demanded equality of expression between words and music; but as his compositional self-confidence grew and Schopenhauer began to dominate his intellectual horizon, Wagner began to place more and more emphasis on music. (Nietzsche, however, later dismissed Schopenhauer's mystical interpretation of music: "No music is in itself deep and full of meaning. It does not speak of the 'will' or the 'thing in itself.' The intellect itself has *projected* this meaning into the sound, as it has also read into the relationship of lines and masses in architecture a meaning that is, however, actually quite foreign to mechanical laws."[8] Thanks to Schopenhauer, Nietzsche felt that Wagner had become "an oracle, a priest, even more than a priest, a sort of spokesman of the 'in itself' of things, a telephone of the beyond—from that time on he ceased to talk just music, this divine ventriloquist—he talked metaphysics: is it any wonder that one day he finally talked *ascetic ideals*?"[9]

Schopenhauer also encouraged Wagner's abandonment of his earlier anarchist ideals of joy, love and freedom, with which Nietzsche so identified, and replaced them with a more pessimistic program of salvation through annihilation: Tristan and Isolde consummate their love in death;

Brünnhilde sets the world on fire; Kundry, in *Parsifal*, "falls lifeless to the ground" at the end of the opera—even Wagner, as Cosima's diaries continually reiterate, longed for death. All this disappointed Nietzsche:

> Half his life, Wagner believed in the Revolution as much as ever a Frenchman believed in it. He searched for it in the runic writing of myth, he believed that in Siegfried he had found a typical revolutionary.
>
> "Whence comes all misfortune in the world?" Wagner asked himself. From "old contracts," he answered, like all revolutionary ideologists.
>
> Siegfried continues as he has begun: he merely follows his first impulse, he overthrows everything traditional, all reverence, all *fear*.
>
> For a long time, Wagner's ship followed *this* course gaily.... What happened? A misfortune. The ship struck a reef; Wagner was stuck. The reef was Schopenhauer's philosophy; Wagner was stranded on a *contrary* world view. What had he transposed into music? Optimism. Wagner was ashamed.
>
> So he translated the *Ring* into Schopenhauer's terms. Everything goes wrong, everything perishes, the new world is as bad as the old: the *nothing*, the Indian Circe beckons.[10]

Philosopher of Pessimism: **Arthur Schopenhauer (1788–1860). Engraving by Martin Moritz Lämmel, Leipzig, 1890 (Ontologistics).**

Critical though Nietzsche was of Wagner's change of direction and its betrayal of life-enhancing optimism, he never ceased to be astounded by Wagner's ability to express psychological realities; and Nietzsche was himself as much of a psychologist as a philosopher. Without calling Wagner by name, he obviously meant Wagner in this passage from *The Gay Science*:

Here is a musician who, more than any other musician, is master at finding the tones from the realm of suffering, dejected, tormented souls and at giving speech even to the mute animals. Nobody equals him at the colours of late autumn, at the indescribably moving happiness of a last, very last, very briefest enjoyment; he knows a tone for those secret, uncanny midnights of the soul, where cause and effect seem to have gone awry and something can come to be "from nothing" at any moment; more happily than anyone else, he draws from the very bottom of human happiness and so to speak from its drained cup, where the most bitter and repulsive drops have merged, for better of for worse, with the sweetest ones; he knows how the soul wearily drags itself along when it can no longer leap and fly, nor even walk; he has the shy glance of concealed pain, of understanding without solace, of taking farewell without confession; yes, as the Orpheus of all secret misery he is greater than anyone, and he has incorporated into art some things that seemed inexpressible and even unworthy of art, and which could only be scared away and not be grasped by words in particular—some very small and microscopic features of the soul: yes he is a master of the very small. But he doesn't *want* to be! His *character* likes great walls and bold frescoes much better![11]

This observation, later reiterated, that Wagner was a master *miniaturist*, is true, despite the vast orchestrations and mythic grandeur. Two or three bars of *Parsifal* can indeed provide a fascinating evening's study, extracting, as they do, the psychological essence of the words they set in a way that few other composers can match. Kundry's disjointed ejaculation at the beginning of Act II, provides us with an excellent example: "Tiefe Nacht ... Wahnsinn ... Oh!—Wuth ... Ach! Jammer! Schlaf ... Schlaf ... tiefer Schlaf ... Tod!" ("Gloomy night—Frenzy—Oh! Rage—Ah! Wailing! Sleep ... sleep ... deeper sleep ... death!") Not only is this a new approach to operatic dialogue, its disjointed, psychologically condensed style brilliantly expressive of Kundry's schizophrenic somnambulist condition, but Wagner also accompanies these words with equally schizophrenic harmonic effects: unrelated chords, chromatically altered chords, unexpected modulations and wide vocal intervals.

Nietzsche fully recognized the power of Wagner's music for *Parsifal*. Of the *Parsifal* prelude, he observed "on purely aesthetic grounds has Wagner ever done anything better? This music reveals the very highest psychological consciousness.... I wonder whether any painter has ever depicted such a sad look of love as Wagner has given us in the last accents of his overture."[12]

The Prelude announces Wagner's complex, highly perfumed conflation of the medieval poem of Wolfram von Eschenbach, Buddhism, Schopenhauer, Meyerbeer, the racist writings of Count Arthur Gobineau, and memories of a Good Friday morning in the refuge provided for him many years earlier by the industrialist Otto Wesendonck, whose wife Wagner seduced—a morning of such transcendent beauty that it later inspired

Parsifal's transcendent "Good Friday Spell." Wagner also employed another memory of the Dresden Amen cadence he had heard in the Frauenkirche of that baroque Saxon city, long before the high explosives of the Second World War shattered it to rubble. In *Parsifal* it becomes the leitmotif of "the Grail." It had previously been used by Mendelssohn in his otherwise rather perfunctory "Reformation" symphony of 1830, and in retrospect it now stands out in that work almost as though in the beam of a searchlight. Consequently it seems somehow out of place, *Parsifal* having so completely claimed it. (It is also supremely ironic to modern ears, given the terrible destiny of the Jewish Mendelssohn's music and reputation in Wagner-loving Nazi Germany.) Nietzsche, like so many other decadents (Proust, Debussy, Delius, D'Annunzio) never fully escaped from the magic of the *Parsifal* prelude with its rising, syncopated theme: A flat, C, E flat, then the added sixth: that infinitely sorrowful, sad smile of soaring strings, shimmering like the haze over a lonely sea, which Wagner labeled "Love-Feast." This is followed by "the Grail," as discussed. "Faith" then takes over: a simple scale—three notes, growing through augmentation till, *fortissimo*, mere Faith seems, rather, Certainty; but then a tremolo slips onto an F, and over it comes "Love"—now troubled. The semitone fall, symbolic of man's sin, is emphasized with harsh *sforzandi*, drifting through a perfumed and chromatic cloud. It writhes and twists through swirling fogs of doubt, a yellow haze of guilt and pain; but out of sin it flows ethereal and *pianissimo*, to end upon an unresolved, soft dominant—the seventh lingering like a prayer.

The somewhat D'Annunzian style of my description here is appropriate, for Nietzsche recognized that he was himself a decadent and responded to the music as a decadent. We have already encountered his conviction that "the world is poor for him who has never been sick enough for this 'voluptuousness of hell,'" but crucially, he added the clarification that "I am strong enough to turn even the most questionable and most perilous things to my own advantage and thus to become stronger."[13] Nietzsche aimed to cure himself of his own decadence, along with that of the whole of Europe. "I am a *décadent*," he confessed in *Ecce Homo*, adding, "I am also its antithesis. My proof of this is, among other things, that in combating my sick conditions I always instinctively chose the *right* means: while the *décadent* as such always chooses the means harmful to him."[14]

So, though Nietzsche may have disagreed with what Wagner stood for philosophically, he never failed to acknowledge the psychological profundity of his music—not to mention its overwhelming sublimity. "My objections to Wagner's music," he clarified, "are physiological objects: why

4. The Case of Wagner

A nineteenth-century postcard of Wagner's *Parsifal* (author's collection).

disguise them with aesthetic formulas? My 'fact' is that I stop breathing easily once this music starts affecting me; that my *foot* immediately gets angry at it and revolts—it has need for tempo, dance, march; it demands chiefly from music the raptures found in *good* walking, striding, leaping, and dancing."[15]

Psychological profundity and sublimity were acceptable, but Wagner's art was, according to Nietzsche, fundamentally pessimistic, "Romantic" and therefore dangerous. Being a Wagnerite was, Nietzsche confessed, "an extremely dangerous experiment, and now I know I have not been ruined by it I also realize what it has meant for me—it was the severest test of character I could have had."[16]

> There are two types of sufferers: first, those who suffer from a *superabundance of life*—and they want a Dionysian art as well as a tragic outlook and insight into life; then, those who suffer from an *impoverishment of life* and seek quiet, stillness, calm seas, redemption from themselves through art and insight, or else intoxication, paroxysm, numbness, madness. All romanticism in art and in knowledge fits the dual needs of the latter type, as did (and do) Schopenhauer and Richard Wagner, to name the most famous and prominent romantics that I *misunderstood* at the time.[17]

Thus it was possible for Nietzsche to love but simultaneously to criticize Wagner's music. One of his most perceptive descriptions of Wagner's music combines profound admiration with perceptive censure:

> Richard Wagner's overture to the *Meistersinger:* it is a magnificent, overladen, heavy and late art which has the pride to presuppose for its understanding that two centuries of music are still living.... What forces and juices, what seasons and zones are not mixed together here! Now it seems archaic, now strange, acid and too young, it is as arbitrary as it is pompous-traditional, it is not infrequently puckish, still more often rough and uncouth—it has fire and spirit and at the same time the loose yellow skin of fruits which ripen too late. It flows broad and full: and suddenly a moment of inexplicable hesitation, as it were a gap between cause and effect, an oppression producing dreams, almost a nightmare—but already the old stream of well-being, of happiness old and new, *very* much including the happiness of the artist himself, which he had no desire to conceal, his happy, astonished knowledge of the masterliness of the means he is here employing, new, newly acquired, untried artistic means, as his art seems to betray to us. All in all, no beauty, nothing of the south or of subtle southerly brightness of sky, nothing of gracefulness, no dance.[18]

Like Goethe before him, and the Swiss symbolist artist Arnold Böcklin (1821–1901), Nietzsche craved the south as a cure for German solemnity, gravitas and pessimism. He craved the company of "some one who can laugh with me and who has cheerful spirits."[19]

> I shall say another word for the most select ears: what I really want from music. That it is cheerful and profound, like an afternoon in October.... I myself am still sufficient of a Pole to exchange the rest of music for Chopin; for three reasons I exclude Wagner's Siegfried Idyll, perhaps also a few things by Liszt, who excels all other musicians in the

nobility of his orchestral tone; finally all that has grown up beyond the Alps—*this side* ... I would not know how to get on without Rossini.... And when I say beyond the Alps I am really saying only Venice. When I seek another word for music I never find any other word than Venice.[20]

But, of course, the flight into Italy never really banished Nietzsche's emotional bond with Wagner's music and the ideals he thought he had once shared with him. Or, to put it another way, as he did at the end of his own career:

A psychologist might add that what I in my youthful years heard in Wagnerian music had nothing at all to do with Wagner; that when I described Dionysian music I described *that* which *I* heard—that I had instinctively to translate and transfigure into the latest idiom all I bore within me. The proof of this, *as strong a proof as can be*, is my essay "Wagner in Bayreuth": in all the psychologically decisive passages I am the only person referred to—one may ruthlessly insert my name or the word "Zarathustra" wherever the text gives the word Wagner.[21]

This is disingenuous to say the least, and masks a disappointment with Wagner as a human being, rather than a misunderstanding of what Wagner wrote. Nietzsche took exception to the nationalistic element in Wagner's redemptive ideals, placing himself firmly in the position of "good European" rather than nationalistic German. To his mother and sister, he confided his concern that the Franco-Prussian War was hardly a step in the right direction: "I am gradually losing all sympathy for Germany's present war of conquest. The future of German culture seems to me now more in danger than it ever was."[22] Nietzsche knew all about the horrors of war, having served as an ambulance orderly amid the carnage, filth and disease. To his mother in August 1870 he had written of "the terribly devastated battlefield, strewn with countless sad remains and smelling strongly of corpses."[23] So, when he employs his characteristic military vocabulary, it should not necessarily be interpreted as bloodthirsty, but rather as metaphoric of the intellectual war he is waging against bad ideas. He speaks of how "a great opportunity was lost of making a truly German Educational Institute for the regeneration of the German Spirit and for the total extermination of what has hitherto been called 'culture.' War to the knife! or, rather, to the cannon!" For "present day Germany," he wrote in 1887, "I no longer have any respect. It represents the stupidest, most depraved and most mendacious form of the German spirit that has ever existed," so different from "the different things we have in mind" in his new location in in sunny Italy."[24]

After Wagner's "mortal insult," which made Nietzsche's onanism semi-public property—not to mention the further implication of homosexuality—Nietzsche could no longer endure to recognize a kinship with

Wagner. He now reserved the term "Dionysian" for himself alone. Having recognized himself as a decadent, woefully prone to the Wagnerian disease ("Is Wagner a human being at all? Isn't he rather a sickness? He makes sick whatever he touches—*he has made music sick*"[25]), Nietzsche now attempted to cure himself and the rest of Europe of the monomania of *Wagneritis*. The infection was deadly precisely because it was so seductively beautiful. Indeed, the imagery of the vampire becomes almost inevitable. It was not only that Nietzsche's nightmares transformed Wagner into a vampire, like the one in Herzog's *Nosferatu*; Nietzsche also railed that there was "too much blood" in *Parsifal*, "especially at the Last Supper, which was far too full-blooded for my taste."[26] *Parsifal* is irresistibly seductive like an operatic vampire, and the vampire women in Bram Stoker's *Dracula* (1897), are, in effect, a Gothic variant of Wagner's super-seductive flower maidens. Stoker's hapless hero, Jonathan Harker, quivers in anticipation as "the skin of my throat began to tingle as one's flesh does when the hand that is to tickle it approaches nearer—nearer. I could feel the soft, shivering touch of the lips on the supersensitive skin of my throat, and the hard dents of two sharp teeth, just touching and pausing there. I closed my eyes in a languorous ecstasy and waited—waited with beating heart."[27] Stoker's soft-porn style, with its distinctly decadent longing for what is unhealthy, is also matched by Parsifal's lines in his dialogue with Kundry in Act II:

> die Lippe, ja so zuchte sie ihm,
>   so neigte sich der Nacken,
>   so hob sich kühn das Haupt;
>   so flatterten lachend die Locken,
>   so schlang um den Hals sich der Arm—
>   so schmeichelte weich die Wange;
> mit aller Schmerzen Qual im Bunde,
>   das Heil der Seele
> entküsste ihm der Mund!
>   Ha! diese Kuss![28]

> (These lips too, yes they tempted him, thus she bent her neck toward him, thus boldly rose her neck toward him, thus boldly rose her head, thus fluttered her tresses around him, thus she twined her arms round his neck—so tenderly caressing his cheek; with all the powers of pain united, her lips once kissed away his soul's salvation! Ha!—that kiss!)

Nietzsche laughs off Kundry ("I can't abide hysterical females"), but takes the intoxicating perfume of the work as seriously as Van Helsing takes the cult of vampirism: "as for the situations and their succession—are they not in the highest sense poetical? Do they not constitute a last challenge to music?"[29]

Languishing like one of Dracula's victims, Nietzsche's outrage at Wagner's treatment of him grew into an epic conflict between good and evil, despite the philosopher's aim to move beyond such distinctions. Like Lucy Holmwood in Hammer's 1958 film adaptation of *Dracula* (dir. Terence Fisher), Nietzsche guiltily lay down on his bed and adjusted his negligée, trembling with erotic ecstasy whenever he heard Wagner's music, while simultaneously waving a crucifix at it, despite his increasingly obsessional hatred of Christianity. Indeed, one might compare Nietzsche's tirades against Christianity with Wagner's antisemitism. As Nietzsche knew well, Wagner feared that he might have been a Jew himself—the illegitimate product of a liaison between his mother and a Jewish actor called Ludwig Geyer. To silence these fears, Wagner's antisemitism reached hysterical proportions. Similarly, Nietzsche's translator, R. J. Hollingdale, suggests that Nietzsche's anti–Christian philosophy is really a kind of mirror image of the faith in which he was brought up. (His father was a Lutheran pastor.) Nietzsche's concept of *Amor fati*, or the love of one's own fate, thus equates to the very similar Lutheran sin of hating life. Nietzsche's concept of eternal recurrence and the supreme affirmation of life, is paralleled by Christianity's belief in eternal life. "Will to Power" equates with the Christian command: "Thy will be done," "power" substituting God's glory. Nietzsche's famous phrase "Live dangerously!" is Nietzsche's version of Christ's command to "take up thy Cross, and follow me." Even the Superman is a kind of God: "What the Christian says of God, Nietzsche says in very nearly the same words of the Superman, namely: 'Thine is the kingdom, and the power, and the glory, for ever and ever.'"[30]

The connection between Nietzsche, Wagner and vampirism exists on an even more intimate level with regard to that letter Wagner wrote to Nietzsche's doctor. Wagner, like many "Victorians" equated masturbation with degeneracy. His letter to Nietzsche's doctor makes this quite plain: "I have been thinking for some time of identical and very similar experiences which I recall having had with certain young men of great intellectual ability. I saw them being destroyed by similar symptoms, and discovered only too clearly that these symptoms were the result of masturbation."[31] Similarly, Stoker's description of Count Dracula is one of a blood-gorged vampire, metaphoric of an onanist's penile tumescence: "There lay the Count.... Even the deep, burning eyes seemed set amongst swollen flesh, for the lids and pouches underneath were bloated. It seemed as if the whole awful creature were simply gorged with blood; he lay like a filthy leech, exhausted with his repletion."[32]

And it is significant that Wagner made Hagen, the villain of *Götterdämmerung*, exhausted and pale, depressed, enervated, prematurely aged and worn out. As Marc A. Weiner explains, "For Wagner, and for his contemporary culture, masturbation was the terrible, reprehensible sexual activity of the Outsider par excellence, for not only was it an act deemed morally indefensible but one that purportedly led to severe physiological degeneration resulting in the emergence of distinctive corporeal features connoting degeneration that may be discerned in Hagen."[33] Hagen, we must remember, is the illegitimate offspring of a Teutonic woman and the evil dwarf Alberich, the villain of the *Ring* cycle as a whole, whom many commentators (including Gustav Mahler) have interpreted as a Jewish caricature. Wagner believed that the intermarriage between Jews and Gentiles resulted in the degeneration of the "more noble" Gentile blood, and Weiner points out that the result of this apparent degeneration can be found in the Hagen's physical attributes: His blood is cold, "different from both that of Siegfried and his own half-brother, Gunther.... The textual description of Hagen's anemia is reinforced by the halting, sputtering, increasingly slow rhythmic pulse and sparse instrumentation employed [in the oath of bloodbrotherhood scene]."[34] Stoker's Dracula also has cold hands "more like the hand of a dead than a living man,"[35] and gives the general impression of "extraordinary pallor.... Strange to say, there were hairs in the centre of the palm," and the backs of his hands were "rather white and fine."[36]

Leonard Wolf, in his annotations to Stoker's text, wonders "whether Stoker knew the American boy's entrapment game in which one boy says, 'if you masturbate, you'll grow hair on your palms,' and watches to see which of his listeners looks guiltily down at his hands."[37] Wolf adds a quotation from William Acton's *Functions and Disorders of the Reproductive Organs* (1857):

> However young children may be, they become thin, pale and irritable, and their features assume a haggard appearance. We notice the sunken eye, the long, cadaverous-looking countenance, the downcast look which seems to arise from a consciousness in the boy that his habits are suspected, and at a later period, from the ascertained fact that his virility is lost.... Habitual masturbators have a dank, cold hand, very characteristic of vital exhaustion; their sleep is short, and most complete marasmus [wasting of the body] comes on; they may gradually waste away if the evil passion is not got the better of, nervous exhaustion sets in, such as spasmodic contract, or partial or entire convulsive movements, together with epilepsy, eclampsy, and a species of paralysis accompanied with contraction of the limbs.[38]

Nietzsche, who loathed antisemitism, knew what Wagner's Hagen and Alberich implied. (His sister was a particularly vigorous adherent of Wagner's racial creed, even to the extent of following her own husband to Paraguay to set up a pure-blooded community free of Jewish blood. Nietzsche consequently nicknamed her "Llama.") Coupled with the "mortal insult," Wagner's antisemitic Christian imagery in *Parsifal* with its hypocritical advocacy of celibacy, caused Nietzsche almost spontaneously to combust with indignation. To defuse the dynamite in his soul he delighted in such ironic observations such as "Parsifal is the father of Lohengrin. How did he do it?—Must one remember at this point that "chastity works *miracles*"?—*Wagnerus dixit princeps in castitate auctoritas* ("Said by Wagner, the foremost authority on chastity").[39] Behind the acid wit, however, the argument was serious: "'Parsifal' is a work of rancour, of revenge, of the most secret concoction of poisons with which to make an end of the first conditions of life, it is a bad work. The preaching of chastity remains an incitement to unnaturalness: I despise anybody who does not regard 'Parsifal' as an outrage upon morality."[40]

The music remained supreme, of course, but the message it promoted was, as Mina Harker shouts in *Dracula* when the holy wafer burns her polluted flesh, " Unclean! unclean!"[41] The decadence Nietzsche identified in *Parsifal* is all about blood—vampiric in the case of the flower maidens and Kundry with their fatal kisses, but also racial in the case of Amfortas, the wounded leader of the grail community on Montsalvat, who has been infected with a kind of mythological, semitic AIDS. His outburst in Act III is not unlike that of Mina Harker's:

> O, Strafe! Strafe ohne gleichen
> des, ach! gekränkten Gnadenreichen! ...
> des eignen sündigen Blutes Gewell,
> in wahnsinniger Flucht
> muss mir zurück dann fliessen,
> in die Welt der Sünden sucht
> mit wilder Scheu sich ergiessen.[42]
>
> (O punishment, unparalleled punishment of—ah!—the wronged Lord of Mercy!—The ebb of my own sinful blood in a mad tumult must surge back into me, to gush in wild terror into a world of sinful passion.)

Amfortas, one could say, is here suffering from the classic consequences of an attack from a vampire. Like Mina, he is also the "einz'ger Sünder unter allen"—the only sinner amongst the group opposing the forces of evil, who, again, like Mina, will be redeemed at the end of the story after the destruction of Klingsor/Dracula and the restoration of the spear/phallus into the hands of responsible members of the community who practice neither self-mutilation, self-abuse nor illicit sex. These practices were much associated with Jews in Wagner's mind. Jews were the ultimate vampires for Wagner, draining the blood of the pure race and infecting it with their own poison. *Parsifal* is awash with vampires, if not in a literal, at least in a metaphoric sense: Kundry, the arch-seductress and corrupter-through-kisses; Klingsor, the magician, who has castrated himself to gain a sinister power over others with the ultimate ambition of claiming the grail and its blood for his own nefarious purposes; the flower maidens who ensnare the hero with what that good friend of Wagner's Uncle Adolf, Ludwig Tieck, in his 1823 vampire story "Wake Not the Dead," called their "violet breath."[43] Neither should one forget that Titurel, the former grail king, is a vampire in all but name, whose undead condition is maintained by regular infusions of divine blood from grail itself. There are also zombie grail knights under the control of Klingsor. Indeed, the cast list of *Parsifal* would not be out of place in a horror film. As Thomas Mann pointed out in his essay, "The Sorrows and Grandeur of Richard Wagner":

> The cast list for *Parsifal*—what a bizarre collection at bottom! What an assemblage of extreme and repellent oddities! A sorcerer emasculated by his own hand; a desperate woman of split personality, half corrupter, half-penitent Mary Magdalene, with cataleptic transitions between these two states of being; a love-sick high priest...: together they remind one of that motley bunch of freaks packed into Achim von Armin's famous coach—the ambivalent gypsy witch, the dead layabout, the golem in female shape and the field marshall Cornelius Nepos, who is really a mandrake root grown beneath a gibbet."[44]

All in all, there are 21 specific references to bleeding and blood (divine or others) in the text of *Parsifal*, to say nothing of the frequent mention of wounds. No wonder "too much blood" was Nietzsche's comment on the new Wagnerian communion. This cornerstone of voluptuous, melancholy European decadence was everything that Nietzsche recognized in himself and the times in which he lived, and which he aimed to purge. He perceptively pointed out that the first person truly to recognize Wagner's decadence was a decadent himself—Charles Baudelaire (1821–1867). The poet's "Métamorphose du vampire" appeared in 1857 (the year in which Wagner began to compose *Tristan und Isolde* and only three years before the expanded, super-erotic and highly perfumed Venusberg scene from the revised *Tannhäuser*, which made such an impact on Baudelaire himself at its Paris première in 1861). Baudelaire's female vampire is described as possessing "a strawberry mouth,"[45] which serves a function similar to Kundry's spectacularly powerful lips.

As the century progressed, such imagery became more pronounced. Placed in their cultural-historical context, both *Dracula* and *Parsifal* inhabit a typical *fin-de-siècle* world. Robert Gutman went so far as to suggest that the temple scenes in *Parsifal* "are, in a sense, Black Masses, perverting the symbols of the Eucharist and dedicating them to a sinister god. And the Black Mass, so fascinating to *fin de siècle* decadents, was but one of their obsessions weaving its spell around the aging Wagner and his *Parsifal*."[46] Félicien Rops' frontispiece for Rodolphe Darkens' play *L'amante du Christ* (published in 1888) presents a similarly irreverent approach to the passion of Christ, making the erotic connection between blood and semen, sex, religion and death. *Parsifal* is likewise concerned with these juxtapositions, but it was not the discussion of sex that concerned Nietzsche so much as Wagner's negative attitude to it in his final work, which, like the composer's ambivalent collapse at the foot of the cross, seemed to be such a contradiction to Wagner's former life and opinions. Nietzsche considered Wagner's prurient and hypocritical censure of sexuality to be unhealthy—to say nothing of the racial undertones of a work so drenched in blood ("pure" and "contaminated" alike). Nietzsche was the first to call Wagner a *décadent*, his preferred French orthography firmly linking the composer with the literary movement Baudelaire inaugurated. For Nietzsche, the *décadent* Wagner "*est une nèvrose*": "Wagner represents a great corruption of music. He has guessed that it means to excite weary nerves—and with that he has made music sick."[47]

Nietzsche thus proposed an antidote.

5

The Antidote

Nietzsche met Wagner for the last time in Sorrento on October 27, 1876. Wagner was there on vacation, recovering from the rigors of the *Ring* cycle, which had received its première at Bayreuth a few months earlier. He took rooms of suitable splendor at the city's Hotel Vittoria, and was not a little disconcerted to find that Nietzsche was staying in "a very big high room, with a terrace outside it"[1] at the nearby Villa Rubinacci, rented by the German author and fellow Wagnerian, Malwida von Meysenbug. It overlooked Mount Vesuvius, which was highly appropriate, for Nietzsche, who would soon be preaching the value of living dangerously and building one's house on the slopes of that very volcano,[2] was also about to unleash a torrent of linguistic lava over Wagner's musical Pompeii. In self-imposed intellectual exile, he had no intention of returning to Germany. He was finished with "*German* art! The *German* master! *German* beer!"[3] Switzerland in the summer and Italy in the winter were to be the locations of his life from now on—until, that is, his final illness swept him back to the arms of his ghastly sister in Weimar.

It was highly appropriate that the former friends should meet in Sorrento, that archetypal Mediterranean resort, for Nietzsche's aim was now to Mediterraneanize music, purge it of Wagnerian fog and make it *dance*. Cosima recorded the meeting in her diary, as one would expect, but left no impression of its significance: "Nice day, bathing with the children. In the afternoon took a little walk with R. and the children, then sat for a long time with R. on our terrace and looked at the sea. After that, a visit from Malwida, Dr. Rée, and our friend Nietzsche, the latter very run down and much concerned with his health."[4] Though the Wagners were not to see Nietzsche again, his friend Paul Rée did put in another appearance a few days later, but Cosima complained that his "cold and precise character does not appeal to us, on closer inspection we come to the conclusion that he must be an Israelite."[5] And that was that. Exactly

5. The Antidote

what was spoken between Wagner and Nietzsche on that melancholy coastal walk in late October has not been recorded in detail, but as Robert Gutman explains, Wagner "suddenly began to speak of *Parsifal* in terms of his own religious experience, dumbfounding to someone well aware of the depth of his atheism.... 'Why are you so silent, my friend?' asked Wagner. The two never met again."[6] But Nietzsche should not have been so surprised by Wagner's "religiosity," as religion had played a vital role in several of his earlier works—*Tannhaüser* and *Lohengrin* particularly, and Wagner did make perfectly clear that *Parsifal* was a work *about* religion rather than a traditionally sacred piece. Nietzsche was also shocked by Wagner's flippant inscription on the copy of the libretto he sent to "his dear friend Friedrich Nietzsche, Richard Wagner, Ecclesiastical Councillor," which caused him to wonder if *Parsifal* was not intended to be taken seriously. Was it somehow offered to the public as a satyr play, in the manner of the ancient Greek festivals, which always ended on a laugh after the main meal of the tragedy: *Parsifal* as the pudding course, so to speak, after the Ring's main dish? The idea is absurd, as Wagner was quite able to use religion like any other aspect of culture, without being po-faced about it—or even personally believing in it. He did, in fact, regard himself as a kind of Aryan Christian, in which Christ was not a Jew and God did not literally exist, but that is another story. In "Religion and Art," the essay which accompanied the composition of *Parsifal*, Wagner explained: "One might say that where Religion becomes artificial, it is reserved for Art to save the spirit of religion by recognizing the figurative value of the mythic symbols which the former would have us believe in their literal sense, and revealing their deep and hidden truth through an ideal presentation."[7]

Wagner may not have held orthodox beliefs, but he regarded Christ as a redemptive figure, as he did Buddha, both of whose teachings he interpreted along Schopenhaurian lines. Nietzsche himself was an admirer of Jesus, if not of Christianity, and though disagreeing with Schopenhauer's pessimism, still regarded the philosopher's atheism as an important first step on the road to the Superman; so, once again, one suspects that it was not so much the idealogical differences that caused the break between Wagner and Nietzsche, as the clash of personalities. Nietzsche also thought he could hear the clash of something more metallic. When Wagner sent him a copy of the *Parsifal* text, it crossed in the post with Nietzsche's *Human, All Too Human*, in which the philosopher's assault on Wagnerism began in earnest. "This crossing of the two books—it seemed to me to make an ominous sound. Was it not as though two *swords* had crossed?" he reflected later in life.[8] In fact, the damage had already been done, and

Nietzsche's veritable Amfortas-wound from Wagner's "mortal insult" was never to heal. His lamentations were fully as eloquent and emotional as those of the hapless grail king. He needed a secular Parsifal to redeem him, and he hoped to find him in Italy. In fact, the redeemer came from France.

Nietzsche began his famous attack on his former idol in *The Case of Wagner* by praising, of all people, Georges Bizet (1838–1875). In his quest to Mediterraneanize music, *Carmen*, which had first appeared in 1875 one year before the première of the *Ring* cycle at Bayreuth, seemed the perfect antidote. Of course, depending on one's perspective at the time, this could have been seen as another Nietzschean irony, for Bizet was by no means an anti–Wagnerian. "Wagner is Verdi," he once said, "with the addition of style."[9] Also, Bizet was accused by French critics of imitating Wagner, whom Bizet championed even during the challenging period of the Franco-Prussian war: Wagner's music was not, according to Bizet, the music of the future but rather "the music of all time, because it is admirable."[10] *Carmen* was even considered by some French critics of being Wagnerian in its apparent surrender of the voices to the orchestra.[11]

Georges Bizet (1838–1875). Photograph by Étienne Carjat, Paris, 1876 (Wikimedia Commons).

Nietzsche's tongue was no doubt somewhat in his cheek when he pronounced the virtues of Bizet over Wagner, but a large part of his enthusiasm was serious. In Bizet's opera, instead of drowning in Wagner's addictive and decadent music-dramas, he could find his way back to musical health, for, according to his analysis, Bizet's music knew how to *dance*. A sense of rhythm was of supreme importance to Nietzsche, and he devoted several pages to the subject in *The Gay Science*. In the ancient world, Nietzsche argued, rhythm "was supposed to make a human request impress the gods more deeply after it was noticed that humans remember a verse better than ordinary speech.... Above all, one wanted to take advantage of that elemental over-powering force that humans experience in themselves when listening to music: rhythm is a compulsion; it engenders an unconquerable desire to yield, to join in; not only the stride of the feet but also the soul itself gives in to the beat."[12] According to Nietzsche's interpretation, rhythm was the most useful thing in the world: it could work magically, invoke gods, purge emotions and even had the ability to transform an ordinary human being into a god himself. Apparently, we still feel that a thought is truer "when it has a metric form and presents itself with a divine hop, skip, and jump."[13] Rhythm was therefore preeminent among Nietzsche's demands of music, and, his observations here constitute a prophecy of commercial pop music, in which reassuringly diatonic melody and infectious rhythm are united to usually optimistic effect; but this is somewhat leaping ahead of our theme.

Nietzsche is more specific in the final aphorism of *The Gay Science*, in which he contrasts Wagnerian solemnity with a more plebeian idiom: "even plain, rustic bagpipes would be better than the mysterious sounds, such bog-cries, voices from the crypt, and marmot whistles with which you have so far regaled us in your wilderness, my Mr Hermit and Musician of the Future! No!" he continues, this time paraphrasing Schiller's "Ode to Joy," "Not such sounds! Let us rather strike up more pleasant, more joyous tones!"[14] The vulgar element in music, which Nietzsche acknowledges in Italian opera, did not offend him "because there is no shame.... Bad taste has its right just as good taste does—and even a prior right if it answers to a great need...; good taste ... is not and never was popular!... So let them all continue to go their way, all those masklike elements in the melodies and cadenzas, in the leaps and gaieties of the rhythm of these operas!"[15]

Rhythm promotes dance, and the joyful, life-enhancing consequences of dance are everywhere to be seen in Nietzsche's writings, particularly in *Zarathustra*, where Zarathustra comes upon a group of maidens dancing in a meadow. The passage is entitled "The Dance Song," later described as "a mocking-song on the Spirit of Gravity":

> Do not cease your dance, sweet girls! No spoil-sport has come to you with an evil eye, no enemy of girls.
> I am God's advocate with the Devil; he, however, is the Spirit of Gravity. How could I be enemy to divine dancing, your nimble creatures? or to girls' feet with fair ankles?[16]

Nietzsche as the prophet of disco? Perhaps even of the "ecstasy"-fueled rave scene? We shall see. For now, Nietzsche combined dance and ecstasy in Sicily, whither he journeyed perhaps to enjoy the cavortings of naked young fishermen. Like gods, these youths, "dancing, are ashamed of all clothes."[17] In his exposé of Nietzsche's homosexual subtext, Joachim Köhler observes that the photographs of naked Sicilian boys photographed by the homosexual Wilhelm von Gloeden (1856–1931), which Nietzsche much admired, are often shown dancing. They were "raised by Nietzsche to the heroic status of gods who spurn all clothes and are often said to congregate on the slopes of Monte Ziretto at night to celebrate Bacchanalian rites." Köhler also records that when the philosopher's mind finally disintegrated, his landlady observed her tenant, through the keyhole of his bedroom door, singing and "capering around in the nude."[18]

Was Nietzsche singing the "Ride of the Valkyries" or the "Toreador's Song" from *Carmen*? Perhaps snatches of both, but, as we have seen, he accused Wagner's music of having nothing of the dance about it. There are rhythms aplenty in Wagner's oeuvre, of course (think of the exciting prelude to Act II of *Die Walküre* not to mention the Dance of the Apprentices in *Die Meistersinger*), but once Wagner had become a symbol of what was wrong, Nietzsche regarded Wagner's music as a form of "paralysis, arduousness, torpidity"[19]—in other words "decadent," "full of glances, tendernesses, and comforting words in which nobody has anticipated him, the master in tones of a heavy-hearted and drowsy happiness"[20]—but quite the opposite of "the apotheosis of the dance," which, ironically, was how Wagner had described the finale of Beethoven's Seventh Symphony (while choreographically interpreting—fully clothed—Liszt's rendition on the piano. One laments that home movies did not exist at the time).

However, *Carmen* undeniably overflows with dance rhythms: march, habanera, séguedille, tarantella, to name but four. Despite its Spanish sunshine, Nietzsche insists, *Carmen* "does not *sweat*. 'What is good is light; whatever is divine moves on tender feet': first principle of my aesthetics." Nietzsche also found the traditional "number-opera" approach of Bizet healthier than Wagner's "infinite melody." Bizet achieves all this "without grimaces. Without counterfeit. Without the *lie* of the great style." He believed he "became a better human being when this Bizet speaks to me."[21] Nietzsche also found time to praise the prose style of the author on whose story the opera is based. In *The Gay Science*, Nietzsche placed Prosper Mérimée in the company of the Italian lyric poet Giacomo Leopardi (1798–1837), the American "Transcendendalist" Ralph Waldo Emerson (1803–1882) and the Englishman Walter Savage Landor as "masters of prose."[22] Together, Mérimée and Bizet formed a powerful compound with which to blow up Wagner: "It looks as if the French were on the road to better

5. The Antidote

things in dramatic music," he exclaimed ecstatically to Peter Gast, "and they are far ahead of the Germans in one important point; passion with them is not such a very far-fetched affair (as all passion is in Wagner's works)."[23] Nietzsche kept going to performances of *Carmen*. He caught one in Genoa in March 1883 and confessed that "when this music is played some very deep stratum seems to be stirred in me, and while listening to it I always feel resolved to hold out to the end and to unburden my heart of its supremest malice rather than perish beneath the weight of my thoughts."[24] And Nietzsche much enjoyed hearing music in his new surroundings: "I have just returned from a big concert which really produced upon me the *strongest* impression I have ever experienced at a concert in my whole life,"[25] he wrote from Turin. Among works by Beethoven, Schubert, Bizet and Liszt he praised the Hungarian composer Karl Goldmark's overture to *Sakuntala*, an opera based on the Indian epic *Mahabharata*, as "a thousand times better than anything of Wagner's,"[26] which rather puts one in mind of Tchaikovsky's remark that Delibes' *Sylvia* was a thousand times dearer to him than the *Ring* cycle.[27] For Nietzsche, Turin was, musically speaking, "the soundest city I know"[28]—no doubt because not a note of his loathed yet still-beloved Wagner was played at the concert.

Despite all these other musical enthusiasms, Bizet remained Nietzsche's totem pole for the new esthetics around which his Superman would dance. It became all the more appropriate when, to his delight, he learned that Wagner hated Bizet's music: "Gersdorff saw Wagner in a transport of rage against Bizet, when Minnie Hauck [sic] was in Naples and sang *Carmen*. In view of the fact that Wagner has taken sides in the matter, too, my malice in a certain important passage [of *The Case of Wagner*] will be felt all the more keenly."[29] Ironically, the American singer, whose name is properly spelt "Hauk" was the last person to occupy Haus Tribschen before it was bought by the city of Lucerne and turned into a museum in 1931. Hauk visited Wagner when he was on vacation in Naples in 1880. Cosima recorded that she did not displease him, "but he finds it all a burden," before adding that the Meister then talked about "adopting vegetarianism,"[30] so long after he had disparaged Nietzsche's feelings on the subject!

Nietzsche's friend, Georg Brandes, enquired if he knew Bizet's widow: "You ought to send her the brochure [*The Case of Wagner*]. It would delight her. She is the loveliest, most charming woman, with a chronic tic that, curious to say, is most becoming, but she is quite genuine, full of sincerity and fire."[31]

Meanwhile, musical life in Paris was developing a Wagner cult of its own. Ernest Chausson, Debussy, Paul Dukas, Fauré, and Vincent d'Indy were all "infected" (to use Nietzsche's metaphor), and thanks to the short-lived but influential periodical, the *Revue Wagnérienne*, which ran from 1885 to 1887, Wagnerianism in a more general sense pervaded the thinking of French writers and intellectuals. The ideal of artistic integration—that synesthetic union described by Baudelaire in his poem "Correspondences" (1857)—now became the holy grail of the symbolist generation. Catulle Mendès, who had visited Wagner at Tribschen, promoted Wagnerian theory to French artists. He prophesied "a great name" who would, like Parsifal himself, redeem French opera and rid it "of the mass of outmoded and ridiculous shackles which now hold it in thrall. He will achieve an intimate unity between poetry and music, for the sake of the drama and not for mere brilliance. The poet in him will boldly reject literary ornament, the musician all those vocal and symphonic beauties which can hinder the flow of dramatic emotion. He will reject recitatives, airs, strettos, even ensembles, unless these are demanded by the dramatic action, to which everything must be sacrificed."[32]

"Wotan puts Brünnhilde to sleep." A nineteenth-century postcard of Joseph Hoffmann's stage design for the final scene of Wagner's *Die Walküre*, sent by an enthusiastic Wagnerian by the name of Heinrich: "This was really splendid. I have quite exhausted my stock of adjectives over the Ring. We have a day off today—tomorrow Tannhauser and on Sat: Parsifal. Heinrich Aug 18 '04" (author's collection).

Had Nietzsche read this call to arms, he would not have been surprised but would nonetheless have been alarmed at so rapid a spread of the Wagnerian bacillus. Having dispensed with his former enthusiasm for Wagnerian music drama, Nietzsche now regarded Wagnerian "infinite melody" as a "polyp in music," as opposed to Bizet's approach, which he regarded as "precise. It builds, organizes, finishes."[33] In fact, Nietzsche's recantation was merely a return to former convictions that had been expressed in his early notebooks, and which cast doubt on the advisability of opera as a whole. As we have seen when discussing Beethoven, the youthful Nietzsche had doubted the ability of music to express ideas at all:

> The concept of opera demands from music not an improper use, but—as I have said—an impossibility! Music *can* never become a means to an end, however much one may squeeze, wrench and torture it: even in its rawest and simplest stages, as mere sound, as a drum roll, it overcomes poetry and reduces it to a reflection of itself.... Although music can never become a means in the service of the text and in any case overcomes the text, it certainly becomes bad music if the composer breaks every Dionysian force rising in him by an anxious glance at the words and gestures of his marionettes.[34]

Music has its own logic—and attempts to Wagnerize it therefore destroy its autonomy. However, this is not to say that music is "absolute." As Nietzsche points out, music in the ancient world was always *occasional* never absolute—it was only sounded in relation to drama or divine service.[35] Music is needed in such situations because of its idealizing power, "in which all things look transfigured."[36] But attempts to destroy its autonomy by means of "infinite melody" corrupt its Dionysian power. Hence, Bizet's "number-opera" *Carmen* is closer to the ideal of Greek Tragedy than the *Ring* cycle.

Such jottings made around the time that Nietzsche first encountered Wagner suggest that a fault line underlay their relationship even before Nietzsche had fully discovered what kind of man Wagner was. The seduction of Wagnerian sonority and Wagnerian harmony might, from the start, have been only superficial attractions. Vienna's foremost music critic, Eduard Hanslick, whom Wagner had maliciously caricatured in *Die Meistersinger von Nürnberg* as the musically uninspired (and presumably Jewish) town clerk, Sixtus Beckmesser, had put forth similar esthetic beliefs about the autonomy of music in a book entitled *On the Beautiful in Music* (1854):

> Its nature is specifically musical. By this we mean that the beautiful is not contingent upon nor in need of any subject introduced from without, but that it consists wholly of sounds artistically combined. The ingenious co-ordination of intrinsically pleasing

> sounds, their consonance and contrast, their flight and reapproach, their increasing and diminishing strength—this it is which, in free and unimpeded forms, presents itself to our mental vision.
> To the question: What is to be expressed with all this material? The answer will be: Musical ideas. Now, a musical idea reproduced in its entirety is not only an object of intrinsic beauty but also an end in itself, and not a means for representing feelings and thoughts. The essence of music is sound and motion.³⁷

In his early notebooks, Nietzsche was really only reiterating Hanslick's argument, adding his own infusion of ancient Greek principles, such as the conviction that drama and music spring from the *people*—from folk impulses, not from erudition and study.³⁸ The notebooks comment: "Absolute music and everyday drama: the two parts of musical drama torn apart"³⁹—but this does not necessarily mean that their only possible reunification must take the form of Wagnerian music drama. It seems that Nietzsche, even during this period of his thinking, already believes in the union of drama with traditionally structured music. His eventual discovery of and enthusiasm for *Carmen* suggests the fulfillment of this dream. Bizet is the antithesis of Wagner because he acknowledges those earlier convictions that "music can never become a means in the service of the text," and that if a composer "breaks every Dionysian force rising in him by an anxious glance at the words and gestures of his marionettes," the music becomes "bad music."⁴⁰ By the time of *The Gay Science*, when he was an unrepentant Wagnerian apostate, he argued that the opera texts over which Wagner took such pains, were hardly important at all. "One shouldn't believe the words of characters in opera," he claimed, "but rather their sound! That is the difference, that is the beautiful *unnaturalness* for the sake of which one goes to the opera."⁴¹

Nietzsche's disappointment with Wagner spilled over into a general disappointment with Germany as a whole—even the German language came in for blame. Nietzsche complained that German was incapable of a *presto* pace. On the contrary, German was "staid, sluggish, ponderously solemn, ... long-winded and boring."⁴² Nietzsche intended to do something about that by developing what is now generally regarded as the most elegant, witty and graceful prose style of any German author. But to do that—and to discover not only his Superman but also the music to which the Superman would dance—he had to travel south. There he would dream "of the redemption of music from the north and have in his ears the prelude to a deeper, mightier, perhaps wickeder and more mysterious music, a supra-German music which does not fade, turn yellow, turn pale at the sight of the blue voluptuous sea and the luminous sky of the Mediterranean, as all German music does." In Italy, he hoped to imagine "a music whose rarest magic would consist in this, that it no longer knew anything of good and evil."[43] Such music would make him dance, inspire laughter, enhance life and shout "Yes!" to the heavens. He might well have been disappointed by the music of those composers who were inspired by him.

6

Richard Strauss

In 1886, that very German composer, Richard Strauss (1864–1949), soon to be known as "Richard II," also went to Italy. (Wagner had, of course, been "Richard I.") He spent two months there, traveling through Bologna, Florence, Mantua, Pompeii, Rome, Naples, Pompeii—and, most significantly of all, perhaps, Sorrento, where Nietzsche and Wagner had parted company ten years earlier. When in Rome, he was guided around by Franz von Lenbach, the artist who had painted Wagner's portrait in 1872, and like Goethe, Böcklin, Wagner and Nietzsche before him, Strauss was bowled over by the country as a whole—the sunshine, the architecture and the sense of freedom. Echoing Nietzsche's sentiments, Strauss later complained to Romain Rolland that Germany, with its "horrible grey on grey [… and] phantom ideas with no sun," drained him of the ability to compose. This was actually in 1892, after a tour of Greece, Egypt and Sicily while recovering from pneumonia. Rolland, who met the composer on an icy April day in Berlin's Charlottenburg, claimed that Strauss' nostalgia for Italy "penetrated his music, in which one feels one of the most tormented souls of deep Germany and, at the same time, an unceasing yearning for the colors, the rhythms, the laughter, the joy of the South. Like the musician dreamt of by Nietzsche, it seems as if 'he must have in his ears the prelude to a deeper, mightier, and perhaps more perverse and mysterious music, a super-German music…'" and so on, quoting Nietzsche's recipe for musical heaven from *Beyond Good and Evil*, which we have already encountered. Rolland added in a footnote: "I hope I will be forgiven for annotating this essay with Nietzsche's ideas, which are constantly reflected in Strauss, and throw such sharp light on the soul of the modern German."[1]

The fruit of Strauss' first visit to Italy was his first symphonic poem, *Aus Italien* (op.16), in which he filled four conventionally constructed symphonic movements with evocations of his Italian holiday, the whole work being dedicated to his mentor, Hans von Bülow, whose piano transcription of *Tristan* had inspired Nietzsche to become a Wagnerian. The first movement summons the natural beauty of the Campagna. The second evokes the sombre majesty of Roman ruins. In the plangent third movement, "Am Strande von Sorrent," Strauss perfectly captures the melancholy beauty of the scene, which must, for so well-read a musician as he, have suggested Nietzschean associations. Flutes and clarinets open the movement with sustained chords under which harps and trilling strings soon start to cascade, imitate the surging of waves on the shore. A Wagnerian luster is suggested (but not actually attained, it has to be said), in the high tessitura of the string writing, suggestive, as it is, of the prelude to *Lohengrin*. Then, sea breezes are called to mind by more trilling flute figurations over the first appearance of the main melody in the strings, characterized by wide and plunging intervals, which were already a fingerprint of Strauss' style. Things then grow more agitated in the middle section, marked "più mosso," suggesting a slight change in the weather with a slightly more agitated mood, before returning to the opening serenity.

"Richard II": Richard Strauss (1864–1949) (Société des Auteurs Photographes, Paris). Taken from J. Cuthbert Hadden, *Modern Musicians* (London: T. N. Foulis, 1913) (Wikimedia Commons).

The finale quotes the popular song "Funiculi, funicula," which had originally been composed to celebrate the opening of a new funicular railway. Strauss' orchestra, amused by the apparent incongruity, burst out laughing when they first rehearsed the movement, but Strauss calmly responded by informing everyone that "there has never been a great artist yet, who thousands of people didn't think was mad."[2] Critics were less amused. The pianist Joseph Giehrl suspected that Strauss had been inspired by a Neapolitan cholera epidemic. In Vienna, critics argued that listening to *Aus Italien* would put anyone off from visiting the country that had inspired it. All this is quite incomprehensible now.

Strauss' finale anticipated the stupendous scherzo of the extravagantly eccentric five-movement piano concerto by Busoni, whose connection with Nietzsche I will be exploring in chapter 14. Busoni's concerto caused caused outrage at its première in 1904 due to the perceived vulgarity of the riotous Neapolitan tarantella in the fourth movement. (Here we should pause to recall what Nietzsche had to say about "vulgar" Italian music in *The Gay Science*). Headed "All' Italiana," it was labeled an "atrocity" by critics who regarded the appearance of Italian popular songs and military marches as a desecration of a hall sacred to the name of Beethoven (Berlin's Beethoven-Saal). The *Tägliche Rundschau* decried the tarantella as a musical depiction of "the orgies of absinthe-drinkers and harlots.... It was frightful," while the critic Adolf Weissmann summed up the proceedings as a whole as a "Höllenspektakel," which Busoni's biographer Edward Dent translated as "Pandemonium let loose."[3] Obviously everyone had forgotten the consternation caused by Strauss' Neapolitan finale to *Aus Italien*.

Though well-read (he worked his way through the complete works of Goethe twice), Strauss was not an intellectual, as his attempt to translate *Thus Spoke Zarathustra* into music demonstrates with both orchestral ingenuity and dubious taste. To be fair, Strauss himself confessed that he "did not intend to write philosophical music or portray Nietzsche's great work musically": "I meant rather to convey in music an idea of the human race from its origin, through the various phases of development, religious as well as scientific, up to Nietzsche's idea of the Übermensch. The whole symphonic poem is intended as my homage to the genius of Nietzsche, which found its greatest exemplification in his book *Also Sprach Zarathustra*."[4]

His translation was composed in 1896, and he wrote on the title page, "Symphonic optimism in *fin de siècle* style, dedicated to the twentieth century." Already, one detects a suitably ironic tone, which echoes Nietzsche's own approach to philosophy. Strauss' sense of humor however seems more Wagnerian. In the autograph sketch, he wrote under the final notes of the piece: "When? When? When?... Never, never, never, will the weather improve," which reminds one of Wagner's inscription of his *Parsifal* poem to Nietzsche as "Ecclesiastical Councillor." As Nietzsche was shocked by that, Strauss' flippancy might have caused him to wonder just how seriously Richard II was taking the musical transformation of his magnum opus. Nietzsche was, in fact, still alive in 1896, but hardly in a condition to know anything much about it, being, by then, quite insane.

The opening bars of Strauss' tone poem are, of course, the most famous fragment of "Nietzschean" music ever composed, thanks mainly to their appearance in Stanley Kubrick's film *2001: A Space Odyssey* (1968). Those bars are in fact a sublime evocation of the sunrise described in the opening lines of Nietzsche's book, and Kubrick sensibly used the same imagery to accompany the music in his film. The famed musical supervisor of Hammer Film Productions, Philip Martell, once told me that he was instrumental in exposing Kubrick to the repertoire pieces eventually used in the film, and Strauss' superlative musical statement was the perfect choicer the opening titles. The fact that the rest of the symphonic poem that it introduces fails to live up to the impact of these introductory bars is proved every time this section is played as a separate entity on classical music radio stations, not to mention Liberace's celebrated use of it to introduce his medley of Viennese waltzes by the other (totally unrelated) Strauss. The Brazilian composer Eumir Deodata released a funk/jazz version of the piece in 1972, which appeared in Hal Ashby's 1979 film *Being There*, starring Peter Sellers. Synthesizers accompanied the London Symphony Orchestra on Douglas Gamley's arrangement of "the theme from *2001*" for a now rather obscure LP called *Sounds Astounding* in 1974, and so famous is the segment through its adoption by popular culture that many people have no idea that it is by Richard Strauss, still less that it is based on Nietzsche's *Thus Spoke Zarathustra*. After its use as the theme tune for the BBC's coverage of the Apollo 11 Space Mission in 1969, it become all-purpose "space" music. It is indeed a quintessential main title cue, an archetypal advertising jingle, a tailor-made sci-fi convention or corporate launch event fanfare. Concise, dramatic, memorable, highly dramatic, it remains Strauss' most celebrated and performed creation, and it is therefore easy to forget what it was originally meant to suggest to the listener:

> One morning [Zarathustra] woke with the dawn, stepped before the sun, and spoke to it thus:
>> Great star! What would your happiness be, if you had not those for whom you shine!
>> You have come up here to my cave for ten years: you would have grown weary of your light and of this journey, without me, my eagle and my serpent.
>> But we waited for you every morning, took from your superfluity and blessed you for it.
>> Behold! I am weary of my wisdom, like a bee that has gathered too much honey; I need hands outstretched to take it.
>> To that end, I must descend into the depths: as you do at evening, when you go behind the sea and bring light to the underworld too, superabundant star![5]

It is often the case that the most successful musical statements are the simplest. Over the centuries a great many melodies have been generated from a simple major triad; but Strauss' big theme is no more than a rise through a fifth to the octave above the note he began with. Consequently, the impact is entirely lost when this is played on the piano (as it often was in the days before recordings). Just as Wagner made an E-flat major triad a thing of magical wonder through instrumental wizardry in the prelude to *Das Rheingold*, Strauss relies on his orchestral mastery to create something out of next-to-nothing. However, the orchestra employed is quite the opposite of nothing, involving 14 wind players, six horns, four trumpets, three trombones and four tubas, timpani, triangle, cymbals, organ and a large string section. He chooses the simplest key, C major, to begin with, and like Wagner, casts his spell by first holding the tonic note in the deep registers of his darkest instruments—in this case, contra-bassoon, organ, double bass and timpani. The main three-note theme is then announced by four trumpets, marked "feierlich," ("solemn"), which was also one of Wagner's favorite terms. The following two devastating chords drop from major to minor (the second chord flattening the E of the C major triad) and these are succeeded by portentous oscillations between C and G on the timpani. There would hardly be any point in describing all this were it not to demonstrate that this is all musical gesturing—a mere rumination on C major—raised to the level of genius by the inspired way in which Strauss orchestrates his meagre material. Its melodic and harmonic simplicity, high-impact orchestration and brevity are what recommend its use in film, advertising and corporate events. In its success as a soundbite it has left Nietzsche far behind; but that was not Strauss' intention.

The rest of the tone poem attempts to provide a musical equivalent to selected aspects of Nietzsche's main ideas. The next section is entitled "Von den Hinterweltlern"—"Of the Afterworldsmen," in which Zarathustra attempts to dispel the obfuscating mists of religious belief. Once Zarathustra cast his "deluded fancy beyond mankind, like all afterworldsmen," he realized that "this God, which I created was human work and human madness, like all gods!"[6] Appropriately, Strauss plunges us into a fumbling world of shuffling string tremolos, pizzicato gropings in the dark, and a motif resembling a Gregorian-chant scored for the horns, over which he inscribes the words "Credo in unum deum"—"Believe in one God." (The blending of a plainchant theme with a late–Romantic orchestral texture here is reminiscent of Wagner's imitation of a Lutheran chorale in the opening scene of *Die Meistersinger*.) This leads to a sugary-sweet, highly sentimental melody, introduced by the kind of muted strings that would eventually underscore Hollywood love scenes. Strauss, of course, intended to satirize the religiosity of a composer like Gounod, who famously made sanctimonious candy-floss out of Bach's first C major Prelude from the 48 Preludes and Fugues. Max Steiner accompanying Bette Davis weeping in *Now Voyager* (dir. Irving Rapper, 1942) was only a matter of time.

Cutting his way through this musical meringue comes the opening "Zarathustra" theme, and gradually the battle between them grows in intensity. "My Ego taught me a new pride," Zarathustra exclaims, "I teach it to men: No longer to bury the head in the sand of heavenly things, but to carry it freely, an earthly head which creates meaning for the earth!" Strauss, egocentric and proud atheist that he was, wholeheartedly agreed with this, and he ends the section, after much chromatic wailing from the Afterworldsmen, with a whimper rather than a bang: "Listen rather, my brothers, to the voice of the healthy body: this is a purer voice and a more honest one.... Thus spoke Zarathustra."[7]

The problem with all of this is that if one listens to the work without bothering to find out what it is meant to be describing, the cloying sentimentality of the "Afterworldsmen" theme ceases to be satirical, and becomes simply ... sentimental, and consequently, something of a musical emetic. It really is sickly sweet, and Strauss himself was well aware of it. "What suits me best, South German bourgeois that I am," he confessed, much later in life, to Stefan Zweig, "are sentimental jobs; but such bull's eyes as the *Arabella* duet and the *Rosenkavalier* trio don't happen every day. Must one become seventy years old to recognize that one's greatest strength lies in creating kitsch?"[8] (Strauss' most celebrated collaborator, Hugo von Hofmannsthal, agreed whole-heartedly, regarding the composer as "an incredibly unrefined person," with "a frightful bent towards triviality and kitsch."[9])

After the defeat of religion, Strauss now turns his attention to Zarathustra's praise of Science, wildly skipping from the third section of part one to the 16th section of part four. "Air! Let in good air!" Zarathustra commands, echoing Goethe's dying words "Light! More light!" He has just ejected the "evil old sorcerer" from his cave—in other words, old Klingsor himself, Richard Wagner, whose poetic style Nietzsche parodied in the preceding section. "You are making this cave sultry and poisonous!" "Woe to all free spirits who are not on their guard against *such* sorcerers. Their freedom is done with: you teach and lure back into prisons, you melancholy old devil, a luring bird-call sounds from your lamenting you are like those who with their praise of chastity secretly invite to voluptuousness!"[10] This is precisely what Nietzsche had against *Parsifal*. Instead of illusions, Zarathustra praises the virtues of science—all that is intellectual and courageous, "adventure and joy in the unknown, the unattempted."[11]

To suggest all this, Strauss created something truly breathtaking: Behold! the "Science Fugue," which introduces a 12-tone theme on imperious trombones, well over 20 years before Schoenberg composed his first dodecaphonic piece (in fact, the little waltz that concludes his *Five Piano Pieces*, Op. 23). But there the similarity with Schoenberg ceases, for Strauss does nothing "serial" with his theme, developing it along entirely conventional late-Romantic harmonic lines. The theme itself consists of four versions of the opening "Zarathustra" theme, which we might usefully compare to the theme that opens Liszt's 1857 *Eine Faust-Symphonie.* (Liszt's theme consists of four arpeggiated augmented triads, which also use up all 12 notes of the chromatic scale.) After everything chases its own tail ("fugue" after all means "flee" or "flight"), the main theme thunders back, echoing in musical terms Nietzsche's constant reiteration of "Thus Spoke Zarathustra!" A quieter section gradually builds up to a frenzy, with the most extraordinary orchestral effect of oscillating flutes and high pitches in all departments suggestive of Nietzsche's desire for weightlessness—his assault on gravity; and sure enough, this all leads up to the Tanzlied (Dance Song), in which such qualities are celebrated. Here, Strauss might seem to be guilty of yet another lapse in taste by using a Viennese waltz idiom to suggest Nietzsche's attack on gravity, but it is a perfectly appropriate idiom, being quintessential dance music. The melody here also has various things in common with the Dance of the Apprentices from Wagner's *Die Meistersinger.* (Most notably, both begin with a rising triplet on the upbeat.)

Those who nonetheless feel that a Viennese waltz is still inappropriate, might support their argument with Nietzsche's opinion that while it was perfectly fine for Italian music to be vulgar, the same did not apply to the German variety: "A vulgar turn in Northern works, for example in German music, on the other hand, offends me unspeakably. Here there is *shame;* the artist has lowered himself in his own eyes and could not even help blushing: we are ashamed with him and are so offended because we suspect that he believed he had to lower himself for our sakes."[12] One suspects, however, that Strauss, for whom composition came as naturally as apples from a tree, was temporarily forgetting all about Nietzsche and simply enjoying himself here; but it was this perceived kitsch element in Strauss' style that the novelist Thomas Mann couldn't abide. In his novel

Doctor Faustus, to which I will be returning in chapter 15, he attacked Strauss for turning his back on dissonances and "affronts," in favor of "appeasing the philistine and telling him no harm was meant."[13]

Having danced himself into a euphoric state of collapse, like Elektra at the end of his later opera of that name, Strauss brings his *Zarathustra* to an ecstatic if somewhat understated close by juxtaposing two contrasting keys: C-major, representing nature, and B-major representing humanity. It was at this moment that he made his comment about the weather.

Romain Rolland, who knew Strauss well, was both an admirer of and troubled by his music. He fully understood the Nietzschean ideas that underpinned much of it, and even traced Nietzsche's quest for a "supra-German" music that combined Italian and German elements in Wagner's *Tristan*: "There was already something Italian in *Tristan*; how much more there is in the work of this follower of Nietzsche [i.e., Strauss]. Constantly the phrases are Italian, and the harmonies ultra-Germanic. Not one of the least attractions of this art is that of seeing, amidst the storms of German polyphony, the veil of lowering clouds of heavy thoughts being rent and the smiling line of Italian shores appearing with dances taking place by the seaside."[14] One observes a similar combination of the Latin and Teutonic in the music of Liszt, particularly in his operatic paraphrases; but Rolland worried that Nietzsche's praise of Will to Power and instinct in the context of his dream of a world beyond good and evil, was a dangerous influence on Strauss' vulgar, technically impeccable, egocentric music. "How his laughter stings and lashes in *Zarathustra*! How his will crushes and slashes in *Heldenleben*!"[15]

Ein Heldenleben was Strauss' sixth symphonic poem, premièred in 1898. A musical self-portrait, it presents Strauss as a mighty musical hero reviewing his past works of peace (quotations of former symphonic poems) and taking on the withering, complaining critics. Strauss identified one of them as Dr. Theodor Dehring, a music critic of the *Sammler* journal. (Tubas in parallel fifths intone the syllabic stresses of "Dok-tor Dehring.") As we have seen, Wagner had similarly lashed out at Eduard Hanslick in *Die Meistersinger*, but Strauss actually wrote Dr. Dehring's name into the score, and the music Strauss conceived to suggest the bickering of music critics is very like that of the argumentative Jewish priests in his opera *Salomé*. (In his own defense after the Second World War, Strauss admitted, "I had adversaries in the Jewish press ... but my worse and most malicious enemies were 'Aryans.'"[16])

Strauss took from Nietzsche a sense of individualism and heroism against the forces of convention. To depict an inflated ego in musical terms one requires an equally expansive theme, and this one virilely launches itself through two octaves. It is surely just as much a symbol of Zarathustra as of the composer who so identified with Nietzsche's free-thinking hero. The hero's critics, whose motif on woodwind is marked "scharf und spitzig" (sharp and spiky), represent exactly those moral conventions and "*résentiments*" with which Nietzsche was at such odds. Strauss' hero is aided by the "Helpmeet," a musical portrait of the shrewish Pauline de Ahna, Strauss' testy wife, whom he loved and feared in equal measure. *Heldenleben's* love theme unsentimentally and really rather weirdly demonstrates this odd relationship with its highly chromatic and somewhat schizophrenic writing for solo violin, before the hero takes on his critics in the ensuing musical battle. This cacophonous onslaught is of course intended to be entirely symbolic of the individual asserting his right to say and compose what he pleases, but the means used, like Nietzsche's own metaphors in his struggle against religion, morality and public opinion, is distinctly militaristic. Nietzsche spoke of bayonets, dynamite and war, Strauss uses their musical equivalents: snare drums, dotted rhythms and trumpets. The (possibly Jewish) critics are thoroughly overcome in a manner that later historical events have made much more disturbing than when they were first heard. Like Holst's "Mars" from *The Planets* Suite this section of *Ein Heldenleben* is also something of a premonition of the mechanized slaughter of the trenches, Strauss' technical mastery anticipating the application of technology to the so-called "art of war" in 1914. The opening theme of Strauss' *Also Sprach Zarathustra* is later quoted as one of the Hero's "Acts of Peace," along with quotations from Strauss' other works, but it is really the flavor of war that remains in the listener's imagination when the work ends in apparent tranquility: It is, after all, the tranquility of *victory*.

Rolland found all this both fascinating and worrying, and was well-aware of the connection it all had with Nietzsche's vocabulary, even if Nietzsche's actual message was rather more subtle:

> Through victory he [Strauss] has become conscious of his power: now, his pride no longer knows any limits; he becomes hysterically uplifted, like the nation which it reflects he can no longer distinguish the reality in his immoderate dream. There are morbid germs in present-day Germany: a mania of pride, a belief in itself and a contempt for others which are reminiscent of France in the seventeenth century. *Dem Deutschen gehört die Welt* (The German owns the world) pictures displayed in shop-windows in Berlin calmly state…. Germany had scarcely reached the mastery of the world when she found the voice of Nietzsche and of his hallucinated artists from the *Deutsches Theater* and of the *Secession*. And now here is the grandiose music of Richard Strauss.[17]

In Rolland's view, such mastery leads to boredom; and boredom quite often leads to war. "I see an heroic nation, intoxicated with its triumphs, with its immense wealth, with its numbers, with its power, which clasps the world with its huge arms, and stops, crushed by victory,—wondering, 'Why have I conquered?'"[18]

War, as we know only too well, eventually came. Some saw no reason for the enthusiasm all the European nations expressed but the desire for a "holiday from life" as the German writer Franz Schauwecker put it. Admittedly, Schauwecker went on to be very popular during the Third Reich, but even the respectable playwright Carl Zuckmayer regarded the war as representing "liberation from bourgeois narrowness and pettiness." And in the midst of a conflict, which one German student, no doubt speaking for many, regarded as being about "poetry, art, philosophy, and culture,"[19] came Strauss' *Eine Alpensinfonie*.

Significantly, Strauss started to work on this, perhaps his most characteristic and revealing work, out of boredom too, while waiting for Hofmannsthal to send him a detailed synopsis of *Die Frau ohne Schatten*, the next opera on which they were to collaborate. He began in 1911, but it wasn't finished until February 1915. He claimed no longer to be amused by writing symphonies, but was actually rather proud of this one. "You must hear the *Alpine* Symphony. It really is quite a good piece!"[20] he wrote Hofmannsthal. This work, once described by the musicologist Gerald Abraham as consisting of no more than "diatonic platitudes," and "his weakest composition,"[21] is actually one of Strauss' most enjoyable and successful works. Superficially, it describes a sturdy walk up and down a mountain—probably the Zugspitze, which Strauss could see from his villa at Garmisch, in the Bavarian Alps, though it could also recall an expedition when he was 14 years old and climbed the Heimgarten near Ohlstadt in the Bavarian Prealps. On that occasion he got lost, was drenched by a thunderstorm and spent three hours climbing back to safety. Immediately after this "interesting and pleasant change,"[22] as he described it, he sat down and depicted the experience at the piano, unknowingly warming up for the much larger *Alpine* Symphony 34 years later.

Strauss' childhood adventure had also involved taking refuge in a peasant's hut, which is significant because Nietzsche also took refuge in a similar storm when he was 22. Describing the event in a letter to his friend von Gersdorff, Nietzsche wrote:

> Yesterday, a heavy storm hung in the sky, and I hastened up a neighbouring hill, called Leusch (perhaps you can explain the word to me?). On the summit I found a hut and a man killing two kids, with his son looking on. The storm broke with a mighty crash,

Ex Libris plate by Alfred Soder for Friedrich Bertold Sutter, fancifully showing Nietzsche naked in the mountains (author's collection).

discharging thunder and hail, and I felt inexpressibly well and full of zest, and realized with singular clearness that to understand Nature one must go to her as I had just done, as a refuge from all worries and oppressions. What did man with his restless will matter to me then? What did I care for the eternal "Thou shalt" and "Thou shalt not"? How different are lightning, storm and hail—free powers without ethics! How happy, how strong they are—pure will untrammeled by the muddling influence of the intellect![23]

Here we have, in essence, the whole of Nietzsche's philosophy, with its acceptance of Nature's amoral violence and joy, along with the need to confront it head on, rather than avoid the issue with morality and religion. Strauss very probably had Nietzsche's letter in mind when he composed his *Alpine* Symphony. If not, he certainly had Nietzsche's philosophy in mind, and was fully aware of the mountain imagery that Nietzsche so often employed. Just before beginning work on *Zarathustra*, Nietzsche wrote a note to himself, which encapsulated the connection he made between mountains and freedom: both are to be found "6,000 feet beyond man and time."[24] Alpine altitudes cleansed Nietzsche of Bayreuth and all it stood for. They were, to rephrase Mary Shelley's description of Frankenstein's laboratory, the healthy workshop of creation in which he was able to construct the Superman. That Strauss chose a Wagnerian model for his musical tribute to the philosopher in *Eine Alpensinfonie* might at first seem inappropriate, but only if we ignore the complexity of Nietzsche's feelings for Wagner and fail to separate the "mortal insult" from his undying, but increasingly tortured love affair with Wagner's music.

At the beginning of *Ecce Homo*, Nietzsche wrote one of his most characteristic passages:

> He who knows how to breathe the air of my writings knows that it is an air of the heights, a *robust* air. One has to be made for it, otherwise there is no small danger one will catch cold. The ice is near, the solitude is terrible—but how peacefully all things lie in the light! how freely one breathes! how much one feels *beneath* one!—Philosophy, as I have hitherto understood and lived it, is a voluntary living in ice and high mountains—a seeking after everything strange and questionable in existence, all that has hitherto been excommunicated by morality.[25]

Strauss' biographer Kurt Wilhelm suggests that "there is no symbolic symphonism in the *Alpine* Symphony, by contrast with *Zarathustra*,"[26] but this is surely to ignore what Strauss himself had to say on the subject, which Wilhelm, rather contradictorily, quotes in the same book:

> The Jew Mahler could still be uplifted by Christianity. The hero Richard Wagner descended to it again as an old man, under the influence of Schopenhauer. It is absolutely clear to me that the German nation will only find new strength through liberation from Christianity.

> I will call my *Alpine* Symphony the Antichrist, because in it there is: moral purification by means of one's own strength, liberation through work, worship of glorious, eternal nature.[27]

Nature of a particularly Wagnerian kind is indeed abundant in *Eine Alpensinfonie*, which critics, as if to lend it a respectability it really doesn't require, are always keen to remind the listener is composed in a modified sonata form, but the musical form really isn't the issue here. This is descriptive music *par excellence*, and as such, it is one of the important cornerstones of classic Hollywood film style. Indeed, in the section known as "Durch Dickicht und Gestrüpp auf Irrwegen" ("On the wrong track through tickets and undergrowth"), it really does seems as though Errol Flynn is hacking his way through the undergrowth in a swashbuckler with music by Erich Wolfgang Korngold.

Eine Alpensinfonie begins with a sustained discord, held very quietly, creating a cushion of dark sound. This represents "Night." Over it, arpeggio figurations ripple with increasing agitation as dawn emerges. This is reminiscent of what Thomas Mann called the "acoustic idea" of Wagner's prelude to *Das Rheingold*.[28] The "Entritt in den Wald" ("Entering the forest") has so many semiquavers in the string section, rising up and down through two octaves, that all the long stems on the score actually look like a pine plantation. Here are all the musical effects we might expect: birdcalls, a glittering waterfall (orchestrated with truly Klingsorian sorcery), flowery meadows, babbling brooks, cow bells, rising mists, typically Straussian plunging intervals, and, most important of all, a storm, which is surely the most graphic depiction in all music of such a phenomenon, reducing Beethoven's *Pastoral* Symphony to a mere storm in a teacup by comparison, Berlioz's comments on Beethoven's storm, which I quoted earlier, now seem to be a premonition of Strauss' piece. Wind machines, chromatic scales, immense forces, including an organ, and the most ingenious way of depicting in musical terms the purely visual effect of lightning, followed by thunderous timpani. Strauss' storm exactly summons the mood Nietzsche described in his letter to von Gersdorff so many years before: violence, joy, instinct, freedom. No wonder Strauss considered calling his symphony "The Antichrist," while no doubt realizing that such a title would be entirely misunderstood; but this symphony really is a celebration of natural forces and Strauss' positively pagan response to them. As such, it is deeply anti–Christian.

A popular manifestation of all this can be found in Robert Wise's 1965 film adaptation of Rogers and Hammerstein's musical *The Sound of Music*. Wise's film version begins with a high-altitude shot of clouds with nothing but wind noise on the sound track, echoing the mountain films of Arnold Fanck and Leni Riefenstahl (a popular genre in pre-Nazi Germany). We are indeed in Nietzsche's ideal territory here, where one can breathe freely and so much appears beneath one. (That *The Sound of Music* later became such a gay icon might also have intrigued Nietzsche.) As Wise's camera plunges ever lower, it eventually picks out Julie Andrews walking through an alpine meadow, and, as soon as she is in close up, she begins to sing the title song, the melody of which is based, like the descending "Sunrise" motif that emerges from "Night" at the beginning of *Eine Alpensinfonie*, on a descending scale. "The Hills Are Alive with the Sound of Music" is actually set to a descending minor scale. Strauss chose a major scale for his musical sunrise, with more note repetitions and reversals than Rogers' melody, but both motifs are intended to convey moods of Nietzschean ecstasy and freedom. To this, one might add that "Climb Every Mountain" is also something Nietzsche put personally into practice while thinking out his books. Foreshadowing Wise, a film version of *Eine Alpensinfonie* was made in April 1941, in which shots of Strauss conducting the work were intercut with comparable mountain imagery.

Also Sprach Zarathustra, *Ein Heldenleben* and *Eine Alpensinfonie* represent Strauss at his most flamboyantly Nietzschean, and are also among his most characteristic works; but towards the end of his life, he wrote not only his most moving but also most cryptic piece: *Metamorphosen*, for 23 solo strings, which is usually interpreted as a lament for the destruction caused by the Second World War. There are those, however, who see more to it than that, principally due to Strauss' enigmatic quotation of the Funeral March from Beethoven's *Eroica* Symphony right at the end of the piece. Strauss' unfortunate involvement with the bureaucracy of the Third Reich as President of the Reichsmuiskkammer, not to mention his composition of the Olympic Hymn for the Berlin Olympic Games in 1936, provide two clues as to why he did this. His involvement with the Nazis is a complex one, with its defenders and detractors. Those who wish to remove Strauss from any ideological complicity point to the many statements Strauss made against Hitler, his collaboration with Jewish librettists such as Stefan Zweig, his political naivety, the difficulty of emigration and of standing up to ruthless tyrants, his own belief that, as Germany's most important composer, he should be involved in the "reorganization" of music under the new regime, etc., etc. All of these things are true, but the fact remains that Strauss was also a close friend of the infamous, but nonetheless highly cultured Nazi war criminal, Baldur von Schirach, and, in the early years, had been an admirer of Hitler.

He also wrote a contentious little song about a brook, "Das Bachlein," which includes the now red-hot words "Mein Führer sein" ("Be my Leader"). The words are attributed to Goethe, but Strauss might well have written them himself, in which case the word "Führer" takes on an added resonance not to be found in Goethe. In the poem, it is the river itself which is speaking: "He who has called me forth from the stone, he, I think, will be my leader." The song was dedicated to Goebbles, whose name was later scratched out after the war, rather as the name of Napoleon was scratched out of the title page dedication of Beethoven's "Eroica"—scratched out with such force, indeed, that Beethoven ripped the manuscript paper.

So, here we have an intriguing dilemma: Strauss' name also means "ostrich" and "a small posy of flowers." Does Strauss' reputation suggest that he stuck his head in the shifting sands of the Third Reich or did he come up smelling of roses? Timothy Jackson, whom I interviewed for a BBC Radio 3 program in 1999, has his own interpretation of these facts. With regard to Strauss' late opera *Capriccio* (1941), the sextet of which was first performed in March 1942 in von Schirach's Vienna residence, Professor Jackson suggested:

> If you look at Nazi art, you will see that the focus on the naked body, in a certain way, a chaste nakedness—a return to nature—things that were already implicit in Weimar culture but were emphasized: the body beautiful (the nordic body beautiful) in Nazi art. These things, I think, are translated into Strauss' later style. Gone is all the intensity of dissonance in his early expressionist period. If you look at the beginning of the sextet of *Capriccio*, you'll see that from a technical perspective, there are hardly any dissonances or suspensions introduced in the first measures of this piece. It's very euphonious. This style corresponds very clearly to the esthetics that the Nazi's were propagating at that time.

Does this suggest that Strauss was in sympathy with what he believed the Nazis stood for? Again, Timothy Jackson offered a possible explanation:

> You know, when the piece was first performed, there was an uproar in Holland about the citation from the *Eroica* Funeral March at the end of the *Metamorphosen*, because one of the early critics had said that the piece was really in memoriam of Hitler. This, of course, prompted fierce denials from the Strauss camp, because it was maintained that Strauss had been vehemently opposed to Hitler, which may well be true: by late 1944 I think that Strauss had in fact turned against Hitler; but my idea about this is that it does in fact refer to Hitler, but it also refers to Hitler through quotation from Beethoven, and that quotation has the connotation of Beethoven repudiating Napoleon whom *he* had once admired. You'll recall that the "Eroica" was originally dedicated to Napoleon, and then Beethoven violently crossed out the dedication and wrote "to the memory of the great man" even while Napoleon was still alive, and I think this is true also of the *Metamorphosen*, that the ending was penned before the capitulation, before Hitler's suicide; so I think that Strauss was prematurely burying Hitler here.[29]

To explain the phenomena of the Third Reich is, obviously, too large a task to embark upon here, but one important aspect of it is deeply relevant to my argument here. The immense importance of esthetics in Hitler's regime made it quite unlike any other regime in modern history. One might even argue, as Walter Benjamin has suggested, that esthetics was its entire *raison d'etre*: Not so much the esthetization of politics but the politicization of esthetics. Racism, after all, is all a matter of appearance; but on a deeper level, Hitler exploited the promise of Nietzsche (and despite the contradiction, of Wagner too) to achieve a transformation of society through the application of art. Hitler suggested to many Germans who had been nurtured by late-Romantic culture that art was indeed about transfigure existence, that it really was possible to fulfill Nietzsche's desire to "found a state upon music."[30] It was perhaps Strauss' wholesale belief in Nietzsche's anti–Christian, instinct-loving, nature-worshipping agenda of Kunst über Alles, that persuaded Strauss to believe in the fool's gold of National Socialism.

The Norwegian novelist Knut Hamsun (1859–1952) and Hamsun's compatriot, the composer Christian Sinding (1856–1941), both fell into the same trap, along with many others. The most notable example of this tendency among the minor German musicians was the conductor and composer Sigmund von Hausegger (1872–1948). A friend of Strauss, who did much to establish his reputation, Hausegger similarly toppled into the Nazi maelstrom, only to fall out of favor with the regime when later distancing himself from its excesses, and disagreeing with their belief in the artistic value of propaganda. A composer of no small talent, Hausegger was similarly responsive to the Nietzscheanism that was in the air in the early years of the twentieth century. His early *Dionÿsische Fantasie (Dionysian Fantasia)*, completed in 1897 was directly inspired by Nietzsche's

Siegmund von Hausegger (1872–1948). Taken from *Monographien Moderner Musiker 1*, C.F. Kant Nachfolger (Leipzig, 1906), p. 128 (Musicalics).

Birth of Tragedy, along with the "Ja-Sagender" philosophy of *Zarathustra*, with its affirmation of life regardless of pain and suffering. Hausegger even wrote his own program note:

> The hero sees the clash of combat and eagerly joins in. While in the fray, he sees a vision of Death, which he tries to banish. He wanders through an arid valley, full of the miasma of death. Amidst the desolation, he sees a pathway out, blocked by the Specter. Yet, a renewed inner life force flares; he will defy Death. It crumbles at his challenge. He walks the shining path, which broadens as he ascends, a song of victory rising from his heart. From the summit, even if dying in ecstasy, the hero can cry "Thou world, I love thee!"[31]

Similarly, in Hausegger's Symphonic Poem, *Barbarossa* (1888–1889), a Germanic equivalent of the King Arthur myth promising the return of an ancient warrior in the Fatherland's hour of need, there is a Nietzschean resonance in the subtitle of the second movement. This describes the cave in which Barbarossa lies sleeping beneath the Kyffhäuser Mountain. The title Hausegger uses for this section, "Zauberberg" ("magic mountain"), reminds us of the title Thomas Mann's later novel, but it was in fact a term originally coined by Nietzsche in *The Birth of Tragedy* ("Now it is as if the Olympian magic mountain had opened before us and revealed its roots to us"[32]). Alas, all this late-Romantic nationalism played readily into the hands of the Nazis, who even named their ruthless invasion of Russia after the same hero who had inspired Hausegger's symphonic poem. It was perhaps only because Hausegger fell out of favor with the Nazis that this work did not become a staple in the concert halls of the Third Reich.

Hausegger's masterpiece, the *Natursymphonie* (Nature Symphony, 1911), reaches its climax with a setting of lines from Goethe's *Proömium* rather than Nietzsche's *Zarathustra*, but the mountain symbolism of the philosopher is there, along with its redemptive associations of freedom, heroism, and all that Nietzsche implied by his exclamation: "how freely one breathes how much one feels *beneath one!*"[33] Under such circumstances it might indeed be tempting to believe, as Nietzsche had suggested that "It is only as an *aesthetic phenomenon* that existence and the world are eternally *justified*."[34]

It may have been Hitler's hijack and betrayal of these ideals that Strauss was lamenting in *Metamorphosen*: It could all have been so beautiful, but it was not. How could it have been so under Hitler? How could racism, censorship, genocide and terror ever have been beautiful? But the dream to found a state on music? That dream surely was and is. With suitably Nietzschean irony, it was Strauss' tragedy to have hoped for the best.

7

Gustav Mahler

Strauss wrote about his intention to call *Eine Alpensinfonie* "The Antichrist" on May 11, 1911, the day that Mahler died. Mahler (1860–1911), though Jewish, had converted to Christianity for pragmatic reasons: The only way he could succeed as a musician in Vienna was to become a Catholic. The ruse instantly aroused enmity amongst the antisemites, Cosima Wagner being the most notable. Mahler was never invited to conduct at Bayreuth, despite his pre-eminence as an interpreter of Wagner, simply on grounds of race rather than religion. According to Cosima, if religions can be changed, race cannot. These antisemites; one is tempted to adapt Nietzsche's comment (in fact about Christians) with regard to them: "It spoils my love of life to live among such people."[1]

Mahler was not Nietzschean by instinct, and his sympathies with the philosopher waxed and waned. One thing he particularly identified with was Nietzsche's vehement disdain for antisemitism. To clear up any doubt on the matter, Nietzsche argued that "it was the Jewish free-thinkers, scholars, and doctors, who, under the harshest personal pressure, held fast to the banner of enlightenment and intellectual independence, and defended Europe against Asia; we owe to their efforts not least, that a more natural, rational, and in any event unmythical explanation of the world could finally triumph again, and that the ring of culture which now links us to the enlightenment of Greco-Roman antiquity, remained unbroken."[2] Antisemitism drove a wedge between Nietzsche and his fanatically antisemitic sister, Elisabeth, who, as we have seen, even went to Paraguay with her husband Dr. Bernhard Förster, a leading antisemite of the day, with the aim of founding a colony of pure Aryans.

Ironically, Wagner's deeply-held and unshakeable antisemitic views did nothing to damage Mahler's admiration of Wagner's art, but certain other of Nietzsche's ideas later caused him to break with the philosopher.

Principally, Mahler did not fully accept Nietzsche's entirely human account of the world. Creeds certainly did not matter to Mahler, but he did feel that undiluted atheism fell short of the truth, as the Christian agenda of the *Resurrection* Symphony (No. 2) suggests. Mahler's unorthodox spiritual views led Otto Klemperer, for one, to regard him as "a thoroughgoing child of the nineteenth century, an adherent of Nietzsche and typically irreligious,"[3] but it was more complicated than that. Mahler was not irre-

"*I conduct to live. I live to compose*": Gustav Mahler (1860–1911). Caricatures by Otto Böhler (1847–1913). Taken from *Dr. Otto Böhler's Schattenbilder* (Vienna: Wilhelm Lechner, 1914) (Wikimedia Commons).

ligious, nor an adherent of Nietzsche. "He was deeply religious," remembered the stage designer Alfred Roller:

> His faith was that of a child. God is love and love is God. This idea came up a thousand times in his conversation. I once asked him why he did not write a mass, and he seemed taken aback. "Do you think I could take that upon myself? Well, why not? But no, there's the credo in it." And he began to recite the credo in Latin. "No, I couldn't do it."
>
> But after a rehearsal of the Eighth in Munich he called cheerfully across to me, referring to this conversation: "There you are, that's my mass."
>
> I never heard a word of blasphemy from him. But he needed no intermediary to God. He spoke with Him face to face. God lived easily within him. How else can one define the state of complete transcendency in which he wrote?[4]

Mahler also took Nietzsche's attack on Wagner as heresy. Wagner was supreme in Mahler's pantheon, and Mahler simply couldn't agree with Nietzsche on this subject, failing, perhaps, to recognize the emotional agenda that underpinned Nietzsche's diatribe, which only disguised a similar love and respect for the music. Mahler did agree with Nietzsche's insistence that life was to be lived in the here and now, and that every moment mattered, without feeling the need also to agree with Nietzsche's conviction that the here and now was all there is. Both men were mountain hikers and both shared a credo of joy, humanity, natural beauty, and, above all, personal freedom. Mahler also sympathized with Nietzsche's belief that art redeems us (though he might have drawn back from Nietzsche's other suggestion that it saves us from suicide). When creating or experiencing art, Nietzsche suggested, "we then feel that we are carrying a *goddess*, and are proud and childish in performing this service. As an aesthetic phenomenon existence is still *bearable* to us, and art furnishes us with the eye and hand and above all the good conscience to be *able* to make such phenomenon of ourselves."[5] Art transfigures the individual, and the artist teaches us "to value the hero that is hidden in each of these everyday characters and taught the art of regarding oneself as a hero, from a distance and as it were simplified and transfigured—the art of 'putting oneself on stage' before oneself. Only thus can we get over certain lowly details in ourselves. Without this art we would be nothing but foreground, and would live entirely under the spell of that perspective which makes the nearest and most vulgar appear tremulously big and as reality itself."[6]

Mahler, who conducted to live and lived to compose, had little success with his symphonies in his life-time. Indeed, it was not until the 1960s that his music became part of the repertoire. That Mahler was by no means a thorough-going Nietzschean, in superficial terms at least, is clear from this passage from his wife, Alma's reminiscences. On one occasion, she visited the poet Max Burckhard:

> Mahler had always been jealous of him, but only as a spiritual influence. I had always gone to him for advice during the years before I married. In temperament and attitude to life they were complete opposites. Burckhard preached Nietzsche's doctrine of the superman, and he had the right to, for he lived up to it in all his many activities. He ran the Burgtheater, he was a Privy Councillor and judge of the High Court, he loved sailing when the lake was stormy, he was a daring climber. He had no equal in strength and courage, and nothing whatever could stop him. He was a pagan and hated Christianity. He could live among brigands in Sicily, disguised as one himself, and pick up any dialect so quickly that he was at home in any company. "Death," he used to say, "exists only for those who believe in it, and therefore it has no existence for me."
>
> It was impossible for Mahler, who saw everything from the opposite point of view, to get on with him, and Burckhard felt the same about Mahler.[7]

There is, of course, more to Nietzsche's Übermensch than these poster-paint stereotypes. His imagery is symbolic not literal, so Alma may be missing the point somewhat here. However, from an early age, she too had been interested in the philosopher. She played Strauss' *Also Sprach Zarathustra* on the piano ("Suddenly I felt a strange sensation in my stomach.... The power of music, it transpires, extends as far as the bowels"[8]), and it is amusing to see Nietzsche and Wagner appear amid the more feminine items in Alma's list of Christmas presents, duly recorded against their givers' names in her diary:

> Ernst—picture of Wagner
> Horovitz—handbag
> Gretl H.—handbag
> Flora—handbag
> Pollack—two volumes of Nietzsche
> Xando—perfume.[9]

Well, this is not so incongruous perhaps, given Wagner's penchant for attar of roses; not, of course, that Nietzsche, grand misogynist that he was, would have had much time for quite so many handbags.

When Mahler first met Alma, he was horrified to learn that she was reading a book by the great philosopher whom he had by then apparently turned against. "He demanded abruptly that it should be cast there and then into the fire."[10] This might seem curious, because only five years earlier he had completed his most "Nietzschean" Third Symphony, but the interim seemed to have clarified his position—or perhaps the distorted editions of Nietzsche's writings issued by his sister, which were growing more fashionable, had corrupted Mahler's view of the philosopher. One might also interpret his violent reaction to Alma's library as an example of his chauvinism. After all, he insisted that Alma stop composing and literally bury what she had composed hitherto. Mahler was firmly of the opinion that women were subservient and should not be allowed too much independence. "You must understand that I could not bear the sight of an untidy woman with messy hair and neglected appearance," he insisted. "I must also admit that solitude is essential to me when I am composing; as a creative artist I require it without conditions. My wife would have to agree to my living apart from her, possibly several rooms away, and to my having a separate entrance.... Finally, she should not take offense or interpret it as disinterest, coldness or disdain, if, at times, I had no wish to see her."[11] Undaunted by this ultimatum, Alma went ahead with the marriage; but though he was certainly a chauvinist, Mahler was not a misogynist like Nietzsche.

The fact remains that Mahler set Nietzsche's words in his Third Symphony, the whole of which he contemplated calling it *Die fröhliche Wissenschaft* (*The Gay Science*) after Nietzsche's book. The attraction in Nietzsche's title lay in its implication of playfulness and unconventionality. Mahler's symphony is likewise both playful and unconventional (the first movement owes very little to traditional sonata form), but he also considered other titles, including *A Summer Night's Dream* and *Pan*.

These alternatives are significant, for alongside Nietzsche's Dionysian revival, there was something of a cult of Pan in Europe around this time, which lasted at least until the First World War. During the gestation period of the Third Symphony, Knut Hamsun wrote his novel *Pan* (1894), which contains many almost aphoristic but rapturous descriptions of nature along the pantheistic lines of Mahler's approach. Hamsun invokes Pan by name, but Pan never actually appears in this otherwise naturalistic novel. He is, however, carved on the narrator's powder horn, as a symbol of his spiritual presence throughout the story. Indeed, at one stage, he wonders if Pan is "sitting in a tree, watching to see how I would act."[12] Arthur Machen's story, *The Great God Pan* was also published in 1894, while the German art nouveau magazine, *Pan*, started publication in 1895. Pan, like Nietzsche's Dionysus, was very much in the air at the time.

In the end, Mahler eventually rejected all these titles in favor of the straightforward designation of "Third Symphony." Like Strauss, with his "Antichrist" option for *Eine Alpensinfonie*, Mahler decided against so confining a title. Also, at the time, Nietzsche's book was not so well known, so perhaps Mahler considered that that particular title would have involved too many explanations. Such a proposal, however, suggests that the Nietzschean setting in the fourth movement is part of an overall Nietzschean agenda. Alma records that Mahler did work out various subtitles for the individual movements, all of which he also later rejected. However, in the program of the first performance of the second movement in Berlin in 1896, which was conducted by Arthur Nikisch, Mahler did print a list of the symphony's programatic content as a whole. Donald Mitchell has listed these in a footnote to his edition of Alma's reminiscences:

> (1) Introduction: *"Pan erwacht"* ["Pan awakens"]: followed by *Der Sommer marschiert ein* ["Summer marches in"]; (2) *Was mir die Blumen auf der Wiese erzählen* ["What the flowers in the meadow tell me"] (Minuet); (3) *Was mir der Kuckuckerzählt* ["What the cuckoo tells me"] (Scherzo)—this movement was also known as *Was mir die Tiere im Walde erzählen* ["What the animals in the forest tell me"]; (4) *Was mir der Mensch erzählt* ["What man tells me"]; (5) *Was mir die Engel erzählen* ["What the angels tell me"]; *Was mir dir Liebe erzählt* ["What love tells me"] At one stage Mahler contemplated a seventh movement: *Was mir das Kind erzählt* ["What the child tells me"]. This was his setting of a *Wunderhorn* poem, *Das himmlische Leben*, for soprano and orchestra, which existed as an independent song and eventually became the finale of the Fourth Symphony. Indeed, it was *into* this song that the Fourth was, so to say, composed.[13]

Mahler also suggested that this seventh movement could more appropriately be called "What God tells me"—and this was where he and Nietzsche would have parted company, but Mahler's use of Dionysian imagery in his explanatory letter to Richard Batka does suggest that for the symphony's overall meaning was distinctly Nietzschean:

> That this nature hides within itself everything that is frightful, great, and also lovely (which is exactly what I wanted to express in the entire work, in a sort of evolutionary development)—of course no one ever understands that. It always strikes me as odd that most people, when they speak of "nature," think only of flowers, little birds, and woodsy smells. No one knows the god Dionysus, the great Pan. There now! You have a sort of program—that is, a sample of how I make music. Everywhere and always, it is only the voice of nature! ... Now it is the world, Nature in its totality, which is, so to speak, awakened from fathomless silence that it may ring and resound.[14]

Just as Nietzsche believed that one must encompass both pain and pleasure, joy and sorrow and affirm them all, so Mahler's approach to Nature was never selective. He confronts both the horror and beauty of existence in a very Nietzschean way; and Mahler's imagery of Dionysus banishing winter, the appearance of Helios and the bursting forth of spring leading to summer, which conquers everything in its path, seems to reflect Nietzsche's preface to the second edition of *The Gay Science*: "It seems to be written in the language of the wind that brings a thaw: it contains high spirits, unrest, contradiction, and April weather, so that one is constantly reminded of winter's nearness as well as of the *triumph* over winter that is coming, must come, perhaps has already come."[15]

We encounter similar pantheistic moods in Hamsun's *Pan*. In brief lines, such as "I gaze into the earth's inner brain, see its workings, how it seethes!"[16] "I roamed about and noticed how the snow was turning to water and how the ice was breaking up.... A slight fragrance rose from the earth and the sea; there was a sweet sulfurous smell from the old leaves rotting in the woods, ... the whole forest was in ecstasy.... I feel a strange sense of gratitude, everything reaches out towards me, blends with me, I love all things," and perhaps most significantly of all he describes summer bursting out in blossom one night "when everyone is asleep, and in the morning there it is,"[17] which perfectly parallels Mahler's phrase "Summer marches in." Hamsun also describes the forest in a way that reminds one of the subtitles and emotional moods of the second and final movements of Mahler's symphony ("What the Animals in the Forest Tell me" and "What Love Tells Me"): "I was happy and languid; all creatures came near and regarded me, insects sat on the trees, and beetles crawled on the path. Well met! I thought. The mood of the forest suffused my senses through and through; I wept for love of all things, and was utterly happy, I yielded myself up in thanksgiving."[18] The great Adagio that brings the Third Symphony to its cathartic conclusion is a similar kind of thanksgiving, to nature and to love.

This is all in contrast to the imperious trumpet call in the first movement, which is one of the chilliest and most frightening of all Mahler's musical motifs. It is no more than a broken A-minor chord leading up to the sharpened seventh of the scale, but it is full of winter's icy grip. In his film of Mahler's life in 1974, Ken Russell brilliantly visualized this music as a human chrysalis (in fact, the Alma Mahler of actress Georgina Hale), emerging from its sleep and drawn to a stone with Mahler's features. Mahler's music is no winter wonderland: It is a bleak, deadly and terrifying world, out of which summer does indeed come noisily marching in in military style, the martial rhythms, woodwind and snare drums providing a musical parallel to the similarly martial imagery of Nietzsche's writing. Even less than was the case in Strauss' *Ein Heldenleben*, such martial sounds should not be taken literally. Mahler was far from being militaristic, but the musical imagery is nonetheless one of conflict between winter and summer, old ideals and new freedoms, respectively.

In a conversation with the Viennese critic and musician Bernard Scharlitt, later printed in the *Neue Freie Presse* on May 25, 1911, Mahler explained that both he and Strauss had set Nietzsche to music because "we both, as musicians, sensed what might be called the 'latent music' in Nietzsche's mighty works. You once called Nietzsche, not without justification, an 'unachieved' composer. That he was, in every deed. His *Zarathustra* inborn of the spirit of music, absolutely 'symphonic' in its construction. By the way, Nietzsche's talent as a composer was far greater than is generally assumed."[19]

In his setting of Nietzsche's "O Mensch gib acht" from *Zarathustra*, Mahler looked once more to Wagner for his inspiration. The opening rumination for cellos and basses of this second movement of the Third Symphony, followed as it is by the alto solo, is strongly reminiscent of Brünnhilde's "Ruhe, ruhe, du Gott" ("Rest, rest, you god") from the end of *Götterdämmerung*. In Mahler's symphony, the cellos and basses oscillate between a low A and the B above it. In *Götterdämmerung*, much the same thing happens between an E-flat and the F natural above. A sense of deep reverence and tranquility is the result in both.

The setting of "O Mensch gib acht" in the fourth movement of the Third Symphony is a "Night Piece" in all but name. Nietzsche designates the original text as "The Second Dance Song," and it is structured around the tolling of a midnight bell, which Mahler replicates in his orchestration with a harp.

> *One!*
> O Man! Attend!
> *Two!*
> What does deep midnight's voice contend?
> *Three!*
> "I slept my sleep,
> *Four!*
> "And now awake at dreaming's end:
> *Five!*
> "The world is deep,
> *Six!*
> "Deeper than day can comprehend.
> *Seven!*
> "Deep is its woe,
> *Eight!*
> "Joy—deeper than heart's agony:
> *Nine*
> "Woe says: Fade! Go!
> *Ten!*
> "But all joy wants eternity,
> *Eleven!*
> "—wants deep, deep, deep eternity."
> *Twelve!*[20]

Mahler places his setting at the crossroads between summer marching in and "What Love Tells Me"—in other words, this is the voice of Man, the intermediary between Nature and God. He also interprets the word "eternity" rather differently from how Nietzsche intended. Nietzsche's theory of "eternal recurrence" was a kind of test, as much as a belief. He suggests that one should so affirm life that one should be prepared to accept all its sufferings as well as all its joys, over and over again throughout eternity. This test of total affirmation has nothing much to do with an actual belief in literal eternal recurrence, still less in the idea of the eternity of heaven, which latter is how Mahler seems to have interpreted the lines. Mahler travelled with Nietzsche as far as affirmation but parted with him on the road to heaven—even if that particular Mahlerian heaven had very little to do with the established church, and rather more to do with pantheism.

A similar mood is found in the two "Night Pieces" of the Seventh Symphony, which counterbalance the distinctly Nietzschean positivity and sensuality of the first movement. Indeed, the Seventh has been described by Ferenc Skodnitz as "dithyrambic music," raising echoes of Nietzsche's lines: "Absolute music and everyday drama: the two parts of musical drama torn apart. The happiest stage was the dithyramb as well as the early Aeschylean tragedy."[21] Skodnitz refers to Mahler's "strong inclination to the superlative," the work's "shining major brilliance" and the "illuminating sound of the orchestration."[22] The Night Pieces counterbalance this, and fit well with Nietzsche's own Night Pieces in *Zarathustra*, "The Night Song," with its exquisite lines:

> It is night: now do all leaping fountains speak louder. And my soul too is a leaping fountain.
> It is night: only now do all songs of lovers awaken. And my soul too is the song of a lover.
> Something unquenched, unquenchable, is in me, that wants to speak out. A craving for love is in me, that itself speaks the language of love.
> Light am I: ah, that I were night! But this is my solitude, that I am girded round with light.
> Ah, that I were dark and obscure! How I would suck at the breasts of light.
> And I should bless you, little sparkling stars and glow-worms above!—and be happy in your gifts of light.
> But I live in my own light, I drink back into myself the flames that break from me.[23]

Mahler acquired still further Nietzschean resonance posthumously with Visconti's 1971 film version of Thomas Mann's novella "Death in Venice," which was largely responsible for the surge of popularity in Mahler's music around that time. Mann had originally had Mahler in mind when creating the character of the fictional writer Gustav von Aschenbach, whom Visconti transformed into a composer played by Dirk Bogarde. Taking the "Adagietto" from Mahler's Fifth Symphony as the film's musical theme, Visconti also included the setting of "O Mensch, gib acht!" as a musical equivalent of Aschenbach's prose response to his emotions on observing the young boy Tadzio on the Lido in Venice. Mann describes this passage as "the page and a half of choicest rose, so chaste, so loftily, so poignant with feeling, which would shortly be the wonder and admiration of the multitude."[24] It is the expression of the merging of feeling and thought, "an emotion as precise and concentrated as thought: namely, that nature herself shivers with ecstasy when the mind bows down in homage before beauty."[25]

Inspired by the Apollonian/Dionysian antithesis of Nietzsche's *The Birth of Tragedy*, and strongly suggestive of the homosexual subtext of Nietzsche's philosophy, this scene captures the one moment in Aschenbach's life when he becomes truly "Dionysian" in the sense of Nietzsche's later sense of the term, in which the Dionysian impulse of beauty has been contained and sublimated by Apollonian restraint. Mahler's setting of "O Mensch!" is therefore the perfect musical equivalent of Aschenbach's prose. Alas, Aschenbach fails to sustain this balance, representing as he does, the dilemma of an Apollonian artist who has failed to confront and absorb the Dionysian elements within his own psyche. Triggered by his

Poster for Visconti's *Death in Venice* (1971).

infatuation with youthful beauty in Venice, Dionysus erupts from his subconscious and destroys him.

Mann based the appearance of his hero on Mahler. He describes Aschenbach as "somewhat below middle height, dark and smooth-shaven, with a head that looked rather too large for his almost delicate figure. He wore his hair brushed back; it was thin at the parting, bushy and grey on the temples, framing a lofty, rugged, knotty brow—if one may so characterize it. The nose-piece of his rimless gold spectacles cut into the base of his thick, aristocratically hooked nose. The mouth was large, often lax, often suddenly narrow and tense; the cheeks lean and furrowed, the pronounced chin slightly cleft."[26] Bogarde's Aschenbach was originally intended to resemble Mahler but more by accident than design ended up looking more like Mann. The original make-up failed to work, and so, in desperation, Bogarde's partner and manager Anthony Forward handed him a "bushy, grayish" mustache.

> In another box of buttons, safety pins, hair grips, and some scattered glass beads he disentangled a pair of rather bent pince-nez with a thin gold chain dangling. I placed the hat back on my head, took up a walking stick from a bundle of others which lay in a pile, and borrowing a walk from my paternal grandfather, heavily back on the heels, no knee caps, I started to walk slowly round and round the room.... From a long way away [I] suddenly heard Visconti's voice break the almost unbearable silence. "Bravo! Bravo!" it cried. "Look, look, all of you! Look! Here is my Thomas Mann!"[27]

When Ken Russell directed his own film tribute, *Mahler*, in 1974, he in turn paid tribute to all this by including a pastiche of Visconti's film, in which a Tadzio-like character appears on the platform of a train station through which Robert Powell's Mahler is passing. The boy moves seductively around the columns of the platform canopy while a snatch of the Adagietto duly accompanies the action on the soundtrack. Thus spoke Nietzsche unto the cinema.

8

Alexander Scriabin

Scriabin (1872–1915) started his career as a composer of Chopinesque piano music but gradually evolved an idiosyncratic style characterized in particular by polyrhythms and harmonies constructed from fourths (both the perfect, augmented and diminished varieties). He simultaneously moved into the arena of orchestral music with five symphonies, the last three of which have increasingly theosophical programs. When I first discovered Scriabin's orchestral works during my student days, I enjoyed listening to recordings of them in very hot baths. It was the perfect way to be absorbed by this profoundly sensual music. Languorous heat and clouds of steam would swirl around me during Eugene Ormandy's performance of *The Poem of Ecstasy* with the Philadelphia Orchestra (still one of the best); and as I lay there soaking, my heart beating so fast I was surely close to cardiac arrest, soap and bubbles perfumed the other side of the tape: *Prometheus—The Poem of Fire*. Nothing I ever subsequently heard in a concert hall approached these synesthetic sessions in the tub, and they still seem to me to be the ideal circumstances in which to experience Scriabin's music. What is more, I am convinced that Scriabin himself would also have enjoyed the experience if he could have envisaged portable stereo, as it was in those distant cassette-player days of the early 1980s.

As we have seen, Wagner, one of Scriabin's most important musical influences, similarly summoned a mood conducive to composition with perfume. Later in life, the perfume was supplied by his last mistress, Judith Gautier, to whom he wrote: "The little bottle of rose-water was completely ruined by cold water; and in my clumsiness I dropped the larger bottle as I was trying to arrange it with the alcohol: it broke, and its contents went all over the carpet; what really surprised me, however, was how little effect the smell had, since I would have expected it to have given me 1000 headaches. Send me some more of it."[1]

Alexander Scriabin (1872–1915), circa 1914. Photographer unidentified (Blogspot).

Wagner required the stimulation of satins, silks and velvets, and deliberately arranged the layout of his Bayreuth villa, "Wahnfried," so that his study lay directly above his bathroom. He liked "to smell the perfumes rising"[2] from below while coaxing the intricate, and, as Nietzsche would have it, decadently neurasthenic details of his score for *Parsifal*. Scriabin went further than Wagner in his desire to combine music with scent, light and physical sensations, but his "clavier de luce" (keyboard of light) in *Prometheus* never really achieved the psychedelic impact of later rock concert light shows, which it anticipated. Subsequent attempts to flood concert halls with pulsating, ever changing colors have also seemed relatively tame and well-mannered, while the atomization of perfumes throughout the performing space could never really work in a large auditorium. A confined bathroom, its door shut against the outside world, is much better.

But there are other reasons why my bath-time experiences of Scriabin are appropriate. Scriabin developed into one of the most insular, ego-centric composers who ever lived. Wagner, perhaps an equal egomaniac, at least engaged actively with his public. Hugh Macdonald, one of the less tolerant biographers of Scriabin's idiosyncrasies, observed that towards the end of Scriabin's life, "humanity at large had almost ceased to exist for him."

> The kinds of matter which most composers encompass—heroism, national fervour, religious ritual, human love, not to mention time-honoured musical principles such as concerto or fugue—were totally excluded from his imaginative world. He could expand his language by advancing in style and technique but not by moving away from himself. He lived in a mirrored gallery of tiny dimension where his own image seemed to him to stretch far in every direction. He lacked common humanity as a man and universality as a musician. He was monarch of all he surveyed, deluded into believing that what he surveyed was the universe itself.[3]

I gradually came to realize that the same could be said of King Ludwig II, who anticipated my own preference of watching DVDs alone at home when he commanded performances of Wagner's *Ring* cycle at Bayreuth to take place in an otherwise empty auditorium, where he would not be disturbed or distracted by the gawp and gaze of his subjects.

Perhaps there is nothing intrinsically wrong in the idea of the world being our own creation, an idea that, after all, has a venerable philosophical lineage stretching back to Plato's cave in *The Republic*, via Schopenhauer and Hegel. Schopenhauer claimed that the world is only one's own representation of it; Hegel suggested that our only reality is indeed the Mind: "Mind, therefore, sets out only from its own being and is in relationship only with its own determinations."[4] Philosophically speaking, it is possible to argue that we inhabit an insular world of the imagination, because on so many levels we merely "imagine" the world.

Scriabin's egocentric outlook was, however, extreme. His poetic effusions, which so often accompanied the creation of his music, are testament to that:

> I am the instant illuminating eternity
> I am the affirmation.
> I am Ecstasy.[5]

Inevitably, he also claimed to be God; but this need not be delusional. Creating the world by means of one's own representation of its essentially unknowable phenomena—those things in themselves of which Kant spoke and which remain forever beyond our reach—is an essentially God-like process. Certainly, a creative artist of Scriabin's magnitude, who created such self-contained musical universes, had just claim to such feelings.

Scriabin's first important Nietzschean work, his Third Piano Sonata in F-sharp minor, Op. 23, first appeared in 1900. Scriabin himself claimed that Nietzsche's ideas lay behind the work,[6] which he subtitled "états d'âme" (soul-states). He even provided a program for it:

> I
> The free, untamed Soul plunges passionately into an abyss of suffering and strife.
> II
> The Soul, weary of suffering, finds illusory and transient respite.
> It forgets itself in song, in flowers
> But this vitiated and uneasy Soul invariably penetrates the false veil of fragrant harmonies and radiant rhythms.
> III
> The Soul floats on a tender and melancholy sea of feeling. Love, sorrow, secret desires, inexpressible thoughts are wraithlike charms.

IV
    The elements unleash themselves. The Soul struggles within their vortex of fury. Suddenly, the voice of the Man-God rises us from within the Soul's depths.
    The song of victory resounds triumphantly.
    But it is weak, still…
    When all is within its grasp, it sinks back, broken, falling into a new abyss of nothingness.[7]

The key ideas here is "Man-God," which is Scriabin's response to Nietzsche's Übermensch. Scriabin's associates understood this, among them his brother-in-law and biographer, Boris Schloezer, who identified this Sonata as an expression of Scriabin's Nietzschean joy. This joy "flickered, then went out.… In short, this is the tragedy of a personality unable to bear his own deification into the Man-God. At the very moment he sounds his song of triumph, he sinks into the abyss. The world is deserted. The winds blow the dust of supermen into space."[8] The parallel with Mann's "Death in Venice," which appeared 12 years later, is intriguing, almost as though Scriabin (and Schloezer) had anticipated Mann's main theme, albeit with a cosmic/mystical gloss. Like Aschenbach, the Third Sonata is unable to integrate the Dionysian within the Apollonian—hence its heroic but oddly inconclusive finale, the final bars of which indeed end on the tonic chord of F-sharp minor but in its third inversion, emphasizing the C-sharp of the triad. This creates a subtly less definitive conclusion than a first inversion, especially as the melody note is a C-sharp as well.

Scriabin's biographer, Faubion Bowers, described this sonata as reverberating "with proud, ponderous, noble emphases of heavy chords. It spreads widely over the keyboard with large intervals of space—windows for the sound to be heard through. Mixed into this voyage of Soul are whiplashes of tempestuous winds and waves, out of which bursts the Man-God."[9]

Nietzschean symbolism also informed Scriabin's ultimately aborted plans for an opera. Bowers explains that the hero of this work was to be another manifestation of the Man-God of the Third Sonata "and the *Übermensch*, Superman, the 'Beyond Man' of Nietzsche.… He asserts his 'I will' as an absolute, and so loves the world he absorbs it, fuses it with himself."[10] One of the proposed sections was to be a "Dance Song," surely echoing Nietzsche's use of that term in *Zarathustra*. The text Scriabin wrote for this acknowledges that while "life is suffering," art gives solace (thus paraphrasing the message of *The Birth of Tragedy*.)[11] Bowers also points out that in Scriabin's vision of the work, "there is no good or evil, no duty or purpose in unifying the world, nothing but mere capricious will exerting itself towards bliss."[12] In this Nietzschean world "beyond good and evil" there is consequently no conventional dramatic action, which is one of the reasons why the project never came to fruition.

In his Third Symphony—the "Divine Poem" (completed in 1904), Scriabin conflated Nietzschean imagery with the occult agenda he was developing in the wake of his interest in the Theosophical Society set up by Madame Blavatsky (1831–1891); and to make sure the message was clear, his wife, Tatyana wrote an explanatory program note covering its three subtitled movements, for the first performance in 1905:

> "The Divine Poem" represents the evolution of the human spirit, which torn from an entire past of beliefs and mysteries which it surmounts and overturns, passes through Pantheism and attains to a joyous and intoxicated affirmation of its liberty and its unity with the universe (the divine "Ego").
>
> *Struggles.* The conflict between the man who is the slave of a personal god, supreme master of the world, and the free, powerful man—the man-god. The latter appears to triumph, but it is only the intellect which affirms the divine "Ego," while the individual will, still too weak, is tempted to sink into Pantheism.
>
> *Delights.* The man allows himself to be captured by the delights of the sensual world. He is intoxicated and soothed by the voluptuous pleasures into which he plunges. His personality loses itself in nature. It is then that the sense of the sublime arises from the depths of his being and assists him to conquer the passive state of his human "Ego."
>
> *Divine Play.* The spirit finally freed from all the bonds which fastened it to its past of submission to a superior power, the spirit producing the universe by the sole power of its own creative will, conscious of being at one with the Universe, abandons itself to the sublime joy of free activity—the "Divine Play."[13]

There does indeed seem to be more Nietzsche than Blavatsky here. For a start, the human spirit has "overturned" past beliefs and mysteries, paralleling Nietzsche's statement in *The Gay Science*, that "we have killed God."[14] The terms "man-god" and "slave of a personal god" echo Nietzsche's "master" and "slave" terminology. The program also speaks of "individual will," which must be strengthened to rise above itself (echoing Nietzsche's dictum that man is something to be overcome—that he is a bridge, not a goal). Through sensual freedom, the Ego awakens and man becomes fully himself, at one with the universe, and approximating, in mystical terms, the Nietzschean Superman.

Scriabin suggests the power of this triumphant Ego—the individual who raises himself to become his own god—right at the outset of the symphony with a theme called "Divine Grandeur." Midway through it plunges down a major seventh from F-natural to G-natural, suggesting an affinity with Wagner's equally phallic sword motif "Nothung" in the *Ring* cycle (which is actually a full octave plunge). The second theme of the Prologue, a rising minor sixth from F-natural to D-flat, reverses the process, and is subtitled "The Summons to Man." These themes, combined with the sensual extravagance of the second movement, ultimately bring the symphony to its conclusion, as humanity, free of God, becomes its own god, at one not only with itself but with the entire universe.

In the poem that accompanied his next symphony, *The Poem of Ecstasy*, Scriabin continued this train of thought:

> And thus the universe resounds
> With joyful cry
> I AM![15]

While admiring the music, Macdonald dismisses such sentiments as "cosmic hocus-pocus"[16] and even "worthless,"[17] but this is surely to miss the point. Though Scriabin also wanted people to respond to the music as music, if one removes the philosophical ideas that informed and elucidate it, it is like listening to Wagner's music-dramas without paying any attention to the words.

The Poem of Ecstasy is Scriabin's most Nietzschean symphony. To become a god sufficient unto oneself, and to be raised into a state of physical and spiritual ecstasy by the action of one's own creativity (what Scriabin called "Creative Play"), has a great deal in common with Nietzsche's program of total affirmation of life through joy—a joy so intense that one would be willing to experience all of life's pain and terror through eternity to experience even one moment of that ecstasy again and again and again. Nietzsche's most celebrated twentieth-century champion, Walter Kaufmann, explained that the the Will to Power is essentially "a creative force," arguing that the powerful man is the creative man who breaks the rules, every creation being "*a creation of new norms.*"[18] But Nietzsche's egoism was to some extent ironic in a way that Scriabin's surely was not. Nietzsche's chapter-headings for *Ecce Homo* ("Why I am So Wise" and "Why I write Such Excellent Books") are half jests at his own expense, written, as they were, at a time when few people had read his works and he felt often intolerably isolated. Scriabin, on the contrary, had no doubt that he was the source of ultimate wisdom and that his music was not only excellent but made all other music redundant. Though it is wise to exercise caution when interpreting the similar language they employed, they did both praise self-reliance. In *Zarathustra*, Nietzsche claimed that the death of God had freed humanity to become its own god. "You Higher Men, this God was your greatest danger.... God has died: now *we* desire—that the Superman shall live."[19] The Superman takes responsibility for himself, rather than resting on God's shoulders: The situation is much more precarious but infinitely more liberating.

Can one have too much freedom? Certainly, if it is pursued without responsibility, and this is why Nietzsche reiterated than humanity as it is at present is something that must be *overcome*. "How shall man be *overcome*?" he asks.[20] The answer lies in the courage to become who you really are: "Overcome, you Higher Men, the petty virtues, the petty prudences, the sand-grain discretion, the ant-swarm inanity, miserable ease, the 'happiness of the greatest number'!"[21] This is entirely in accord with Scriabin's vision, even though that vision was expressed in mystical terms. In the libretto of his unfinished *Preparatory Act*, Scriabin wrote:

> I am the final achievement
> I am the bliss of dissolution
> I am the diamond of the galaxy
> I am freedom, I am ecstasy![22]

Scriabin also shared Nietzsche's dream of defying gravity. The ecstasy Scriabin described as dematerialization and unity with the cosmos, is the mirror image of Nietzsche's description of Higher Men as "aeronauts of the spirit,"[23] and his defiance of "the Spirit of Gravity":

> He who will one day teach men to fly will have moved all boundary-stones; all boundary-stones will themselves fly into the air to him, he will baptize the earth anew—as "the weightless."
>
> The ostrich runs faster than any horse, but even he sticks his head heavily into heavy earth: that is what the man who cannot yet fly is like.
>
> He calls earth and life heavy: and so *will* the Spirit of Gravity have it! But he who wants to become light and a bird must love himself—thus do *I* teach.[24]

Nietzsche's dance imagery also suggests the ecstasy of freedom and the freedom of ecstasy: "Lift up your hearts, my brothers, high! higher! And do not forget your legs! Lift up your legs, too, you fine dancers: and better still, stand on your heads!"[25] Similarly, Scriabin himself literally attempted to fly. Alexander Pasternak, brother of the more famous novelist Boris, knew Scriabin when he was a boy, and in his memoirs he recalled how his father had observed the composer in the road, "bounding down, flapping his arms like a vulture or eagle trying to take off. If it hadn't been for the rigidly straight course he followed, you'd have thought he was drunk, his gesticulations were so peculiar."[26] Scriabin really wanted to fly, and if that ability was denied him physically, he made sure that his music defied gravity. Pasternak recalled that "the spiritual lightness so characteristic of everything he did was reflected in his playing, as in his way of walking, gesticulating, and tossing his head in conversation. It was natural and instinctive to him, not a theatrical affectation.... At the piano he always sat further than usual from the keyboard, leaning with his head tilted back. Hence the impression that his fingers did not drop on to the notes, but fluttered above them. Everything together created that light sound which was the chief beauty of his playing."[27]

Both Nietzsche and Scriabin wanted to fly because this was an image of the ultimate freedom, a freedom that had many psychological implications. The Soviet Union often heralded Scriabin as a pioneer of space flight, and made sure that *The Poem of Ecstasy* accompanied television transmissions of Yuri Gagarin's first space mission, just as Nietzsche's *Zarathustra*, as set to music by Strauss, became the ultimate "space music" for *Apollo 13*. Of course, all this was an over-simplification of what Scriabin, Strauss and most of all Nietzsche stood for, but, the gravity-defying connection between them remains.

Scriabin was not the only mystic to be impressed by Nietzsche's fundamentally atheistic agenda. Madame Blavatsky, Scriabin's other intellectual interest, had called for the abolition of Christianity, admittedly in favor of occult ideas alien to Nietzsche, but these apparent contradictions can be reconciled in a variety of ways, starting with Wagner's approach to Christianity, which Nietzsche himself rather misunderstood. I have already referred to Wagner's belief, expressed in his essay "Religion and Art," that it is up to Art to save the spirit of religion by recognizing the figurative value of the mythic symbols which the former would have us believe in their literal sense. In their various ways, it would seem that Blavatsky, Scriabin and Nietzsche were responding to Wagner's challenge to relocate the religious instinct to occult, artistic, atheistic or philosophical arenas. Blavatsky claimed, in a way that parallels both Wagner and Nietzsche, that "belief in the Bible *literally*, and in a *carnalized* Christ, will not last a quarter of a century longer."

> The Churches will have to part with their cherished dogmas, or the 20th century will witness the downfall and ruin of all Christendom, and with it, belief even in a Christos, as pure Spirit. The very name has now become obnoxious, and theological Christianity must die out, *never to resurrect again* in its present form. This, in itself, would be the happiest solution of all, were there no danger from the natural reaction which is sure to follow: crass materialism will be the consequence and the result of centuries of blind faith, unless the loss of old ideals is replaced by other ideas, unassailable, because *universal*, and built on the rock of eternal truths instead of the shifting sands of human fancy.[28]

Nietzsche would have had no time for Blavatsky's idea of "eternal truth," but he did share her concern about what would fill the vacuum left by the departure of God. His solution was not hers, but as we have seen, his translator, R. J. Hollingdale suggested that many of Nietzsche's apparently anti–Christian ideals, like his diatribes against Wagner, are in fact mirror images of his targets. As Hollingdale explains, "in both conceptions the central idea is that a certain inner quality ... elevates man (or some men) above the rest of nature." When Nietzsche speaks of the Great Noontide, at which time the Superman will claim the earth, he is echoing the idea of the Second Coming, with its separation of the wheat from the chaff. Finally, the Superman himself is really only a secularization of God: "What the Christian says of God, Nietzsche says in very nearly the same words of the Superman, namely 'Thine is the kingdom, and the power, and the glory, for ever and ever.'"[29]

Having isolated these parallels, it no longer seems so strange that Nietzsche, who anyway cast *Zarathustra* in a Biblical idiom, should have appealed to Theosophists like Scriabin. Nietzsche also famously appealed to Rudolf Steiner, the founder of that immensely influential breakaway movement from Theosophy, which he called Anthroposophy. Steiner (1861–1925), a occultist rooted in a mystical Christian belief, and apparently the compete antithesis of Nietzsche, nonetheless identified with several of Nietzsche's core ideas. As Colin Wilson points out, Steiner had himself come to the conclusion that a moral view of the world is entirely man-made: "The external world is, in itself, neither good nor bad; it only becomes one or the other through man." Like Nietzsche, Wilson continues, "his fundamental message is that man is far *stronger* than he realizes. The mind itself transforms reality, as the sun transforms the world when it rises in the morning."[30] In his 1895 book *Friedrich Nietzsche—Fighter for Freedom*, Steiner summed up what he found attractive in Nietzsche's approach, even though his own view of the world was very different:

> It is also of no importance whether man intends to become an image of God or whether he invents an ideal of the "perfect human being," and resembles this as much as possible. Only the single human being, and only the impulses and instincts of this single human being are real. Only when he directs his attention to the needs of his own person, can man experience what is good for his life. The single human being does not become "perfect" when he denies himself and resembles a model, but when he brings to reality that within him which strives toward realization. Human activity does not first acquire meaning because it serves an impersonal, external purpose; it has its meaning in itself.[31]

Unexpectedly, certain aspects of occultism appear to be in accord with Nietzsche, particularly its insistence on placing the responsibility for living the right kind of life on Man's shoulders, with the aim of raising him to becoming a god to himself. Other writers on the occult also share certain of Nietzsche's concerns. Israel Regardi, for example, one time secretary to Aleister Crowley and adept of the Order of the Golden Dawn, seems an unlikely champion of Nietzschean philosophy, but though the means by which he believed it could be attained differed from Nietzsche, Regardie also believed in a kind of "Joyful Wisdom." As he put it himself, this "ecstasy and a marvelous outpouring of gladness, wildly rapturous and incomparably holy—is identical."[32] Magical processes aim to reveal man *as* God, in a mystical parallel to the self-sufficient, but simultaneously god-like Superman. For Regardie, we are "sons of God, Gods in all verity."[33] The following passage from Regardi's *The Tree of Life*, is indeed a kind of mystical parallel to Nietzsche's godless ecstasy of self-fulfillment in the Superman:

> Thus the supreme object of all magical ritual is the building of the pyramidal apex, and the installation of the battlements on the intellectual tower in other words, the communion with the Higher Self. For every man is that the most important step, and no other compares with it in importance and validity until this one union has been accomplished. It brings with it new powers, new extensions of consciousness, and a new vision of life. It throws a brilliant ray of illumination on the hitherto dark phase of life, removing from the mind the clouds which inhibit the glory of the spiritual light.[34]

Regardi's words here in effect describe the program of Scriabin's *Prometheus*. The mythological figure of Prometheus had appealed to earlier nineteenth-century Romantics as a metaphor for mankind's struggle against tyranny and his quest for freedom. (We have already encountered Max Klinger's Promethian statue of Beethoven.) Prometheus stole the sparks made by the chariot wheels of the gods as they rode across the sky, and in giving this fire to Mankind he also gave them wisdom, at the expense of his own liberty. Jupiter was outraged by the theft of his most precious element, and in revenge he chained Prometheus to a peak in the Caucasus mountains. Every day a vulture sent by Jupiter consumes Prometheus' liver, which was replaced each night to perpetuate the horrible torture. Shelley, an atheist like Nietzsche, described the terrible agony of this dissident benefactor of mankind in his epic poem *Prometheus Unbound* (1820):

> The crawling glaciers pierce me with the spears
> Of their moon-freezing crystals, the bright chains
> Eat with their burning cold into my bones.
> Heaven's wingèd hound, polluting from thy lips
> His beak in poison not is own, tears up
> My heart.[35]

The highly charged imagery here is similar to the distinctly sadomasochistic vocabulary of Scriabin's own attempts at ecstatic poetry:

> That which frightened
> Is now a pleasure.
> And the bight of panther or hyena
> Is a new caress.
> Another
> And a serpent's sting
> Is but a burning kiss.[36]

But perhaps more to the point is the equation that both Shelley and Scriabin made between Prometheus and Satan. In his *Defence of Poetry* (1821, pub. 1840), Shelley pointed out that Milton's Satan was really the hero of *Paradise Lost*:

> Nothing can exceed the energy and magnificence of the character of Satan as expressed in "Paradise Lost." It is a mistake to suppose that he could ever have been intended for the popular personification of evil.... Milton's Devil as a moral being is far superior to his God as one who perseveres in some purpose which he has conceived to be excellent in spite of adversity and torture, is to one who in the cold security of undoubted triumph inflicts the most horrible revenge upon his enemy, not from any mistaken notion of inducing him to repent of a perseverance in enmity, but with the alleged design of exasperating him to new torments.[37]

Shelley's principle aim here was a political one. Satan is the symbol of rebellion against tyranny: a role model for Shelley himself in many ways. Nietzsche too was drawn to the figure of Prometheus. As a schoolboy he began to write a play on the subject. As his biographer Ronald Hayman has observed, Nietzsche was "especially interested in the end of Zeus, which Prometheus anticipated, in relation to the downfall of the German gods, destroyed by the forces of nature. So, while still a believer, he was already attracted to the death of godhead as a theme."[38] For Scriabin, the parallel was a spiritual one. For several years before composing *Prometheus* he had aspired to emulating Nietzsche's Superman—to become a god himself with no need of a god beyond himself. The attraction of Prometheus and Satan was therefore considerable. Cast out of heaven for pride and disobedience, Satan was a highly suitable role model for Scriabin, the egocentric par excellence: "I am freedom, I am a dream, I am weariness, I am unceasing burning desire, I am bliss, I am an insane passion, I am nothing."[39] Prometheus brought fire—"the flame of wisdom." Satan, who fell as a bolt of lightning from the right hand of God, was the personification of freedom. Scriabin's third luminary, Lucifer, also banished from heaven for his independent spirit, brought light to mankind and still shines as the Morning Star—an appropriate planet, given Scriabin's penchant for sexual imagery, as it is actually Venus. Blavatsky entitled her theosophical journal *Lucifer* for similar reasons, causing Dennis Wheatley, who included her *Studies in Occultism* in his "Library of the Occult," some confusion when he pointed out that the essays included in the volume "are replies to questions sent to her as the editor of a magazine which, for some strange reason, she entitled *Lucifer*."[40]

Scriabin always kept a copy of Blavatsky's *The Secret Doctrine* by his piano, and it is this work, alongside Nietzsche's Superman, that informed *Prometheus—The Poem of Fire*. Blavatsky claimed that the Secret Doctrine originated in Tibet and was promoted by Tibetan monks through psychic and telepathic means. The monk with whom she was in most regular contact was a certain Master Koot-Hoomi. Blavastky claimed her approach to be scientific and that mankind was evolving through seven evolutionary cycles or "Root Races." The first root race had been astral and dwelt in an invisible land. The second were Hyperboreans, who lived and ultimately perished in the arctic. The third was the Lemurian Root Race, which flourished on a continent in the Indian ocean. The fourth was represented by the Atlanteans who were annihilated by the destruction of Atlantis itself due to their misuse of psychic forces. Present day humanity constitutes the fifth race; the sixth will come from North America and the seventh from South America.

The idea of evolution owes much to Darwin, of course, but also foreshadows the evolutionary imagery of Nietzsche's Superman, which will overcome and transfigure humanity: "And this is the great noontide: it is when man stands at the middle of his course between animal and Superman and celebrates his journey to the evening as his highest hope: for it is the journey to a new morning."[41]

In distinctly Nietzschean prose-style, Scriabin claimed:

> Not only to teach have I come, but to love. I bring not truth but freedom. You heard my secret call, you hidden forces of life, and you arise; the waves of my being, light as a dream, arouse the world. To life, to light!
> I awake you to life by my caresses.... Rise up from the secret depths of the creative spirit.[42]

These are the concerns of *Prometheus—The Poem of Fire*. The light of wisdom and the freedom it brings can be achieved only through the liberation of the creative spirit through sexual ecstasy. Sexual activity was, for Scriabin, the ultimate liberator, and his music is erotic for this reason. Trills and cascades of virtuoso piano writing with widely leaping intervals convey not only the liberation of the individual through sexual ecstasy but also the liberation of man's spirit into the cosmos. Reflecting Blavatsky's Root Race system, *Prometheus* describes the evolutionary process from original chaos to the final transfigured reunion of cosmos and spirit. The so-called "mystic" chord, which opens the work, is built from perfect, augmented and diminished fourths, out of which emerge themes associated with the development of man from incarnated to disembodied spirit. The piano represents mankind, the orchestra represents the universe, and through the ravishing and ecstatic interplay between them man evolves into a spiritual Superman, which will unite male and female principles in an ocean of bliss.

After this Creative Play of Spirit, a wordless chorus intones the vowel-like sounds of ah, e, o, ho, reminiscent of those made by a newborn baby, thus symbolizing the birth of the spirit into the universe. A dance of the atoms completes the process as the material world undergoes its final orgasm, shatters and dematerializes. As Prometheus, Satan and Lucifer were all bringers of light, the musical flames of this Poem of Fire were to be enhanced by projected, multicolored light, bathing the concert hall in a psychedelic extravaganza. One might usefully compare the vowel sounds of the final chorus to the imagery of the Star Child at the end of Kubrick's *2001—A Space Odyssey*, which symbolizes much the same process, and, via its connection with Strauss' *Also Sprach Zarathustra*, provides us with yet another link between Scriabin's music and Nietzsche's famous book.

Nietzsche hoped his collision course with Christianity would clear the ground for the Superman. He did not live long enough to witness the First World War, which Germany justified to no small extent by his writings. Nietzsche would have deplored that, for the war was not at all the sort of collision he was talking about, despite the emotive, indeed explosive terminology he used. Scriabin did live to see the war begin, and, like the Italian disciple of Nietzsche, Gabrielle D'Annunzio, was delighted by the prospect. As Lucy Hughes-Hallett observes, for D'Annunzio, who was simultaneously a barbarian and a decadent, "war was music: war was religion. He could not bear to be without it."[43] Scriabin, however, saw the conflict in spiritual terms: "The masses need to be shaken. In this way they can be rendered perceptive of finer vibrations than usual. How deeply mistaken it is to view war merely as discord between nations."[44] If he had lived to see the world after the conflict he may have changed his mind, but he died from blood poisoning in 1915, 15 years after Nietzsche. This sadly deprived him the opportunity of dematerializing the world himself, which had been the ultimate aim of his never-completed *Mystery*. The *Mystery* would again have combined light, perfume, music poetry, drama and philosophy—even bells hung from the clouds above the Himalayas—to unite all the peoples of the world before delivering them from materialism and transforming them into cosmic spirit, by means of what Faubion Bowers aptly terms "galactic orgasms of ecstasy."[45]

Scriabin, concerned that the evolutionary mystical message of his *Prometheus* be fully understood, commissioned his friend, the equally theosophical artist Jean Delville, to illustrate the cover of the score. Scriabin "adored"[46] this picture, which shows the face of Prometheus staring out at the viewer with androgynous intensity. The flame of wisdom burns

Jean Delville's title page design for Scriabin's *Prometheus—The Poem of Fire.*

from his forehead; the lyre of music surrounds him, at the base of which are laced two interpenetrating black and white triangles forming the mystical seal of Solomon—the six-pointed symbol of Lucifer; the sun shines overhead, surrounded by spiraling comets and sheets of flame.

The final gigantic chord of F-sharp major, which brings the work to its conclusion, was more than just a chord for Scriabin. First of all it represented to him a blazing sensation of violet light, and, according to his synesthetic scheme, the key of F-sharp major radiated the symbolism of "Creativity." Liberated from the tyranny of matter, the spirit of the artist attains the peak of creativity, the summit of ecstasy. If F-sharp major really does mean that, then Shelley's *Prometheus Unbound* would appear to end in the same key.

> To defy Power, which seems omnipotent;
> To love, and bear; to hope till Hope creates
> From its own wreck the thing it contemplates.
> Neither to change, nor falter, nor repent;
> This, like they glory, Titan, is to be
> Good, great and joyous, beautiful and free;
> This is alone Life, Joy, Empire and Victory.[47]

Shelley's vision is entirely in accord with Nietzsche's, but Nietzsche really did know his fate. He ended *Ecce Homo* with the question, "Have I been understood?" Well, not entirely.

9

Frederick Delius

There have been many admirers of Delius' music who would much rather he had never been inspired by Nietzsche's writings. Principle among them was his famous and deeply Christian amanuensis, Eric Fenby, who arrived in the sleepy French village of Grez-sur-Loing, where Delius (1862–1934) had been living for many years, with its dreamy river, "old bridge and an old castle in ruins and a quaint old church."[1] He was horrified to discover not only that his employer was dying of syphilis, but was also an atheist. Both these conditions Delius, of course, shared with Nietzsche, who spent his final years of paralysis in Weimar where his fanatically antisemitic sister enshrined him as the incarnation of the antichrist.

It is intriguing to compare Rudolf Steiner's description of Nietzsche, whom he first met when Nietzsche was paralyzed and insane, with Fenby's first impressions when Delius was similarly paralyzed and blind. Nietzsche, of course, was no longer there, so to speak, whereas Delius' mind was still very much intact; but both Steiner and Fenby described their heroes in almost godlike terms, dwelling on their foreheads—the thrones of their respective genius. Steiner wrote:

> The mentally darkened Nietzsche was lying on a couch. His exceptionally beautiful forehead was that of a thinker and an artist. It was early afternoon. His eyes, though dying, were still ensouled; they received the picture of the surroundings, but it no longer reached his mind. One was present there, but Nietzsche was unaware of it. Observing his countenance permeated with spirit, one could believe it belonged to someone who had spent all morning engaged in thought and now wished to rest awhile. The inner shock I experienced led to what I can describe only as insight into the genius of Nietzsche, whose gaze did not see, though directed toward me. The very passivity of the gaze rested upon me for a long time, and it released my inner comprehension through the power of my sight that met no response.
>
> In inner perception, I saw Nietzsche's soul hovering above his head. It was infinitely beautiful in its spiritual light, freely surrendering to the spirit worlds it had longed for so much but had been unable to find before illness clouded his mind.[2]

Here is Fenby's recollection of that his first meeting with Delius:

> Nothing can ever dim the memory of that first meeting.
>
> There was Delius, gaunt, deathly pale, his fine classical head proud and erect as he sat upright in his chair. Round him stretched a great screen so that for a moment it seemed as if some Roman Cardinal was sitting there. He wore a white shirt open at the neck, and a checked rug hung loosely about his knees. With difficulty he extended his arm, as though to compel the life to return into his drooping hand.[3]

However, Fenby's musical hero had contracted much more than syphilis: Nietzsche had infected him too. Delius' early biographer, Arthur Hutchings (1906–1989), one-time professor of music at Durham University, quotes this passage from Fenby's reminiscences in his 1948 study of the composer:

Frederick Delius (1862–1934). Photograph by C. F. Kahnt Nachfolger, 1907 (Wikipedia).

> Already as a youth, when he had left Bradford on his first visit to Florida, Delius was at heart a pagan. A young mind that had been nurtured chiefly on detective stories and penny dreadfuls was not likely to forget that incident he had witnessed in Bradford when [Charles] Bradlaugh had stood, watch in hand, calling on his Creator to strike him dead within two minutes if He existed! One wet day a few years later, Delius was looking for something to read in the library of a Norwegian friend with whom he was staying during a walking tour, and had taken down a book by one Friedrich Nietzsche; he was ripe for it. That book, he told me, never left his hands until he had devoured it from cover to cover—the poison entered his soul.[4]

Fenby's dismissal of Nietzsche's influence by equating it with poison, penny dreadfuls and detective stories, was typical of Hutchings' book as well. Huchings claimed that "Delius was no intellectual; he was incapable of following any speculative thought that did not flatter his own inclinations and rebellions," implying that Nietzsche's ideas were really on the level of an immature schoolboy. Christians, so the sub-text would have us believe, are altogether more grown-up. "Delius went to Nietzsche," Hutchings continues, "for reasons which drive one youngster to Marxism, another to the New Yoga and another to the Buchmanites—it happened to be in the air, as reactions to former hypocrisy or injustice."[5] True, Nietzsche was very much "in the air" at this time, but one might equally ask, "when has Christianity not been so?" Are "youngsters" never driven to Christianity for the same reasons? Hutchings admits, rather begrudgingly, that "if we are to understand the symbolic language used in Delius' master-work, 'A Mass of Life,' which is taken from Nietzsche's *Thus spake Zarathustra*, we are forced to acquaint ourselves with a few of the leading doctrines of that teacher."[6] The vocabulary here suggests that Hutchings would rather we didn't have to bother, and he says as much a few paragraphs later: "There are those who still talk of Nietzsche as the arch-rascal, but the musician wonders what all the pother is about."[7] Putting Nietzsche into a nutshell (or a bucket, as it turns out) he writes: "The Christian says he cannot stand in the bucket and lift himself up; he therefore believes in and appeals to a power outside the bucket. Nietzsche, as tired of the talk of the man in the bucket as he is of any power outside it, denies the external power and condemns as weakness the prayers and appeals. He advises one to enjoy the sinful bucket."[8]

In essence, there is nothing wrong with such a précis, but the tone implies the disdain Hutchings obviously shared with many people, particularly in England, who had just emerged from the Second World War, when Nietzsche's reputation had been distinctly tainted by association with the Nazis. Of course, this very English intolerance also predated the Second World War as I mentioned in the introduction with regard to P. G. Wodehouse, and it continued at least into the 1990s with A. N. Wilson. All the more to his credit, therefore, is the fact that Sir Thomas Beecham was one of the first British conductors to champion the Delius cause. Beecham approached the issue of Delius' Nietzscheanism altogether more sympathetically in his autobiography, which, significantly, was published during the latter stages of the Second World War:

> After a while I discovered that his [Delius's] entire philosophy of life was based upon an ultra-Nietzschean conception of the individual. The individual was all in all, a sovereign creature who perhaps owed certain perfunctory duties to the State in return for mere protection and security, but certainly nothing more to anyone but himself and the vital needs of his task. This, of course, means that Frederick from the Anglo-Saxon point of view must be reckoned a supreme and complete egoist, and so he was, unquestionably.... But this self-centred, self-sufficient, and self-protected spirit had its noble and idealistic side, for it lived on earth but to look steadily into its own remoter depths, bring to the light the best discoverable there, and to translate it into terms of music with hardly a care that it should be acclaimed by others or even noticed at all. Never did I observe any occasion when he lifted a finger to advance the cause of his own work; and not once in our subsequently long association did he ever ask me to play anything of his, although he knew well enough that I was ready to do so at any moment.[9]

In stark contrast to all that, Hutchings' aim was obviously to "rescue" Delius' music from association with Nietzsche: "Since Delius' music is at its loveliest in an autumnal atmosphere," he writes, "we need not worry at the verbiage required by the Nietzschean text to slide past the facts of old age, pain and death." He then quotes the passage from Nietzsche which Delius sets, adding, "Yet of this Delius makes the most glorious music of all."[10] Finally, Hutchings insists that "musicians have no more need to know the doctrinal teachings embraced by Delius than they have to acquaint themselves with the philosophisings behind Wagner's music dramas. They meant something when Shaw first wrote about Wagner; nowadays only the music remains."[11]

Thus spoke Hutchings, none too wisely—for to embark on *A Mass of Life* purely as music with a German text one apparently needn't bother too much about, is surely to miss the point. Delius was *profoundly* anti–Christian in his outlook, and informed the horrified Fenby that "given a young young composer of genius, the surest way to ruin him is to make a Christian of him."[12] But being anti–Christian does not mean one is not "spiritual" in the broadest sense of the term, as the composer Jonathan Harvey has pointed out:

> Spiritual content in music, as my own experience and that of others has shown, is certainly not restricted to works with a specific liturgical purpose or religious themes. Numerous composers, otherwise very disparate, have consistently expressed their desire to serve humanity through music.... Many composers have believed, like Nietzsche, that music should try to recapture the power of ancient ritual. Delius, for example, wrote that:
>
> "Music is a cry of the soul.... Performances of a musical work are for us what the rites and festivals of religion were for the ancients—an initiation into the mysteries of the human soul."[13]

The entire driving force behind *A Mass of Life* is *against* Christianity. Delius loathed Christianity as much as he identified with Nietzsche's antichrist, and he made no bones about it to Fenby:

> The sooner you get rid of all this Christian humbug the better. The whole traditional conception of life is false. Throw those great Christian blinkers away, and look around you and stand on your own feet and be a man. We are all sent into this world, we know not how and we know not why. We each have our own individualities, our own particular and varying natures, and our job is to find ourselves at all costs. Never be afraid of being yourself in spite of everything and everybody. They'll soon get over it. That is the supreme test of a man—his ability to stand on his own. Look to yourself, and don't narrow and hedge in your life with conventional behavior and all these silly moral restrictions. Sex plays a tremendous part in life. It is terrible to think that we have come into this world by some despicable physical act. Don't believe all the tommy-rot priests tell you; learn and prove everything by your own experience.[14]

Delius' words here provide a virtual précis of Nietzsche's entire philosophy. (It also helps explain why Delius was syphilitic.) Without Nietzsche's philosophy, *A Mass of Life* (the title is surely half-ironic in an appropriately Nietzschean manner) would lose half its impact. Indeed Fenby often thought it was Nietzsche rather than Delius who was speaking to him, adding: "It was not until Delius told me that it had been his habit, over a period of a great many years, to open *Thus Spake Zarathustra* at random, take a chapter and ponder over it sometimes for weeks together, then, when he had extracted its essence, turn to another and do likewise, that I realized something of the influence Nietzsche had exercised over him, and something of his disappointment in my polite refusal to follow his example."[15]

One anecdote recorded by Fenby, is positively Zarathustrian. Delius wanted one last glimpse of a sunset before he became blind from his illness. The Australian composer Percy Grainger, Mrs. Delius and two servants hauled the stricken composer up a Norwegian mountain to achieve this, and were disappointed to find the summit covered in clouds; but at the last minute, the clouds parted and the sun burst forth, evoking Zarathustra's prologue in praise of the sun.[16] Ken Russell captured the mood of this eccentric expedition even more powerfully in *A Song of Summer*, his film adaptation of Fenby's book, with Max Adrian as the very incarnation of Delius—and perhaps the incarnation of Nietzsche as well. Nietzsche's world-view affected Delius even in works which did not set the philosopher's words. There are four songs from 1898 that do ("Nach neuen Meeren" ["By New Seas"], "Der Wanderer" ["The Wanderer"], "Der Einsame" ["The Lonely One"], and "Der Wanderer und sein Schatten" ["The Wanderer and His Shadow"]); but the Symphonic *Life's Dance* from 1911 (a revision of the earlier *The Dance Goes On* from 1898) manages merely by its title and compound-duple meter to suggest not only Nietzsche's dance imagery in Zarathustra but also the style of Hollywood film music. The two *Dance Rhapsodies* from 1908 and 1916 also draw on Nietzsche's terpsichorean metaphors, as does *A Song before Sunrise* from 1918, with its dance-like 6/8 lilt, and a title that echoes that of Nietzsche's book *Morgenröte* variously translated as *Sunrise*, *Daybreak* or *The Dawn*. Heinrich Simon's text for Delius' 1914–1916 *Requiem* suggests the ideas of various writers, including Nietzsche's sense of "carpe diem," but without actually quoting any of them. One might even claim the choral work *A Song of the High Hills* as a musical equivalent of Nietzsche's mountain imagery, while *A Song of Summer*, from 1930, which incorporated material from the earlier orchestral work *A Poem of Life and Love*, is similarly Nietzschean in intent, being in praise of the here and now, nature and sensual joy.

Oddly, given his "musician's perspective," Hutchings nowhere mentions how much Wagner in general, and *Parsifal* in particular informed Delius' response to Nietzsche. It is, of course, deeply ironic that *Parsifal* lies behind so much of Delius' deeply anti–Christian *Mass of Life*, but such is the case. Nietzsche always loved the music of *Parsifal* even if he disagreed with what he thought it was about. Delius was fully aware of how much *Parsifal* had influenced Elgar's *The Dream of Gerontius*, which he called "a nauseating work,"[17] but he may have been less aware of the influence of Wagner's last music-drama on his own music. Echoes and sometimes virtual quotations pepper the score of *A Mass of Life* and other works, sometimes even in their original Wagnerian tonalities. Delius quotes the "Nature" motif from *Parsifal*, in the Lento (No. 4) of Part Two of the *Mass*, and the *Parsifal* grail bells in the fourth number of Part One under the baritone's line, "was mien Mitternachtsherz eben denkt." Even more striking is the similarity between the baritone's "Was geschah mir? Horch! flog die Zeit wohl davon? falle ich nicht?" in No. 6 of Part Two ("What befell me? Hark! was it Time that fled from hence? Am I not falling?") to Parsifal's similarly interrogative lines in Act II when he learns of the death of his mother, Herzeleide: "Wehe! Was tat ich? Wo war ich?" ("Woe! What did I do? Where was I?"). Also, during the serene and sombre setting of Nietzsche's "O Einsamkeit aller Schenkenden! O Schweigsamkeit aller Leuchtenden!" ("O solitude of all Givers! O silence deep of all Lightshedders") in the middle of the final number of Part One, Delius accompanies the words "Leuchtenden" with hushed beats from the timpani. These surely echo what Wagner had called "the annihilating sound of the kettledrum: 'Obliteration of the whole being, of all earthly desire,'"[18] during the baptism of Kundry just before the Good Friday Spell in Act III of *Parsifal*. Wagner thought this "the finest thing I have ever done!"[19] Significantly, both Wagner and Delius call for the timpani to be tuned to a G-natural here (Delius going on to ask for a C-natural too), but the effect is remarkably similar. Delius' sighing fall in the strings from a E-flat to a D-natural also echoes Wagner's F-natural to E-natural over this kettledrum moment.

It is not just *A Mass of Life* that is indebted to *Parsifal*. It also informs Delius' "Walk to the Paradise Garden" from *A Village Romeo and Juliet*, which comes to a close with a motif drawn from the final pages of Wagner's work. A more joy-suffused impression of pantheistic serenity it would be hard to find. It is both Nietzschean and Wagnerian—and perhaps the most successful reconciliation of these two sparring geniuses.

But *A Mass of Life* is also indebted to *Tristan und Isolde*. During the

Liebesnacht in Act II, scene 2, Wagner employs a sequence of quavers falling from C to B-flat, then rising up to D-flat, down to C, and again up, this time to E-flat and down to D. They accompany Isolde's words "Doch, unsre Liebe,/ heisst sie nicht Tristan/ und—Isolde?" ("Yet, may we not call this love Tristan and Isolde?") Delius employs a similar effect (in an overall descending motion) in the second number of Part Two in his *Mass*, where the baritone sings "Es quillt heimlich ein Geruch herauf, ein Duft und Geruch der Ewigkeit" ("An odor secret and sweet, an odor, a breath of Eternity"). Perhaps even the mournful English horn melody, that opens the first scene of *Tristan's* third act is recalled in Delius' musical evocation of evening and of Zarathustra walking alone in a forest that opens Part 2, No. 4. Also, the lively quaver activity, which creates the dance mood for the line "Das its ein Tanz über Stock und Stein" ("That is a dance over stick and stone") in Part One, No. 3 of the *Mass*, echoes the similarly strident 3/4 quaver activity in Siegfried's Rhine Journey in *Götterdämmerung*. Most noticeable of all, is the way in which Delius sets the word "Verlangen" in the final section of Part One, for baritone and chorus. "Verlangen" means "longing." "Nun bricht wie ein Born aus mir mein Verlangen!" is the way in which the word appears in Nietzsche's text ("Now burst from out me my longing like a fountain"). For his setting, Delius consequently modifies the "yearning" *Tristan* chord, which we hear in the first bars of Wagner's prelude. He even maintains Wagner's tonality with an F-natural and B-natural in the bass, forming the same tritone harmony as Wagner, with an E-flat two octaves above, also as in Wagner. Delius adds a A-natural above the B-natural, and a D-flat above the E-flat, which are alien to Wagner's chord, but the sound, particularly the Wagnerian manner in which it is scored, leaves no doubt as to the lineage of this detail.

And so the Wagnerian echoes continue, which it would be wearisome to elaborate in their entirety, though one final reverberation is hard to leave out: During the ruminative opening of Part Two, the interplay between horns (one of which Delius specifies as an "echo") is reminiscent not only of Siegfried's horn calls but, even more so of the reveille between horns that opens Act II, scene 3 of *Lohengrin*. Like Debussy, Delius was so drenched in Wagner than Wagnerian droplets dripped out of him without his knowing it. There is much that is not Wagnerian, though these aspects are perhaps less satisfying. There are also equivalent moods to Mahler's Night Pieces during No. 5 of Part One, "Nacht ist es" ("Night Reigns"), but Delius resists tone painting, even at moments where one might expect it, such as the references to Zarathustra's soul being like a leaping fountain, which calls for but does not immediately receive a flourish of harps. Neither is there a Mahlerian harp to suggest the Midnight Bell during his setting of "O Mensch, gib acht!" There is much "la, la, la-ing" and "ah, ah, ah-ing" from the choir and quite a lot of distinctly Gilbert and Sullivan 6/8 rhythm to suggest the spirit of the dance, which some critics do not regard as having quite come off. Peter J. Pirie certainly felt this to be the case:

> *A Mass of Life* is more uneven than *A Village Romeo and Juliet*—Delius' opera, but in a different way; the opera has its weak passages, but is a stylistic whole, while the *Mass* is a mixture of styles.... The best passages are the orchestral interludes and the meditative centre of the work. The two dance choruses have been much criticized; they seem on the surface to be an odd combination of contrapuntal exercises with Delius' characteristic lilting dance style.... The massive choral section that opens the work, "Oh Thou my Will," is rather foursquare and unyielding. Delius was evidently aiming at rock-like strength, and to an extent he achieved it, but at the expense of a certain muscle-bound effect."[20]

Having said that, surely Delius wrote nothing grander and did indeed transmute the emotional drive that lay behind Nietzsche's philosophy into a luminously musical equivalent. The sublimity of mountain solitude, the heroic loneliness, the hushed rapture of midnight, the pagan joy of dancing, and a sensitive setting of the eloquent rhythms of Nietzsche's German which, among other English composers, perhaps only Benjamin Britten would have been able to match.

I first became emotionally involved with, rather than merely intellectually aware of *A Mass of Life* after having recorded a CD review of music by a quite different composer. Emerging into the control room after reading my script in the studio, the producer was playing back one of the other reviews for the following weekend's transmission. Out poured, in all its glory, Richard Hickox's

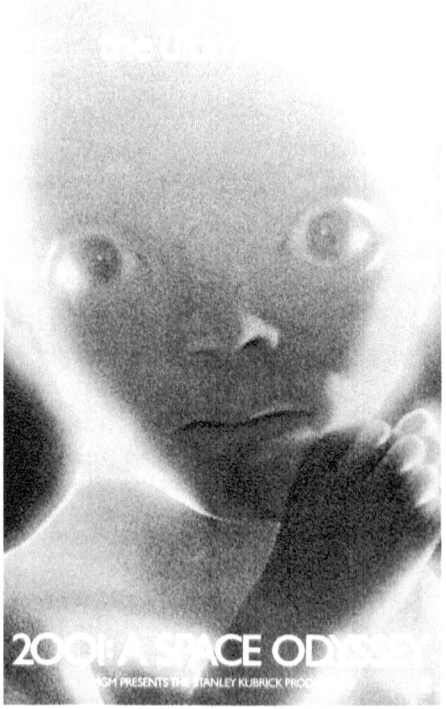

Poster showing the Cosmic Child at the end of Stanley Kubrick's *2001—A Space Odyssey* (1968).

1997 account of the Delius *Mass* with the Bournemouth Symphony Orchestra. From that moment on, I was under Delius' command in a way I had never been before. I had encountered *On Hearing the First Cuckoo in Spring* as a boy, when it had been used in a school play. The pastoral dreaminess had delighted me, as much as the "Sleigh-Ride" had exhilarated me. The Wagnerian echoes of the "Walk to the Paradise Garden" had enchanted me, especially when I heard it in the context of Peter Weigel's dreamy 1992 film adaptation of Delius' opera *A Village Romeo and Juliet* for which it was written. The various evocations of Pan at which Delius excelled struck me as exotic and idiosyncratic—hard to place in a nationalistic sense, but very much an emanation of the fin-de-siècle; but when this musical style was combined with Nietzsche's text, the result, as Nietzsche himself would have said, was "dynamite." Intriguingly, the cover of the Hickox CD depicted an unnerving close-up of a human fetus, again echoing the imagery at the end of Kubrick's *2001*.

But the question remains: Is Delius' *A Mass of Life* the kind of music to which Nietzsche hoped his Superman would one day dance? In his copy of the vocal score of Bizet's *Carmen*, Nietzsche wrote "Ideal aller Castagnetten-Musik"[21] ("Ideal of all castanet music"). Delius did include castanets in the first "Dance Song" of his Mass, but that is about as close he ever got to the spirit of Bizet.

10

Benjamin Britten

With the exception of Delius, who was himself rather an exception, British composers in general seem to have been less influenced by Nietzsche than their continental counterparts. As Colin Wilson once observed, the British have never been particularly interested by ideas, and given England's troubled relationship with Germany throughout the twentieth century, Nietzsche's ideas in particular seemed alien and unwanted, even when they weren't distorted beyond recognition by his sinister sister and her Nazi friends. There were, however, British writers who interpreted Nietzsche along their own lines. One of these was George Bernard Shaw, who, like Wagner with Schopenhauer, took from Nietzsche what he needed to form his own philosophy of life. Before D.C. Comics came on the scene, Shaw's play *Man and Superman* (1901–1903) was largely responsible for popularizing that rather awkward translation of Nietzsche's "Übermensch." The purpose of Shaw's Superman is to enable the Life Force to understand itself: "Are we agreed that Life is a force which has made innumerable experiments in organizing itself; that the mammoth and the man, the mouse and the megatherium, the flies and the fleas and the Father of the Church, are all more or less successful attempts to build up that raw force into higher and higher individuals, the ideal individual being omnipotent, omniscient, infallible, and withal completely, unilludedly self-conscious: in short, a god?"[1]

Shaw thus presented Nietzsche to his countrymen in his own particular way. One of Shaw's musical admirers was the composer Rutland Boughton (1878–1960), whose opera *The Immortal Hour* (1914) was likewise much admired by the playwright. Boughton and Shaw enjoyed a lively correspondence, not all of it complimentary on Shaw's part but ultimately supportive. Boughton, who was a communist, organized music festivals at the Glastonbury Assembly Rooms long before that town became the venue for the famously muddy rock festivals of our own time.

He also described himself as a follower of Nietzsche's ideas, and, as his biographer Michael Hurd explains, Shaw and Nietzsche contributed "to a 'superman' sense of being set apart from ordinary mortals and answerable only to his own vision of what was good, beautiful, and appropriate. They were, in short, admirable fuel for a man intent upon following his own star."[2] In 1921, Boughton wrote, "I intend much more bodily to declare in my work, and so far as possible in my life, the ideas promulgated in Nietzsche's *Zarathustra* and Shaw's *Methusala*." Hurd then usefully points out that Boughton's Violin Sonata from 1921 specifically expresses this intention by means of the quotations that introduce each of its three movements. The first movement quotes from the section called "The Afterworldsmen": "Most honestly and purely the healthy body speaketh, the perfect and rectangular; it speaketh of the significance of Earth." (R. J. Hollingdale translates this as "Purer and more honest of speech is the healthy body, perfect and square-built: and it speaks of the meaning of the earth."[3]) The second movement quotes from "Of Joys and Passions": "Once having passions thou callest them evil. Now, however thou hast nothing but thy passions. Thou laidest thy highest goal upon these passions; then they become thy virtues and delights." (Hollingdale's version is "Once you had passions and called them evil. But now you have only virtues: they grew from out your passions. You laid your highest aim in the heart of these passions: they became your virtues and joys."[4]) The third movement comes from "The Dance Song," which had previously been set by Delius in *A Mass of Life*: "I am the advocate of God in the presence of the Devil. But he is the spirit of gravity. How could I, ye light ones, be an enemy unto divine dances? or unto the feet of girls with beautiful ankles?" (Hollingdale: "I am God's advocate with the Devil; he, however, is the Spirit of Gravity. How could I be enemy to divine dancing, you nimble creatures? or to girls' feet with fair ankles?"[5])

There is little evidence of Nietzsche in Boughton's other work, however. He set none of Nietzsche's writings to music, and the prophet of the Superman would indeed seem rather out of place in mystical Celtic dramas like *The Immortal Hour*, ballets such as *Mystic Dance of the Grail* or, indeed, Boughton's cycle of Arthurian operas. Neither did Nietzsche appeal to Boughton's more famous British contemporaries Elgar, Holst and Vaughan Williams. Though the rather more experimental composer Cyril Scott (1879–1970) quotes from Nietzsche three times in his autobiography, *Bone of Contention* (1969), and H. Balfour Gardiner (1877–1950), who had studied music with Scott in Frankfurt, was also an enthusiast of Nietzschean philosophy,[6] it really wasn't until much later in the twentieth century that Nietzsche found a satisfying response from a British composer in the music of Benjamin Britten (1913–1976).

Ironically given the pun implicit in his name, Britten was a much more cosmopolitan figure, setting French, Italian and German texts to music. One of these was his setting of *Seven Sonnets of Michelangelo* (1940), which he suggested were perhaps a response to Nietzsche's call to "mediterraneanize music."[7] Nietzsche also hovers behind Britten's virtuosic display piece for piano and strings, *Young Apollo* (1939), his response to the brilliant sunshine of America, whither he had fled at the outbreak of the Second World War. This piece might be viewed as a landmark on the way to Britten's most Nietzschean work, *Death in Venice* (1973), for *Young Apollo* is also a peon of praise to the god who forms the antithesis of Dionysus in Nietzsche's *The Birth of Tragedy*. Apollo and the sun form the imagery of *Young Apollo*—the planet of life and the glittering male god of inspiration combining to inspire humanity (but particularly the homosexual Britten) with form, light and intellectual beauty. Brilliantly ascending scalic passages and glissandi on the piano scatter sonic light all around at the beginning of *Young Apollo* before the strings set up a buoyant rhythm fully suggestive of Nietzsche's desire to become weightless. This truly is music of weightlessness and radiance, replete with some of Britten's most gravity-defying orchestral tricks—*col legno* effects on the strings, swirling glissandi up into celestial registers, ecstatic ostinati and lucid timbres created by the combination of percussion and strings, which none other than Britten could have created. Britten might very well have placed these lines from Nietzsche's *Zarathustra* at the head of the score:

> A dance-song and a mocking-song on the Spirit of Gravity, my supreme, most powerful devil, who they say is "the lord of the earth."
> Lately I looked into your eye, O Life! And I seemed to sink into the unfathomable.
> But you pulled me out with a golden rod; you laughed mockingly when I called you unfathomable.[8]

One does not necessarily need to interpret these words along homosexual lines (Nietzsche, after all, refers to dancing *girls*—due, one suspects, to the morality of the time, which prohibited what Nietzsche more likely had in mind), but Britten's perspective undeniably did.

Young Apollo is a musical expression of Britten's own homoerotic but ultimately Platonic ideal, which finds its fullest expression in the character of Tadzio. But another work lay on the road to *Death in Venice*, which was Britten's setting of *Sechs Hölderlin Fragmente* (*Six Hölderlin Fragments*, 1958). What was implicit in *Young Apollo*, becomes explicit in Britten's spare and serene setting of the third Hölderlin fragment, "Socrates und Alcibiades":

> Warum huldigest du, heiliger Sokrates,
> Diesem Jünglinge stets? Kennest du Größers nicht?
> Warum siehet mit Liebe,
> Wie auf Götter, dein Aug' auf ihn?
>
> Wer das Tiefste gedacht, liebt das Lebendigste,
> Hohe Tugend versteht, wer in die Welt geblickt,
> Und es neigen die Weisen
> Oft am Ende zu Schönem sich.
>
> (Why do you, holy Socrates, so revere/ This youth? Do you know nothing greater?/ Why, as if on gods,/ Does your eye rest lovingly on him?
>
> He who thinks most deeply loves what is most full of life,/ Moral philosophy is understood by one who's seen the world/ And in the end, wise men/ Incline, often, to Beauty.)

Though the poem ends with a statement, Britten's music suggests a question, making us wonder if there is not more to this very Apollonian hymn than "only" the worship of Beauty. There is, of course, and Britten explores what is missing here (i.e., Eros, Dionysus and Thanatos) in *Death in Venice*, a work which he described as expressing "everything that Peter [Pears, Britten's partner] and I have stood for."[9]

Based on Thomas Mann's novella "Der Tod in Venedig" (1912), Britten's opera is much more focused on the Nietzschean subtext of the story than Visconti's film version, which had appeared two years before the opera's 1973 première. Visconti stayed mostly on the surface of the narrative, concentrating on mood, fashions, mis-en-scène and personalities, but Britten went to the core of what the story is about, which Mann himself had based on Nietzsche's ideas. The work is, of course, set in Venice, a location with many Wagnerian and Nietzschean connotations. Indeed, Nietzsche had claimed in *Ecce Homo* that the only other word he could think of to replace that of "music" was "Venice."[10] In his 1900 novel *Il fuoco* (*The Flame*), D'Annunzio, another interpreter of Nietzsche's writings after his own fashion, pointed out that Wagner came to Venice to compose the second act of *Tristan*. D'Annunzio's hero, Stelio Effrena, a distinctly autobiographical character if ever there was one, described this historical event as Wagner's "conversation with death," the second act of *Tristan* being "a hymn to eternal night."[11] Now, Wagner has come back to Venice to die. Stelio is later one of the pallbearers of Wagner's coffin; and D'Annunzio himself composed the inscription upon the walls of the Grand Canal's Palazzo Vendramin where the Meister did indeed die:

> In questo palagio
> l'ultimo spiro de Riccardo Wagner
> odono le anime perpetuarsi come la marea
> che lambe i marmi

> (In this place/ the souls hear/ the last breath of Richard Wagner/ perpetuating itself like the tide/ which washes the marble beneath.[12])

Thomas Mann was well aware of these resonances when choosing the location of his novella. It is ultimately Venice itself, the city of Dionysian decadence, that destroys the writer Gustav von Aschenbach; Aschenbach embodies all those Apollonian qualities identified by Nietzsche in *The Birth of Tragedy*:

> Apollo, the god of all plastic energies, is at the same time the soothsaying god. He, who (as the etymology of the name indicates) is the "shining one," the deity of light, is also ruler over the beautiful illusion of the inner world of fantasy. The higher truth, the perfection of these states in contrast to the incompletely intelligible everyday world, this deep consciousness of nature, healing and helping in sleep and dreams, is the same time the symbolical analogue of the soothsaying faculty and of the arts generally, which make life possible and worth living.... We must keep in mind that measure, restraint, that freedom from the wilder emotions, that calm of the sculptor god.[13]

Aschenbach represents all these qualities in Myfanwy Piper's libretto. When he first observes Tadzio on the Venice Lido, Aschenbach believes that he embodies the soul of Greece.[14] Later, he adds that he might even have created him himself out of his own Apollonian ideals[15]; but Aschenbach would have done well to have read Nietzsche's *Birth of Tragedy* first, which offers a warning to those who neglect the Dionysian side of the coin: "Lest this Apollonian tendency congeal the form to Egyptian rigidity and coldness, lest the effort to prescribe to the individual wave its path and realm might annul the motion of the whole lake, the high tide of the Dionysian destroyed from time to time all those little circles in which the one-sidedly Apollonian "will" had sought to confine the Hellenic spirit."[16]

This is exactly what happens to Aschenbach. Too long a slave to Apollo, he has neglected the Dionysian aspects of his own personality, and when his attraction to Tadzio—originally Platonic and inspiring—degenerates into the "hackneyed words 'I love you,'" he finds he is unable to resist the power of "the stranger god." "Overcome by beauty I tried, quite simply, to use the emotion released for my own creation," Piper's Aschenbach explains, "What I wrote was good, quite what was expected of me; to the point, yet poignant. But when it was done I felt degraded—as if I had taken part in an orgy."[17] He has a premonition that this would happen right at the start of the drama, when he encounters one of the several harbingers of death, who are all sung by the same bass-baritone. (These include the gondolier who rows him to the Lido, the hotel manager, the barber who transforms him into a fop and the strolling player who torments him.) In this instance, it is the traveller Aschenbach encounters in the Munich graveyard, who sings of monstrous flowers, distorted trees with naked roots, "milk-white blooms" and "huge birds,"[18] summoning up a nightmare landscape of erotic horror. In his later dream, in scene 13, Dionysus and Apollo compete for his soul. Dionysus urges him to "receive the stranger god," but Apollo cautions him to reject the abyss. Dionysus argues that whoever rejects him in the name of Apollonian reason, beauty and form "denies his nature," and in section 20 of *The Birth of Tragedy*, Nietzsche similarly argues that the overly Apollonian culture of the nineteenth-century was in desperate need for a new Dionysian art—specifically the music-dramas of Richard Wagner and the new world of the Nietzschean Superman, both of which will overthrow old values and inaugurate a new world of moral and sexual freedom. The subtext of all this may well have been Nietzsche's own repressed sexuality.

> But how suddenly the desert of our exhausted culture, just described in such gloomy terms, is changed when it is touched by the Dionysian magic! A tempest seizes everything that has outlived itself, everything that is decayed, broken, and withered, and, whirling, shrouds it in a cloud of red dust to carry it into the air like a vulture. Confused, our eyes look after what has disappeared; for what they see has been raised as from a depression into golden light, so full and green, so amply alive, immeasurable and full of yearning. Tragedy is seated amid this excess of life, suffering, pleasure, in sublime ecstasy, listening to a distant melancholy song that tells of the mothers of being whose names are: Delusion, Will, Woe.
> Yes, my friends, believe with me in Dionysian life and the rebirth of tragedy.... Prepare yourself for hard strife, but believe in the miracles of your god.[19]

This is the writing of a young man, but as Nietzsche grew older he realized the importance and necessity of balance and integration. To be "Dionysian" one has to be strong enough to withstand the life-enhancing but terrifying powers of Dionysus while at the same time Apollonian enough to stop them spiraling out of control.

Taken from a Jungian perspective, this is also what Michael Tippett's 1955 opera *A Midsummer Marriage* is about: a simple case of psychological balance, which both sets of male and female principals use fully to integrate their respective personalities. Significantly, Tippett (1905–1998) applied Jung's anima and animus archetypes, along with other Jungian concepts such as individuation and the collective unconscious, all of which originally derived from Nietzsche in the first place. Jung's biographer Richard Noll is quite clear on this, arguing that after reading Nietzsche's works as a student in the 1890s, Jung (1875–1961) became "intoxicated with the mysteries of blood and sexuality and underground initiation in the ancient cults of Dionysus."[20] The action of *The Midsummer Marriage* takes place on a wooded hill-top before a temple, which imagery also reminds one of Thomas Mann's Nietzschean-inspired chapter "Snow" in *The Magic Mountain* (1924), in which the hero Hans Castorp dreams of walking through an Apollonian landscape of "joyous and winning" youths; but there is also a temple, "massy, weathered to a grey-green tone, on a foundation reached by a steep flight of steps,"[21] in which Castorp witnesses a horrifying Dionsyian ritual of human sacrifice. Mann's imagery here ultimately derives from Nietzsche's stormy mountain experience in which he witnessed a farmer killing a goat; and Tippett's setting for *The Midsummer Marriage* also suggests a Nietzschean origin if only in part. Indeed, he himself referred to Nietzsche in his essay on the opera. Though erroneously regarding Nietzsche's insanity as the result of experiencing the rebirth of an ancient god in Zarathustra (more probably, it was much more prosaically the result of contracting syphilis), he went on: "But it can be shown, I think, that hidden in Zarathustra is an earlier meeting of Nietzsche with yet another god—with Dionysus, the god who came from the East into Greece to force his way like a wild storm into the measured climate of the Olympian system."[22] In the first Act of *The Midsummer Marriage*, the characters Mark and Jennifer are transfigured respectively into archetypes of Dionysus and Athena. (Athena is the feminine equivalent of Apollo.) Mark's reference to young men laughing and dancing "to the springing sap" carries with it echoes of Nietzsche's Dionysian dance imagery of gravity-defying joy. Tippett follows this up with the famous Ritual Dances, which combine Dionysian revelry and Apollonian restraint. Everything ends with marriage, as the title leads us to expect—and hence, from Tippett's Jungian point of view, the integration of the psyche, both male and female, Dionysus and Athena/Apollo.

In Britten's opera, Aschenbach, alas, is not Superman enough to withstand the power of Dionysus and attain this life-saving integration. Instead, he collapses on the sands of the Lido, a hideous travesty of himself after a vain attempt to restore his youth by cosmetic means. And as he does so, Tadzio—the spirit of Apollonian beauty—wades out into a sea that symbolizes artistic inspiration.

Of course, in Visconti's film version of the story, Aschenbach is transformed into a composer, based on Mahler, and Mahler's music accompanies the action in a highly choreographed manner, transmuting Visconti's elegiac images into something far more powerful than they would be without it. The effect is highly Wagnerian. Britten's approach was radically different and it much more closely approaches the musical esthetic argued for by Nietzsche—that lightness, Mediterraneanism, elegance and light-footedness. It is, in fact, far more than mere Mediterraneanism, inspired, as it is, by the indigenous music of the Far East. There is no mighty orchestra in Britten's opera; the overall effect is of chamber proportions with much of Aschenbach's recitative being accompanied by solo piano. Music descriptive of Venice, such as the expansive motif for the sea and for "Serenissima" itself, does suggest a more colorful orchestral palette, but the music for Tadzio is the most radically "different."

Ever since his tour of the Far East in 1956, Britten had been fascinated by the sound of the Balinese Gamelan Orchestra, that evocative percussion ensemble, the timbres, pentatonic scales and rhythms of which also inspired his 1956 ballet *The Prince of the Pagodas*. Britten returned to these exotic sounds for *Death in Venice* using them to suggest the "otherness" of Tadzio and the ideal of Apollonian beauty which he symbolizes. As Michael Kennedy perceptively observes, "rarely can the vibraphone have been used more tellingly"[23] This "otherness" is emphasized by Britten's decision to cast a dancer rather than a singer as Tadzio, who never speaks in the opera and whose big moment is the Pentathlon (in scene 7). This is presided over by Apollo himself, who inaugurates the proceedings with the famous phrase, "He who loves beauty/ Worships me." Harking back to Britten's *Young Apollo*, the chorus refers to the legend of Hyacinthus, "basking in Apollo's rays." (Apollo and Hyacinthus were the archetypes of male love in the ancient world: When Apollo accidentally killed his lover, the Hyacinth flower bloomed from Hyacinthus' blood.) Watching Tadzio and his young friends compete in these athletics inspires Aschenbach to write his Apollonian prose, just as Visconti had him inspired to write Mahler's setting of "O Mensch, gib acht." Britten and Piper instead decided to have Aschenbach compose a Hymn to Beauty based on the *Phaedrus* of Socrates, which Mann had also incorporated into the story. Michael Kennedy quite rightly compares the music for these lines ("But this is beauty, Phaedrus,/ Discovered through the senses/ And senses lead to passion, Phaedrus/ And passion to the pit"[24]) to Britten's earlier setting of the *Michelangelo Sonnets*.

Kennedy claims there are no words to describe the end of the opera, comparing Britten's music here to the late paintings of Turner.[25] With its vibraphone, tam-tams and drifting strings, Britten summons a sound world at the opposite extreme of Wagner's, far beyond even the Mediterranean setting of the opera's action. Reminiscent of the imagery that brings W. B. Yeats' 1930 poem "Byzantium" to a close, with its "dolphin-torn" and "gong-tormented" sea, this music is truly an equivalent of what Nietzsche hoped for—that "supra-European music which holds its own even before the brown sunsets of the desert, whose soul is kindred to the palm-tree and knows how to roam among great solitary beasts of prey": "I could imagine a music whose rarest magic would consist in this, that it no longer knew anything of good and evil, except that perhaps some sailor's homesickness, some golden shadow and delicate weakness would now and then flit across it: an art that would see fleeing towards it from a great distance the colors of a declining, now almost incomprehensible *moral* world, and would be hospitable and deep enough to receive such late fugitives."[26]

There are also deeply personal and somewhat troubling undercurrents in Britten's opera, which is also a kind of musical confessional, and

Benjamin Britten (1913–1976). Photograph by Hans Wild for *High Fidelity* magazine, 1968 (Wikimedia Commons).

Nietzsche may well have sympathized with them if he had lived to experience them. If we are to believe what Nietzsche's biographer, Joachim Köhler believes, Nietzsche was strongly attracted to young boys, whom he may well have sought out in Sicily, inspired by the erotic photographs of Wilhelm von Gloeden. As we have seen, Köhler suggests: "In his photographs we see dancing boys, raised by Nietzsche to the heroic status of gods who spurn all clothes and are often said to congregate on the slopes of Monte Ziretto at night to celebrate Bacchanalian rites. 'There all is dance and high spirits, where the gods seek each other, flee from each other, find each other again, hear each other again, belong to each other again, where all time mocks the passing moment.' Thus spake Zarathustra."[27]

Britten was also interested in young boys, some of whom he employed in his operas such as David Spencer in *Albert Herring* (1947) and David Hemmings in *The Turn of the Screw* (1954). Others he merely enjoyed spending time with. One of these was Robin Long, his "fisherboy friend" known as "the Nipper." Another was his live-in amanuensis James Bernard. Fresh from Wellington College, Bernard assisted Britten on work for *Billy Budd* (1951) before moving on to scoring Hammer horror films. There is not a shred of evidence that any impropriety with any of these boys ever took place. Bernard told me that though he and Britten shared a bath together during his time at Britten's Red House at Aldeburgh, nothing inappropriate ever took place between them, and that whenever Bernard talked about is own "naughtinesses" as he termed them, Britten would "clam up." But despite that, the attraction was there, and the appeal of Mann's novella to Britten was surely more than merely an esthetic one: It was a way of confessing his own psyche to the world. Britten knew all too well the importance of Apollonian restraint and its emotional consequences. The Dionysian art of music no doubt helped him to negotiate all this; not that he was celibate: Bernard also told me that Britten did confess to needing "a lot of sex" when he was composing, and "less sex" when he wasn't, but that was presumably with Peter Pears, and apparently, according to the complete lack of evidence, never with boys. That would have caused Dionysus to have hurled him into the abyss—if not emotionally (one thinks of Aschenbach's line, "I felt degraded—as if I had taken part in an orgy"), then certainly socially. Britten's erotic attraction to male innocence (a subject so fully worked out in *The Turn of the Screw*) might usefully be compared to Nietzsche's response to the putative self-portrait of Hans Holbein: "Lips made for kissing!"[28] This does not say it all, but it says a great deal nonetheless.

11

Béla Bartók

Bartók (1881–1945) often felt lonely. He was also almost pathologically obsessed with privacy and also had a passing interest in the macabre, which to modern ears would seem to chime with his simultaneous interest in Transylvanian folk culture. Indeed, during a visit to Paris in his youth, he much enjoyed visiting the nightclub called *Le Néant* (literally "Nothingness"):

> In this tavern, there are wooden coffins instead of tables, and the walls of the rooms are black and decorated with human skeletons or parts of skeletons; the waiters wear *pompe-funébre* sort of garments; and the lighting makes your skin look wax-yellow, your lips livid and your finger-nails violet (in fact, you look like a corpse); and they entertain you by, for instance, wrapping one of your party in a shroud up to the chin and standing over him—or her—in a coffin where under your eyes, he turns into a skeleton.[1]

If one puts all these factors together—the loneliness, the privacy, the spookiness—it helps to explain why Bartók should have been attracted to compose an opera based on the legend of *Bluebeard's Castle* (1918). In turn, his librettist, Béla Balázs, had been inspired by Maurice Maeterlinck's play *Ariane et Barbe-Bleu* (1906), in which Bluebeard's various imprisoned wives resist the freedom offered to them by Ariane, his latest wife. The idea stemmed from an anecdote about Maeterlinck's mistress, Georgette Leblanc, who was forever rescuing animals, none of which ever showed any gratitude. He subtitled his play "The Useless Deliverance." Paul Dukas, who set the play to music in 1907, explained, "No one wants to be rescued. Rescue is costly because it is the unknown. Men (and women) will always prefer a familiar slavery to the terrifying uncertainty of the burden of liberty."[2] And here is the first Nietzschean resonance of this chapter: the Superman is not for everyone. After all, Nietzsche subtitled his *Zarathustra* "A Book for Nobody and Everyone," realizing that no one in his own time was ready for the freedom he offered them, but from which everyone would benefit if only they had the courage to embrace it. In Bartók's opera, Bluebeard is also very much alone, and also afraid that his latest wife,

Judith, will destroy their love for one another by her annoying habit of winkling out personal secrets and bringing light into his gloomy castle. We are, of course, meant to feel sorrow for him rather than revulsion. Like Wagner's Lohengrin, Bartók's Bluebeard cautions his new bride not to ask too many questions. Just as curiosity killed the cat, Judith runs the same risk. There are seven doors in Bluebeard's creepy castle, all of them barred and bolted, and there is blood on the castle walls; but Judith manages to persuade her husband to give her the keys. As she opens one door after another, Bluebeard's privacy is stripped away. Behind the final door, she discovers all of her husband's previous wives—wives who had asked the same questions as her, and hence destroyed their only chance of happiness, along with Bluebeard's own chances of a loving relationship. She offers to liberate them, but they are so accustomed to their predicament they reject her offer. Bluebeard now realizes that henceforth he will always live in darkness and solitude. The opera is, therefore, a warning against intrusive curiosity.

Béla Bartók (1881–1945). Photographer unidentified, 1927 (Wikimedia Commons).

Bartók, similarly, needed his own privacy; but *Bluebeard's Castle* is also about the inevitability of solitude, especially for those who consider the realities of existence: Bartók was locked in the castle of his own insight into the reality of life's immense solitude. We are born alone, we die alone and all our meetings in-between merely disguise the terror of our predicament—a terror only a Superman can stare at and survive.

Nietzsche was a kind of Judith, spreading light and eradicating delusion in his quest for the Superman. Like Bluebeard, this aspect of his personality brought him little but isolation and incomprehension from others. Nietzsche never found sexual, still less emotional fulfilment in a partner. Syphilis, possibly caught from a prostitute, possibly congenital, later plunged him into the ultimate darkness and solitude of insanity. Like

Bartók, Nietzsche was a dutiful son, but a not uncritical one. Bartók's letters to his own mother reveal a rather hectoring tone, suggesting that he was always going to prefer to be the dominant partner in all his subsequent relationships with women: "As for you addressing me in German, dear Mama—well, not even as a joke do I want this. Speak a foreign language only when absolutely necessary!"[3] He also urges her not to take early retirement, but at the same time insists, "You should not do one iota over and above what is absolutely necessary."[4]

Some of Bartók's over-protective bossiness towards his mother can perhaps be explained by the loss of his father, who died when Béla was only eight. His chauvinistic side certainly seems to have developed quite early in life. He wavered over the issue of women's liberation, originally thinking that women should share the same liberties as men, before changing his mind and coming to believe that "men and women are so different in mind and body that it may not be such a bad idea after all to demand from women a greater degree of chastity."[5] These misogynistic views (hardly unusual for the time) were, of course, taken to an extreme by Nietzsche, whose views on women contemporary Nietzsche scholars have great difficulty in accommodating; but it was far more Nietzsche's atheism and his emphasis on self-reliance in life that really appealed to Bartók. His discovery of Nietzsche along with Richard Strauss' musical interpretation of *Also Sprach Zarathustra* crystalized Bartók's sense of spiritual and emotional loneliness. It also fired him with enthusiasm: "The work was received with real abhorrence in musical circles here, but it filled me with the greatest enthusiasm. At last there was a way of composing which seemed to hold the seeds of a new life. At once I threw myself into the study of all Strauss' scores and began again to write music myself."[6] The immediate result of all this was Bartók's own gigantic symphony based on the life of the Hungarian revolutionary hero *Kossuth* (1903). Later, he got to know and admire Delius' *Mass of Life*, and on a personal level, Nietzsche's philosophy helped Bartók find the strength to come to terms with his sense of emotional isolation, as he confessed to his mother: "I am lonely. I may have friends yet there are times when I suddenly become aware of the fact that I am absolutely alone! And I prophesy, I have a foreknowledge, that this spiritual loneliness is to be my destiny. I look about me in search of the ideal companion and yet I am fully aware that it is a vain quest. Even if I should ever succeed in finding someone, I am sure I would soon be disappointed."[7]

It is hardly surprising, then, that Bartók should have been so attracted to Nietzsche's advocacy of independence and intellectual freedom. In a letter to Irmy Jurkovics, one of his early female friends, Bartók emphasized just how much Nietzsche's point of view had impressed him, even if he doesn't actually mention Nietzsche by name: "Every man must strive to rise above all. Nothing must touch him: he must be completely indifferent. Only thus can he reconcile himself to death and to the meaninglessness of life. And having attained that highest degree of indifference when it's all the same to you whether you can help people or whether you can't, don't you even then still desire one thing, and desire it fervently: that all mankind should rise to that same height?"[8] This is Bartók's paraphrase of Nietzsche's mountain elegy in *Ecce Homo*, where he describes how the ice is near, the solitude is terrible, "but how peacefully all things lie in the light! How freely one breathes! How much one feels beneath one!"[9] Irmy Jurkovics was the daughter of a judge who lived in Bartók's home town Nagyszentmiklós. She idolized Bartók, as did her sister, but apart from writing her some revealing letters and dedicating his Fantasy No. 2 to her, Bartók seems not to have taken things any further. This was a pity, as Irmy would have been delighted to have been Bartók's long-sought-after "ideal companion."

As one might expect, it was music that always came to Bartok's rescue when the glooms were upon him, but it was appropriately a peasant *girl* (Lidi Dósa) who sang him the first folk song which left so strong an impression on him that it sowed the seed of his compulsion to explore Hungarian folk music. In 1907, Bartók thought he might have found a way out of his isolation and discovered an ideal soul mate in the young violinist Stefi Geyer (1888–1956). His two letters to her reveal far more about himself than he ever revealed to again to anyone. In the first letter, he tried to persuade the devoutly Catholic Stefi to embrace his own Nietzsche-inspired brand of atheism, arguing that man created God after his own likeness, rather than the other way round. He confessed that he had been an atheist since his 22nd year and "explained" the soul by insisting it was a mere "functioning of the brain and the nervous system. It is finite—mortal. The body, as matter is 'immortal' indeed, for matter in this world is never lost; it only changes form."

He signed this very long letter "an unbeliever, who is more honest than a great many believers," and he was devastated to learn that Stefi had been horrified by his views. He was almost in tears, but, undaunted, he wrote back, this time advocating the idea of suicide as a rational choice for human beings, and disagreeing with her that it was a cowardly act. As long as his mother and sister were around, he, of course, would not commit such a selfish act. "But beyond that? Once I have no responsibility towards *any* living person, once I live all by myself (never *'wavering'* even then)—why should suicide be a cowardly act?"[10] (Nietzsche had also confessed that the thought of suicide was a solace that had helped him get through many a bad night.[11]) As a consequence of all this, Bartók felt he would never again find any consolation in life save in music.

He then wrote out a line of music, drawing Stefi's attention to what he called "your Leitmotif." He later included this four-note phrase in his first Violin Concerto, the first movement of which expresses his love for the girl who soon found herself locked in Bartók's castle of memory. The score of the Concerto also contains a mysterious footnote commemorating June 28, 1907, which Bartók, as usual, never explained, but Stefi recalled that it was on this day that she, her brother and Bartók had sung three-part canons, written by the composer.[12] Bartók had come to visit Jászberény, where Stefi lived, ostensibly to collect folk songs, but, as David Cooper explains, the area was hardly a rich hunting ground for folk material, so the real reason for the visit appears to have been to visit her.[13]

Stefi's leitmotif cropped up again as the dedication of the Ten Easy Pieces for Piano (Sz. 39) and also in the 14 Bagatelles (Op. 16), so her ghost continued to haunt him. Alas, that was really all she was to him now—a ghost. Having laid bare his Nietzschean soul to her, Bartók had lost her. He knew all too well not only the danger of asking too many questions but also of supplying too many answers; and he began to realize that perhaps he shouldn't aim to find his intellectual equal in a woman at all. In this, he resembled Wagner, who explained that the story of *Lohengrin* represented his own desire for a woman who would love him unconditionally and unquestioningly. Intellectual equality would have soon put paid to that.

No sooner had Stefi been relinquished than Márta Ziegler (1893–1967), one of Bartók's piano pupils, arrived on the scene. She was the simple, unsmiling, and generally rather enigmatic daughter of a Budapest police inspector. Only 15 at the time, she was, however, no fool, being well-read and musical. Bartók dedicated his "Portrait of a Girl" from *Sketches*, Op. 9b, to her. Unlike the highly romantic music that Stefi had inspired, this piece was much more restrained; but Bartók couldn't resist including an inverted version of Stefi's motif in the final phrase.

Bartók still hadn't dragged himself away from his thoughts of Stefi. He wrote a funeral dirge based on Stefi's leitmotif for his First String Quartet as if to say "gone, but not forgotten." Even so, that didn't stop him marrying Márta in 1909. Again, reflecting his obsessive, Bluebeard-like urge for secrecy, the marriage took place in private. Even Bartók's own mother found out about it only by accident. Bartók was giving Márta a piano lesson and informed his mother that the girl would be staying for lunch. At two o-clock that afternoon he continued the lesson. When evening fell, he told his mother that Márta would be staying for supper, adding, almost as an afterthought, that they were married.

Bartók revealed nothing particularly intimate about Márta in any of his letters to her or anyone else. His marriage was another door securely barred and bolted. It seems that Bartók wanted to keep his private life a secret even from Mártha. The fact that he dedicated *Bluebeard's Castle* to her was perhaps by way of a warning.

But now another woman appeared in his life. This was Klára Gombossy (1901–1980), whom he met in 1915 while collecting folk songs in Slovakia. She was a forester's daughter and amateur poet, and, significantly, only 15 when he got to know her. It is rather odd that a young man should be so consistently attracted to 15-year-old girls, and if he were alive today, Bartók, like Britten, might well have found himself in trouble with the authorities. He and Klára went on long walks together through the forest, and Bartók was very impressed by her precocious poetic talent (as well, perhaps, as the more physical yearnings she inspired in him). Four of the five poems in Bartók's Opus 15 song collection are by Klára and they tell us something of the erotic subtext of their friendship—along with a whiff of somewhat Nietzschean paganism: The poet's love is compared to the moon looking down at the water, as well as the sun at midday; a kiss is like a rose, her eyes burn like flaming trees, "and in my body, eternally youthful, a heathen burns."[14]

The song remained unpublished during Bartók's lifetime: another secret perhaps? Illicit love and Nietzschean paganism was certainly too hot to handle in public.

Unfortunately—and the Klára interlude may have been symptomatic of it—Bartók's marriage gradually began to go wrong. Bartók's lips were sealed on the subject, as usual. The violinist Jelly d'Arányi (1893–1966) now drifted into his orbit, whom Bartók apparently admired from a purely musical point of view. She regarded him as "difficult" and "awfully disgusting"[15]—so perhaps Bartók's Nietzscheanism didn't go down too well with her either. But Jelly was a passing interest. A new wife was on the horizon in the shape of Ditta Pásztory (1903–1982), who had been a student at the Music Academy where Bartók taught. Though he revealed little about his personal feelings for her in his correspondence, he did describe Ditta as "a skillful housewife." She was, of course, much more than that, joining her husband on the concert platform for the world-première of Sonata for Two Pianos and Percussion in 1938. He even wrote her a piano concerto (his third) so that she could perform it after his death and make some money. The Adagio of this Third Piano Concerto is rather curiously marked "religioso," which makes one wonder if the committed atheist was being ironic in an Nietzschean manner—not that there is a trace of irony in the music itself. Perhaps Bartók was trying to convey the idea of resignation and acceptance of the end—what that other Nietzschean, Bernard Shaw called "the happiness of yielding and dreaming instead of resisting and doing, the sweetness of the fruit that is going rotten."[16] Even so, Bartók carried on composing until four days before he died. Then he was taken to hospital where the final darkness and solitude descended upon him.

Ditta was so grief-stricken by her husband's death, she too became ill and also had to spend some time in hospital. On recovering, she decided to return to Budapest, but resumed her concert career only in the 1960s. Looking at photographs of Bartók and Ditta together they look just as enigmatic as what remains of their correspondence. In one of them, they devour each other's gaze with vampiric intensity. In a later pose Bartók looks down protectively—one might even say possessively, with Ditta sitting beside him, her lips pertly pursed, her eyes staring into space. It is the same story in other photos of Bartók and his various women: He stands and stares into the camera, while his mother sits obediently beside him with a rather wan smile; in a photo from 1912, Bartók and Márta are both sitting down but they aren't looking at each other; the moon-faced Stefi Geyer, Bartók's unattainable muse, is apparently always on her own. And there's one last photograph of Bartók, taken just before he died: ill, thin, exhausted—his deep dark and penetrating gaze even more unnerving and wide-eyed than usual. It is the gaze of a man who sees the lid of his own coffin coming down upon him the lonely gaze of Bluebeard himself, as he closes that final seventh door…

It is tempting to compare that lost gaze with Nietzsche's vacancy during his final illness, but only, of course, in terms of emotional isolation. Bartók's music was in some respects a mirror image of Nietzsche's dancing metaphors. Because of his interest in folk song, Bartók was inevitably interested in folk dance as well, and his own dance music is strongly characterized by driving rhythms and motor percussiveness. His ballet *The Miraculous Mandarin* (1926) is full of them, but its plot, like that of *Bluebeard's Castle* is also a warning about the dangers of desire and intimacy: Three crooks exploit a girl to lure victims to their lair so that they can rob the unfortunates, but when the eponymous Mandarin appears on the scene, things don't go according to plan. The girl does her best to seduce him, but runs off, terrified, when the Mandarin tries to embrace her. The crooks then take things into their own hands and try to murder him without the preliminary seduction, but like the myth of Rasputin's murder, nothing works: suffocation, stabbing, shooting—even hanging are all to no avail. Only when the girl decides to embrace the Mandarin after all does he die, bleeding to death in a kind of Liebestod, which is also reminiscent of the dénouement to Murnau's and Herzog's *Nosferatu* vampire films. No wonder the story appealed to Bartók.

But all this dancing is hardly life affirming in the Nietzschean sense. It is, in fact, quite the opposite. Indeed, so much of Bartók's other dance music is similarly macabre. Take the *Két Román Tánc* (Two Romanian Dances), Op. 8a, for example. Written for piano in 1910, they are admirably suited to the percussive nature of that instrument, though he later orchestrated them. The first one begins in a very dark low register, with consecutive open fifths, immediately suggesting the grotesque and sinister sound world of Franz Liszt's earlier *Czárdás macabre*, which uses the hollow sound of these harmonies to similar effect. Liszt made the macabre connotation explicit in his title, which Bartók avoids, but there is definitely a macabre quality to this piece. It would appear that Nietzsche's individualism and atheism were more congenial to the composer than the idea of dancing for joy. Bartók's dances are certainly exciting but in the way that dancing skeletons are exciting. The motoric staccato quaver movement of the melody in this first Romanian dance is lively, certainly, but the constricted tessitura in such a low pitch, along with the unpredictable chromaticism create a rather claustrophobic quality. The jerky semiquaver flourishes at the end of the various melodic phrases seem menacing, goading the imaginary dancers as though with a whip. There are also, as is so often the case in Bartók's music, many implied if not overt tritones—those devils in music, which admittedly appear quite innocently in so much folk music but which after a century of use by Romantic composers are almost impossible to divorce from their acquired connotations of evil and unease. It is perhaps a little fanciful to suggest that this is some kind of uncanny premonition of what the Nazi's did to Nietzsche—their barbaric interpretation of joy, as typified by their infamous "Kraft durch Freude" ("Strength through Joy") organization; but perhaps Bartók *did* foresee what would happen to a world in which Nietzsche's imagery was taken literally. Remote, isolated, emotionally withdrawn, even after so many relationships with women, Bartók was well-placed to comprehend the consequences of Nietzschean freedom when divorced from human warmth. And this is what makes his music so very "modern." It is not at all surprising that Bartók was one of Bernard Herrmann's favorite composers: Bartók's frightening music was the ideal model for the terrifying soundtrack of Hitchcock's *Psycho*, a film that demonstrates the dangers of believing that someone who is already dead is still alive. Norman Bates believes in God the Mother, and kills on her behalf. In this there are, of course, disturbing parallels in the history of Christianity; but Norman Bates is also smasher of idols—or, in his case, a film star, who is slaughtered unconventionally half way through the movie. Like Nietzsche, this motel owner ends up insane as well.

Anthony Perkins as Norman Bates in *Psycho* (dir. Alfred Hitchcock, 1960).

12

Karol Szymanowski

After Chopin and before Kryszstof Penderecki, Szymanowski (1882–1937) was Poland's most celebrated, if perhaps less popular composer. Admirer of Chopin though Szymanowski was, he was in no doubt that Chopin "belongs to the past.... We, the living and the free, should be seeking new paths and singing other songs."[1] Though Szymanowski wrote much for the piano, including collections of Preludes, Études and Mazurkas, his style veered much more towards the mystical idiom of Scriabin, with its often wide tessitura, trills and the ecstatic though troubling harmonic characteristics of augmented and perfect fourths. Szymanowski also admired Bartók, whom he called "without doubt one of the most interesting of today's composers."[2] He not only shared Bartók's musico-ethnic interests but also a fascination with Nietzsche's ideas. Nietzsche's cult of the Superman appealed in particular to Szymanowski's aristocratic personality, believing, as he did, that art can only be the result of what he called "Pathos der Distanz" ("Pathos of distance").[3] The term derives from Nietzsche's *Beyond Good and Evil*, where Nietzsche elaborates:

> Without the *pathos of distance* such as develops from the incarnate differences of classes, from the ruling caste's constant looking out and looking down on subjects and instruments and from its equally constant exercise of obedience and command, its holding down and holding at a distance, that other, more mysterious pathos could not have developed either, that longing for an ever-increasing widening of distance within the soul itself, the formation of ever higher, rarer, more remote, tenser, more comprehensive states, in short precisely the elevation of the type "man," the continual "self-overcoming of man," to take a moral formula in a supra-moral sense.[4]

Early piano works such as *Metopy* (*Metopes*, Op. 29), and *Mity* (*Myths*, Op. 30) for piano and violin, are musical responses to his experiences in Italy and Sicily, which he visited in 1910 and 1911. These visits helped consolidate his growing conviction, along the same lines as Nietzsche, that it was necessary to resist Germany's musical dominance and absorb Mediterranean culture. For Szymanowski, a wider cultural and esthetic perspective was necessary, as he explained in a letter to his friend Zdzisław Jachimecki: "If Italy did not exist—I could not exist either. I am not a painter or a sculptor, but when I stroll through museums, churches, even streets, when I contemplate these proud, imperious works gazing down serenely and with an indulgent smile at everything that is base, stupid, soulless—when I think about these generations of the greatest, the most marvelous geniuses, I feel that life and work are worth something."[5]

Further trips to Tunis and Biskra also made their influence felt in his developing musical style, but it was Sicily that inspired *Metopy* (1915).

Karol Szymanowski (1882–1937). Photographer unidentified (Library of Congress).

This is an architectural term referring to the space, often filled by paintings or sculpture, between two triglyphs in a Doric frieze, and it was metopes from the temples of Selinut that inspired the three movements of this suite ("Wyspa syren" ["Isle of Sirens"] "Kalipso" ["Calypso"] and "Nauzykaa" ["Nausicaa"]). The music follows similar paths to that of Scriabin's mystical style, with its ecstatic trills, glissandi, extravagant flourishes over wide ranges of pitch, wandering chromatic lines and harmonies constructed from the three forms of fourths available (most significantly the tritone, of course), which lie behind the synthetic harmony of Scriabin's "Promethean" chord. Indeed, in the Calypso piece, one could be forgiven for thinking one was listening to the first movement of Scriabin's Fourth Piano Sonata (1903), so similar are some of the harmonies and melodic gestures. One of Szymanowski's favorite musical terms in the last two pieces is "risvegliando"—"awakening"—and this music is indeed a wake up call to the twentieth century, a summons to rejuvenate itself and summon the Superman.

Mity suggested the classical legends of "Arethusa's Fountain," "Narcissus" and "Dryads and Pan." Szymanowski's interest in Pan, pagan imagery, Mediterranean culture in general and a musical style that consciously moved away from the German late-Romantic mainstream (again via Scriabin), all tie in with Nietzsche's call for a "supra-European" music in *Beyond Good and Evil*. Szymanowski was also, like so many, deeply impressed by Nietzsche's *The Birth of Tragedy*, which he coupled with Eckermann's *Conversations with Goethe* as "the two most beautiful books in the world."[6] *The Birth of Tragedy* also went on to play an important role in the symbolism of his opera *Król Roger* (*King Roger*, 1927).

Szymanowski referred to Nietzsche on several occasions in his various essays. "Again," he exclaimed in one of them, "I find I have written that famous name!"

> And just in time to remind my readers that fifty years ago that German dreamed of a "wicked, capricious, southern" music, a music that had rid itself completely of the influence of the "fatherland"—"Europas Flachland"—in other words, a music which had escaped from the dull flatlands of Germany, and dull is an especially apt word if we go on to speak of modern German music! Nietzsche centered his yearnings, not altogether aptly, on *Carmen*. It is, indeed, a glorious work, but how much more would he have rejoiced had he heard Debussy's *Ibéria* or *Nocturnes*.[7]

Unlike many musical Nietzscheans, therefore, Wagnerian music drama was not the idiom in which Szymanowski chose to express Nietzschean ideas. His most Nietzschean creation is the aforementioned *Król Roger*, the libretto of which he wrote in collaboration with the poet and dramatist Jarosław Iwaszkiewicz (1894–1980); but Szymanowski also began to write a novel called *Efebos*, which itself contains Nietzschean elements. In the introduction, he explained that it was written "almost accidentally—at first merely for private use, as a solace and sweet remembrance of things past, in order to exorcise the black pit of an endless succession of days, weeks and months spent amidst the most atrocious external conditions by a magic vision of Italy rising in the mind's eye. It is the somewhat unexpected outcome of the personal circumstances of the author's life in the last two years (from the fall of 1917 to 1919), thrust upon him by the scoffing cynical force of brutal facts ... Italy—the homeland of all dreamers about a heightened sense of living—rose slowly within my inner vision, in all her imperious beauty and seductive grace."[8]

If there is any doubt that Nietzsche was homosexual, there is none where Szymanowski was concerned, and this aspect of his personality found its way into the novel to such a graphic extent that he felt unable to publish it for fear of offending his mother. The Second World War then almost completely destroyed the manuscript in 1939; but we do have Iwaszkiewicz' recollections of it, who explained that the hero of the story, Prince Alo Łowicki, visits Italy where he is not only initiated into the mysteries of Italian art and progressive political ideas, but also experiences a sexual relationship with one Marek Korab, a Polish composer. When the two men split up, Alo visits Sicily (just as Nietzsche had done in 1882) and there undergoes a spiritual renaissance. As Alistair Wightman expresses it: "Alo divested himself of all the trappings and props of his previous existence to experience a healing revelation at night amongst ancient ruins, in this case, the temple at Segesta."[9] After this experience and the greater maturity it brings him, Alo is able to resume his relationship with Korab. Korab and Alo therefore represented two aspects of Szymanowski's own personality, and the story consequently became a metaphor of the search for what Jung would have called "individuation." The desire for harmony between two opposing aspects of a single personality has, of course, much in common with Nietzsche's quest for a reconciliation between the Dionysian and the Apollonian, the former being merged with the latter to create the "Dionysian" Superman, in whom all opposites are balanced and sublimated.

Though *Efebos* came to nothing in the end, it sowed the seeds for *Król Roger*, which is similarly set in Sicily (though this time in twelfth century), and it concerns the similar psychological quest of King Roger to balance and integrate his Apollonian personality of control and detachment with the world of Dionysian instinct and emotion represented by a Shepherd, who reveals to him that mere political power is an empty thing: True power lies in becoming who one is. This strongly reflects Nietzsche's ideas concerning the Will to Power, which, as we have seen, he regarded as being only crudely expressed through politics and tyranny. Iwaszkiewicz hoped that Szymanowski would agree with his own idea for the ending of the opera, in which the King follows the Shepherd into darkness, "abandoning everything for him,"[10] but Szymanowski hesitated, unsure that complete abandonment to Dionysus was advisable. After all, he had himself witnessed the horrors of a social revolution, during which the Szymanowski family estate had been burned to the ground and two of his prized grand pianos had been thrown into a lake. And so, instead, of Iwaszkiewicz' ending, Szymanowski has King Roger welcomes the rising sun, celebrating his spiritual development but holding himself back from the brink of the Dionysian abyss.

In his article for the program of the 2015 production of *Król Roger* at the Royal Opera House, London, John Lloyd Davies linked Szymanowski's opera with Bartók's *Duke Bluebeard's Castle* and Scriabin's synesthetic experiments, arguing that they all shared a concern with defending "a poetic, individual reality against the mass power of the outside world. Phenomena such as the composer Skryabin's colour synaesthesia represent an extreme version of an instance on a personal reality opposed to the powers of the massed external world."[11] As such, they are all highly "Nietzschean" in their desire for freedom and personal expression.

After three sombre strokes on a tam-tam, *Król Roger* begins with an impressive choral Sanctus, designed not only to draw the audience immediately into the action but also establish the religious context of the story, which the subsequent action opposes. Perfect fifths in all their archaic, otherworldly purity characterize this orthodoxy, and they resemble Bartók's use of such intervals to suggest the world of Bluebeard's Castle; but in direct contrast to this world of established religious ritual is the way in which Szymanowski accompanies Roger's opening lines and those of his advisor, Edris, who informs him of the strange shepherd who sings strange songs in praise of an unknown god. Here, whole-tone harmonies suggest the Nietzschean forces of individualism, which are soon to cause conflict in Roger's life with the arrival of the Shepherd, whose often highly Scriabinesque music exploits the tritone harmonies implicit in the whole-tone scale. Pentatonic elements also form a significant part of this ambivalent harmonic world. The libretto describes the Shepherd as dressed in a goatskin like Dionysus himself, with eyes like stars and a smile full of mystery. Like Nietzsche's Zarathustra, he comes from the mountains and his god is very much a pantheistic one, residing in "the whisper of distant seas, the thunder of distant storms, on oceans under the sun."[12] The Shepherd's alternative religion of freedom and ecstasy—a kind of anti-religion like Nietzsche's philosophy—is described at length in the middle of the first Act, and it inspires the desire among the people and church authorities to have him put to death; but Roger allows him to go free, while arranging to meet him privately during the night. The Shepherd's description of his alternative religion, with its god who carries a bunch of grapes and whose clothes are "rosy auroras," features those archaic and pastoral timbres of solo flute and oboe. It is also a hymn in praise of night and freedom, what the Shepherd himself describes as "joy at night"[13]; and as such it carries deeply Romantic Wagnerian undertones. The musical style is very different, but as Stephen Downes has observed, the harmony of the opening bars of the song provides the melodic material, just as the "Tristan" chord informs the Liebesnacht.[14]

Act II continues the "Liebesnacht" imagery, converting the nocturnal assignation of Tristan and Isolde with a parallel midnight encounter between the Shepherd and Roger, raising an inevitable homosexual subtext in the proceedings. The stage directions emphasize an almost effeminate opulence:

The eastern softness and the nearly feminine elegance of the elaborately waving multicolored arabesques, the yellow and blue majolica, the richest rugs, form a strange harmony with the granite arches and columns and the huge bronze double doors at the entrance. Here and there glisten marvelous mosaics, the work of artists from Byzantium, depicting mysterious gardens full of unknown wonders and fantastic birds. In the back, a marble fountain murmurs quietly, its basin overflowing in the richness of flowers brought from all parts of the world.[15]

The direction, "It is night. Alabaster lamps are burning, suspended between the columns of the gallery, softly lighting the interior," is reminiscent of the torch that burns by the open door at the beginning of the second act of *Tristan*. Musically, however, the echoes are much more Gallic, in particular the exotic style of Florent Schmitt's 1907 *La tragédie de Salomé*, along with elements of the Bacchanal that concludes Ravel's 1913 ballet *Daphnis et Chloë*. This is particularly the case in the music that accompanies Iwaszkiewicz's lines about jangling tambourines. Szymanowski's frequent "Ah-ing" in the chorus also reflects Ravel's similar usage in that ballet, not to mention Delius' chorus in *A Mass of Life*. There are also echoes of Debussy's *La Mer* in the prelude to this act, which accords with Szymanowski's desire to follow Nietzsche's program of Mediterraneanizing program.

Claude Debussy (1862–1918). Photograph by Nadar, Paris, 1908 (Wikimedia Commons).

Having mentioned Debussy, with whom Szymanowski has a fair amount in common, a slight digression is in order, for of all the composers who struggled with their Wagnerian infatuations, Debussy (1862–1918) was perhaps the most Nietzschean of all, even though none of his music specifically references the ideas of the German philosopher. If Nietzsche's critiques of Wagner were, as Mann termed them "panegyrics in reverse,"[16] Debussy's music was as though the essence of Wagner's music had been sprayed through an atomizer and reconstituted into something that seems very different, even though the elements of which can nonetheless be traced back to the heady perfumes of the

Bayreuth wizard. We have already seen this in the echoes of *Parsifal* that suffuse Debussy's early work, *La damoiselle élue* (1889), where they appear virtually in quotation marks. They are transmuted in Debussy's only completed opera, *Pélleas et Mèlisande* (1902) and transmogrified in the ballet *Jeux* (1913). His attempt to send up Wagner's *Tristan* in the now politically incorrect "Golliwog's Cakewalk," by sandwiching the opera's opening motif between two slices of saucy piano syncopation, is the musical equivalent of Nietzsche's acidly witty attacks (such as, for example, the philosopher's observation, re. Parsifal's siring of Lohengrin, that "chastity can work miracles"[17]).

As Robin Holloway has already suggested in his book on *Debussy and Wagner*, Debussy was in many ways the French equivalent of Nietzsche when it came to Wagnerian criticism. Debussy coped with the overpowering effect of Wagner's music, theory and persona by laughing at them. He referred to Leitmotivs as "calling cards" and agreed with Nietzsche by insisting that Wagner's music, "is worse than obsession. It is possession. You no longer belong to yourself." Like Nietzsche, Debussy referred to Wagner as a sorcerer—a "Klingsor" of music. "If he [Wagner] had been a little more human," he opined, "he would have been great for all time."[18] Both Nietzsche and Debussy were infatuated with Wagner's music at the same time as being disturbed by it and suspicious of its "meaning." Both also regarded Wagner as a miniaturist, who, as Nietzsche put it, "compresses an infinity of meaning and sweetness into the smallest space."[19] Holloway goes on to suggest that "Nietzsche's description of Wagner's "miniaturism" (particularly in *Parsifal*) is actually even more appropriate to describe Debussy approach to composition: "The continuation of the quotation about Wagner as above all a miniaturist should make this clear: 'His wealth of colour, of chiaroscuro, of the mystery of a dying light, so pampers our senses that afterwards almost every other musician strikes us as being too robust.'"[20]

Busoni also regarded Debussy's style of orchestration as a continuation of Wagner,[21] and, like Debussy, Busoni managed to express his own mixed feelings about Wagner in colorful epigrams: The *Siegfried Idyll*, he wrote, is like "a corpse that is beautiful to behold even in death."[22]

Busoni reacted to German Romanticism in his own way, but the Nietzschean strain in Debussy spilled over into the group of composers Jean Cocteau attempted to herd together as the group known as "Les Six" in the 1920s. Their anti-Germanic, ultra-modern musical ironies are another kind of musical Nietzscheanism. Reacting to the "Romantic" nationalist horrors of the First World War, Cocteau searched for an antidote that would re-package Nietzsche's antidote. "Take a commonplace," Cocteau insisted, "clean it, polish it and place it in a light so that it strikes [the listener or reader] by its youth, by the same freshness and power that it originally possessed. That is the work of a poet."[23] On another occasion he pronounced, "Do your best to be banal."[24] Such was his manifesto, so to speak, not that the composers themselves always abided by it and actually resisted being lumped together by the famous poet and publicist. Reacting against Romanticism, the new "Nietzschean" esthetic even extended to food, drink and fashion: rare steaks and dry wine seemed appropriate. Jazz was the new musical *Mediterraneanism*, resulting in Darius Milhaud's tango-inspired negro ballet *La Création du monde* in 1923. Earlier, in 1919, he had set the words of a catalog of farm machinery, following it up with a similarly tongue-in-cheek, but nonetheless poetic setting of descriptions from a seedsman's catalog. Another of Les Six, Arthur Honegger, created the ultimate musical portrait of a steam locomotive in *Pacific 231*. Georges Auric went on to write film scores for Cocteau before moving to England, where he wrote locomotive music of his own for the Ealing Comedy *The Titfield Thunderbolt* (dir. Charles Crichton, 1953). Francis Poulenc composed his ironic *Mouvements perpétuels*, which ended up in Hitchcock's Nietzschean thriller, *Rope* (1948), in which two, presumably gay Harvard graduates attempt to get away with murder, inviting their victim's parents to dine off a chest in which they have hidden the body. Les Six favored wind instruments over strings, small ensembles over large, staccato over legato: Anything to distance themselves from the dangerous infatuations of German Romanticism. As Martin Cooper sums up, "It must have been a relief to the unmusical to have no longer to sit through *The Ring*, but, instead, to be confronted with little chamber works, lasting hardly as many minutes as *The Ring* lasts hours; and to be told that these pleasing and witty creations are the last word in aesthetic modernity."[25]

All this was taking place in France around the same time that Szymanowski was working on his opera. The musical results were very different, but the impetus was shared, and Nietzsche was the axle around which they spun.

Back in Act II of *Król Roger*, the Shepherd inspires what Iwaszkiewicz describes as an enchanted dance, which Szymanowski introduces with the traditionally "exotic" timbres of celesta and harp, echoing Stravinsky's "Danse infernale" from *The Firebird*. Asymmetrical meters drive the dancers along:

> In the dance of love
> in the flames of blood

> the infinite glow!
> In radiant paradise!
> In the secret frenzy
> the divine dance![26]

Dance imagery, is, of course, highly Nietzschean in itself. As was the case with Britten's Pentathlon in *Death in Venice*, we are again reminded here of Nietzsche's dancing girls in *Zarathustra* and all his pleas for a music that inspires us to dance for joy. At one stage, the Shepherd even says, "Divine girls dance!" Roger is appalled by these excesses and calls for the Shepherd to be arrested. The Shepherd, however, breaks his chains and walks away, encouraging Roger to follow him. Roger, who is as ambivalent about the Shepherd as Nietzsche was about Wagner's music, then throws off his crown, mantel and sword and does indeed follow the Shepherd.

Act III is set in an ancient amphitheater, reflecting the theatrical basis of Nietzsche's *The Birth of Tragedy*. Roger's wife, Roxana, explains that the Shepherd is to be found in "the smile of the stars, in the sound of the storm." He is the incarnation of Nietzschean joy. Roxana and Roger throw piles of flowers into the fire to summon him, and it is here that we find Szymanowski's equivalent of Britten's "Stranger god," who inspires the chorus to praise "the land of eternal ecstasy."[27] Ultimately, however, Roger resists the Shepherd's call to throw all caution to the wind, which some critics have regarded as a reflection of Szymanowski's own fear of sexual and emotional involvement; but in fact it is the most truly Nietzschean conclusion there could be, for Roger hopes to transform his own life in the light of the Shepherd's vision. He thus becomes truly "Dionysian" in the sense of the term we find in Nietzsche's later writings, where the Dionysian man is defined as he who has absorbed the Dionysian *within* the Apollonian. The Dionysian impulses have indeed been acknowledged, controlled and sublimated.

13

Alphons Diepenbrock

Many settings of Nietzsche's words have been set by some frankly rather obscure composers. In his bibliography of the subject, David S. Thatcher lists 173 names, many of which are much less well-known than the ones I have concentrated on here. Alexander Schwartz, Rudolf Schiller, Paul Zoll and Aladár Radó are, after all, hardly household names. Neither is Hans Pogge, despite the fact that his setting of Nietzsche's "Die Sonne sinkt" was chosen to accompany the unveiling of Max Klinger's bust of the philosopher in the Weimar Nietzsche Archiv in October 1903.

The Swedish composer Wilhelm Peterson-Berger (1867–1942) is better known in Sweden, where his Romantic piano piece "Sommarsång" (Summer Song) is a familiar musical fixture, even for Swedes with no real interest in art-music traditions. Peterson-Berger composed two sets of Nietzsche settings, along with a three-part "Dionysos-Dithyramb." They are indeed the kind of thing that Nietzsche himself might have composed himself, given more technique and formal musical training. Peterson-Berger even translated Nietzsche's *The Birth of Tragedy* into Swedish, and went on to discuss Nietzsche in his own study of Richard Wagner in 1913.

Austrian composer and conductor Emil von Reznicek (1860–1945) also set lines from Nietzsche's *Dionysus Dithyrambs*, in his *Ruhm und Ewigkeit* for tenor and orchestra. It was first performed at Frankfurt am Main in 1904, but was never published. His Fifth "Dance" Symphony of 1925 again suggests that Nietzsche's call for a terpsichorean approach to music had not fallen on deaf ears, filled, as each of the four movements are, with infectious dance rhythms in the forms of Polonaise, Csárdás, Ländler and Tarantella. That his second symphony of 1905 is subtitled "Ironic" suggests further Nietzschean affinities.)

Hugo Wolf, another musical admirer of Nietzsche, never achieved a Nietzsche setting of his own. He contemplated a choral setting of Nietzsche's "An den Mistral," but illness intervened before work could begin.

(Like Nietzsche, Wolf suffered from syphilis and its accompanying insanity.) He also agreed with Nietzsche's Mediterraneanizing program, composing an *Italienisches Liederbuch* and *Spanisches Lieberbuch* (to the words of other poets), along with an orchestral *Italienische Serenade* (1893–1894), which followed the example of Strauss' *Aus Italien*. (Wolf's biographer, Ernest Newman described the piece as having "the fine-nerved, delicate poetry of the Italian songs, with the added fragrance and warmth of atmosphere that the orchestral coloring gives."[1])

Alas, the choral *Zarathustra* and three song settings of Nietzsche's words by the Carl Orff (1895–1982) are almost as obscure as those settings by less famous composers. Few, if any of Orff's Nietzsche pieces have had any performances, while other big names like Schoenberg and Paul Hindemith (1895–1963) composed only isolated, one-off song settings.

Alphons Diepenbrock (1862–1921) is the most significant of the perhaps lesser-known Nietzsche composers. For Diepenbrock, literature and music were intertwined as much as they were for Wagner, Berlioz and Schumann, those archetypal literary composers. Diepenbrock, however, was not a professional musician at all. Born in Amsterdam to a Catholic family, he studied classical languages. His literary interests led him to set to music the words of many great writers: Novalis, Hölderlin, Goethe, Horace, Verlaine, Baudelaire, and Sophocles to name the most celebrated. He never studied composition at an academy or conservatoire and was largely a self-taught pianist. (His family owned a fine Erard grand piano.) Composition was sandwiched between his professional work as a language teacher, and it was much influenced by a close study of Wagner and Debussy. That he was also a devout Catholic with a specialized knowledge of Nietzsche's writings, matches the ironic appeal Nietzsche's ideas held for mystics such as Scriabin and Steiner. During a three-week visit to Italy, visiting Rome and Florence

Alphons Diepenbrock (1862–1921). Photograph by Willem Witsen, 1890 (Muziek Encyclopedie).

before traveling on by train to Genoa, Diepenbrock intended to follow in Nietzsche's Italian footsteps. Unlike Szymanowski, however, he did not translate this pilgrimage into musical terms. Diepenbrock had no interest in Mediterraneanizing music.

If Strauss represented the heroic side of Nietzsche, and Mahler his sublimity, Diepenbrock expresses the melancholy, for Nietzsche's optimism was indeed born from the spirit of melancholy. Nietzsche recognized himself as a decadent and also as a melancholic. In *Zarathustra* he girds his loins against "The Song of Melancholy" as sung by "the sorcerer" (who is Wagner in all but name). "Thus sang the sorcerer," Nietzsche writes, "and all who were present went like birds unawares into the net of his cunning and melancholy voluptuousness. Only the conscientious man of the spirit was not captured: he quickly snatched the harp away from the sorcerer and cried: 'Air! Let in good air! Let Zarathustra in! You are making this cave sultry and poisonous, you evil old sorcerer!'"[2]

The isolated Nietzsche, who spend a great deal of time on his own, frequently unwell, was particularly prone to this melancholy "poison." But during his long walks in the mountains, he transmuted his melancholy into joy by strength of will. Remember: "the solitude is terrible—but how peacefully things lie in the light! how freely one breathes!"[3] Melancholia is always a danger, against which one should always be on one's guard. Only a melancholic can truly understand the danger of melancholy, and he perhaps experiences joy all the more intensely when it is forged. (Joy is often the product of effort and suffering, like anything else worth having.)

Diepenbrock's sole Nietzsche setting, *Im grossen Schweigen* (*The Great Silence*) was composed immediately on his return to Amsterdam in 1905, though the whole work was revised in May 1918. At the head of his manuscript of the score, Diepenbrock quoted the whole of aphorism 628 from Nietzsche's *Human, All Too Human*, which Nietzsche headed "*Seriousness in play*": "At sunset in Genoa, I heard from a tower a long chiming of bells: it kept on and on, and over the noise of the backstreets, as if insatiable for itself, it rang out into the evening sky and the sea air, so terrible and so childish at the same time, so melancholy. Then I thought of Plato's words and felt them suddenly in my heart: *all in all, nothing human is worth taking very seriously; nevertheless....*"[4]

Nietzsche's description of the sunset at Genoa was based on a genuine experience. In a letter to his mother written from Genoa on 22nd October 1876, whither he had fled from the intolerable surroundings of the Bayreuth Festival, Nietzsche described a "most beautiful evening tranquility and color," conditions which contrasted starkly with the splitting headache and vomiting that had plagued him for two days.[5] Plato's words derive from *The Republic* (Book X, section 604), where the Greek philosopher says, "The law would say that to be patient under suffering is best, and that we should not give way to impatience, as there is no knowing whether such things are good or evil; and nothing is gained by impatience; also, because no human thing is of serious importance, and grief stands in the way of that which at the moment is most required."[6] Schopenhauer, as might be expected, had also quoted Plato's line, "no human thing is of serious importance" in his *Parerga and Paralipomena* (in the section on "Psychological Observations"), and faced with the immensity of Nature, this would indeed seem to be a truth. "Nevertheless," as Nietzsche added, we are human and have somehow to contend with our existence; hence the perhaps undesirable inevitability of thought. That Diepenbrock should inscribe this quotation on his manuscript reminds us of his profound knowledge of Nietzsche's writings, and also helps the listener to understand what the piece is about.

The idea of setting Nietzsche to music had been in Diepenbrock's mind for some time, having no doubt been inspired by the earlier example of Mahler, whose Fourth Symphony he had conducted on April 14, 1910. Mahler, who met him, much admired him. ("Diepenbrock is a delight to me," he confessed in a letter to his wife Alma in 1909. "He has great depth and truth.")[7] Diepenbrock also became acquainted with Schoenberg, who had visited Amsterdam in 1912 for a performance of his *Pelleas und Melisande*. Diepenbrock described him as "a nice and witty fellow, agile but not fatiguing, flexible and modest," though he found *Pelleas* "much too long and too heavy, too German in sound, but with a lot of beauty and very real, not like the work Scriabin makes."[8]

Like Diepenbrock, Schoenberg made only one setting of a Nietzsche text (Op. 6, No. 8 "Der Wanderer"), but Diepenbrock's piece was much grander than Schoenberg's relatively modest song. The text is drawn from the opening of Book V of Nietzsche's *Morgenrote* (*Dawn of Day*):

> Here is the sea, here may we forget the town. It is true that its bells are still ringing the Angelus that solemn and foolish yet sweet sound at the junction between day and night, but one moment more! now all is silent. Yonder lies the ocean, pale and brilliant; it cannot speak. The sky is glistening with its eternal mute evening hues, red, yellow, and green: it cannot speak. The small cliffs and rocks which stretch out into the sea as if each one of them were endeavouring to find the loneliest spot they too are dumb. Beautiful and awful indeed is this vast silence, which so suddenly overcomes us and makes our heart swell.
>
> Alas! what deceit lies in this dumb beauty! How well could it speak, and how evilly,

too, if it wished! Its tongue, tied up and fastened, and its face of suffering happiness all this is but malice, mocking at your sympathy: be it so! I do not feel ashamed to be the plaything of such powers! but I pity thee, oh nature, because thou must be silent, even though it be only malice that binds thy tongue: nay, I pity thee for the sake of thy malice! Alas the silence deepens, and once again my heart swells within me: it is startled by a fresh truth it, too, is dumb; it likewise sneers when the mouth calls out something to this beauty; it also enjoys the sweet malice of its silence. I come to hate speaking; yea, even thinking. Behind every word I utter do I not hear the laughter of error, imagination, and insanity? Must I not laugh at my pity and mock my own mockery? Oh sea, oh evening, ye are bad teachers! Ye teach man how to cease to be a man. Is he to give himself up to you? Shall he become as you now are, pale, brilliant, dumb, immense, reposing calmly upon himself? exalted above himself?[9]

Nature is full of malice because it does not care for mankind. Our esthetic response to its beauties mean nothing to Nature. Beauty can exist only within us, for the concept has no meaning without a cultural context; and faced with beauty's mute sublimity, Nietzsche comes to the conclusion that speaking and thinking about Nature (and the nature of reality) can never produce "the truth." Delusion, lies, imagination, religion, misconception and our eternal, inescapable subjectivity will always obscure any truth we might think we have discovered. As W. D. Williams has put it, any knowledge we might glean "must lead to questions which are themselves questionable": "And, in this *persona*, he visualizes total silence as the only dignified posture, yet cannot escape the conviction that this negates the whole nature and drive of man, who is above all the *speaking* animal. The beauty of nature cannot communicate, man must communicate, otherwise he ceases to be human. Yet the more he tries the more he is led to the circle of self-doubt, and to the realization that all he says is self-contradictory."[10]

Diepenbrock was perhaps attracted to *Dawn of Day* by the many references to music it contains. Nietzsche writes eloquently of the emotional power of music and its ability to transform our response to reality:

It is music, however, more than anything else that shows us what past-masters we are in the rapid and subtle divination of feelings and sympathy; for even if music is only the imitation of an imitation of feelings, nevertheless, despite its distance and vagueness, it often enables us to participate in those feelings, so that we become sad without any reason for feeling so, like the fools that we are, merely because we hear certain sounds and rhythms that somehow or other remind us of the intonation and the movements, or perhaps even only of the behaviour, of sorrowful people. It is related of a certain Danish king that he was wrought up to such a pitch of warlike enthusiasm by the song of a minstrel that he sprang to his feet and killed five persons of his assembled court: there was neither war nor enemy; there was rather the exact opposite; yet the power of the retrospective inference from a feeling to the cause of it was sufficiently strong in this king to overpower both his observation and his reason. Such, however, is almost invariably the effect of music (provided that it thrills us), and we have no need of such paradoxical instances to recognise this,—the state of feeling into which music transports us is almost always in contradiction to the appearance of our actual state, and of our reasoning power which recognises this actual state and its causes.[11]

Nietzsche also emphasizes the very Romantic connection between twilight, night and music, which also echoes the imagery of *Im grossen Schweigen*: "Night and Music.—It was only at night time, and in the semi-obscurity of dark forests and caverns, that the ear, the organ of fear, was able to develop itself so well, in accordance with the mode of living of the timid—that is, the longest human epoch which has ever yet existed: when it is clear daylight the ear is less necessary. Hence the character of music, which is an art of night and twilight."[12] There are profoundly Wagnerian resonances to this passage, particularly the passage in Wagner's Beethoven essay that recalls a memorable night in Venice, the city of music itself, whither Wagner had fled to compose the second act of that very apotheosis of night and music, *Tristan und Isolde*:

> Sleepless one night in Venice, I stepped upon the balcony of my window overlooking the Grand Canal: like a deep dream the fairy city of lagoons lay stretched in shade before me. From out of the breathless silence rose the strident cry of a gondolier just woken his barque; again and again his voice went forth into the night, till from the remotest distance its fellow-cry came answering down the midnight length of the Canal: I recognized the drear melodic phrase to which the well-known lines of Tasso were also wedded in his day, but which in itself is certainly as old as Venice's canals and people. After many a solemn pause the ringing dialogue took quicker life, and seemed at last to melt in unison; till finally the sounds from far and near died softly back to new-won slumber. Whatever could sun-steeped, colour-swarming Venice of the daylight tell me of itself, that that sounding dream of night had not brought infinitely deeper, closer, to my consciousness?[13]

Amid these general observations on music, which would have been of immense appeal to the Romantic and melancholy Diepenbrock, the following passage from Section 144 of Nietzsche's *Dawn of Day* contains what amounts to a commentary on the meaning of the passage he chose in *Im grossen Schweigen*:

> The man who suffers severely looks forth with terrible calmness from his state of suffering upon outside things: all those little lying enchantments, by which things are usually surrounded when seen through the eye of a healthy person, have vanished from the sufferer; his own life even lies there before him, stripped of all bloom and colour.... Once more we look longingly at men and nature and recollect with a sorrowful smile that now since the veil has fallen we regard many things concerning them in a new and different light,—but we are refreshed by once more seeing the softened lights of life, and emerge from that fearfully dispassionate daylight in which we as sufferers saw things and through things. We do not get angry when we see the charms of health resume their play, and we contemplate the sight as if transformed, gently and still fatigued. In this state we cannot listen to music without weeping.[14]

For Nietzsche, seeing things as they *are*, as opposed to the world-view of an idealist, is both painful and transformative, and music—that art form which, in Schopenhauerian terms, reveals the Will beyond the Representation—can only enhance the melancholy effect of reality, which Nietzsche sees in a new light. Diepenbrock, however, was a devout Catholic, and thus provided his own solution to Nietzsche's dilemma at the end of his setting of this profoundly existential text. Consequently, he seriously undermined what Nietzsche was saying.

Diepenbrock's orchestral preludes and interludes are highly descriptive. At the beginning of the piece, he uses contrapuntal techniques to convey the idea of the bustling town from which Nietzsche departs to discover the silence of the sea. This is followed by the motif of the sea itself, a three-note theme, which is repeated many times throughout the piece to suggest the immensity of the ocean. Oceanic imagery, of course, carries very Wagnerian connotations, in particular those of *Tristan und Isolde*, the first act of which takes place on board a ship. The third act is also sea-obsessed, as Tristan awaits the arrival of Isolde over the waves. Wagner employed sea imagery extensively in his theoretical essay "The Artwork of the Future" (1849), where the sea becomes a metaphor of music itself; but for Nietzsche the sea is *silent*. Nature herself is *silent*. Consequently, there is a certain irony in trying to set the text to music at all, and Diepenbrock acknowledges this problem later on. Having spread the baritone's opening line, "Here is the sea," through the wide span of a seventh to suggest the equally wide horizon, he paints the glories of the view with ecstatic, distinctly Debussian style, glittering glissando flourishes from the harp suggesting the evening light on the waves, along with an orchestral imitation of the sound of the Angelus bells. However, the words "now all is silence" initiate a sustained silence in the orchestra, which is followed by a sombre roll from the timpani, and yet more silence. The effect is deeply dramatic and as close to a musical equivalent of Nietzsche's imagery as any composer could achieve.

The sea motif returns, and Diepenbrock demonstrates his Wagnerian credentials by more sophisticated tone-painting: When describing the "small cliffs and rocks which stretch out into the sea," a solo clarinet accordingly meanders in the accompaniment to illustrate the image; the mockery of Nature ("mocking at your sympathy") is similarly evoked by musical laughter from the woodwind (staccato descending scalic passages), in much the same way that Wagner imitated the laughter of the crowd at Beckmesser's expense in *Die Meistersinger von Nürnberg*. Cymbals and shrill, high-pitched manifestations of the sea motif increase the sense of malice.

The suffering caused by our existential alienation from Nature prompts Diepenbrock to suffuse his score with *Tristanesque* appoggiatura and suspensions to convey the yearning of the text. *Parsifalian* melancholy also evokes its emotional and intellectual pain. Nature's laughter at human "error, imagination, and insanity" are brilliantly suggested by Diepenbrock's use of the dry "ironic" timbre of an agitated xylophone along with snarling brass.

But in the final analysis, Diepenbrock betrays Nietzsche's message by quoting the hymn "Ave Maris Stella," which nonetheless nicely combines the idea of the virgin Mary and the ocean:

> Ave, maris stella,
> Dei mater alma,
> atque semper virgo,
> felix cœli porta.
>
> (Hail, star of the sea,
> Nurturing Mother of God,
> And ever Virgin,
> Happy gate of Heaven.)

Nietzsche would surely not have approved, overwhelmed though he may well have been by the melancholy beauty of Diepenbrock's music, in all its post-Wagnerian and oceanic glory. Could it be, as T. S. Eliot would later observe in *Four Quartets*, that human kind cannot bear very much reality?

14

Ferruccio Busoni

Busoni (1866–1924) also combined an interest in the occult with the apparently diametrically opposed world-view of Nietzsche. In 1911, Busoni bought three Indian temple figures, which he described as "my greatest joy and the crowning glory of my apartment. The central one is a dancing Buddha, richly clad—almost Spanish—and wellnigh a Don Giovanni. To his right and left kneel two praying youths. They all look as if of solid gold and are inlaid with colored stones, half life-size."[1]

He also possessed a complete four-volume first edition of the works of Edgar Allan Poe, and he was even more infatuated with the supernatural stories of E. T. A. Hoffmann. "Oh E. T. A Hoffmann!" he enthused, "can it be that thou still livest in the spirit? and takest possession of me by night? I almost believe so."[2] (In a letter to his friend Egon Petri, he equated Poe's "Ligeia" with Hoffmann's "Der Sandman" and the summoning of Kundry by Klingsor in Wagner's *Parsifal*.[3]) He confessed to maintaining an open mind with regard to certain occult phenomenon, such as ghosts ("a phenomenon which one cannot readily shrug off"), arguing that it should be possible for a clairvoyant to perceive an individual from earlier—or even future times.[4]

Such interests were by no means unusual at that or, of course, any other time, but in the years that led up to the First World War, they were particularly fashionable. Another writer whom Busoni much admired, Bernard Shaw, was convinced that such supernatural preoccupations were just another symptom of the decadence of pre-war Europe, and in his preface to the play that dealt with this decadence, *Heartbreak House*, Shaw wrote:

> *Heartbreak House* is not merely the name of the play which follows this preface. It is cultured, leisured Europe before the war.... It was superstitious and addicted to table-rapping, materialization seances, clairvoyance, palmistry, crystal-gazing and the like to such an extent that it may be doubted whether ever before in the history of the world did soothsayers, astrologers, and unregistered therapeutic specialists of all sorts flourish as they did during this half century of the drift to the abyss.[5]

Busoni's interest in Shaw, however, reflected another, more rational side of his character. Busoni was particularly impressed by Shaw's important critical essay, *The Sanity of Art* (1895), subtitled as "an exposure of the current nonsense about artists being degenerate." Busoni was also fascinated by Shaw's social problem play, *Widower's Houses* (1892). He even considered the possibility of asking Shaw for something to set to music, convinced that this could create "a new direction in music-theater."⁶ Nothing came of the proposal, but the words "a new direction in music-theater" were typical of Busoni, reflecting his passionate interest in what was innovative; and it was the unique combination of modernistic innovation with a preoccupation with the occult that gave birth to his most experimental musical works: the *Berceuse élégiaque* (1909), the *Sonatina seconda* (1912), the *Nocturne symphonique* (1912) and the *Gesang vom Reigen der Geister* (1915).

Ferruccio Busoni (1866–1924). Photograph by Varische & Artico, Milan, 1913 (Wikimedia Commons).

In 1906, when he was 40 years old, Busoni published his *Outline of a New Esthetic of Music*, on the opening page of which he quoted lines from one of his own libretto for the opera *Der mächtige Zauberer* : "I wish for the Unknown!/ What I already know is limitless. I want to go/ Still further." All this is very reminiscent of Franz Liszt's well-known desire to "hurl a musical lance as far as possible into the boundless realm of the future." Busoni also much admired Liszt, whom he credited with much more harmonic ingenuity than Wagner. To Busoni, much of Wagner's so-called "Music of the Future" was merely boring: "It seems astonishing that a little, contemptible Saxon, with boring music and some strokes of genius, could call an international society of this magnitude into being."⁷

> Things like the [Wagner's] Forest Murmurs and Magic Fire Music are quite clearly Lisztian piano études, and the Ride of the Valkyries is such a shameless cheap imitation of the form and content of [Liszt's] "Mazeppa" that I was staggered when I heard this piece of kitsch again at the beginning of the year: staggered that the moving spirit of the work,

aped by this almost parodistic imitation, was constantly rejected and despised.—And I coined the following aphorism: Liszt was the foundation stone of all modern tonal edifices and, as foundation stone, he lies deep below the surface and remains invisible.[8]

Perhaps this was why Busoni transcribed "The Ride of the Valkyries" for piano—his only Wagner transcription. The reason why Busoni admired Liszt and disliked Wagner was similar to Nietzsche's approach to the same issue. Busoni was obviously aware of this, as he included a large extract from Nietzsche's *Beyond Good and Evil* at the end of his *New Esthetic of Music*. For both Busoni and Nietzsche, Wagner was too German, whereas Liszt, the cosmopolitan, combined the culture of Italy with forward-looking harmonic experimentation. Responding to Nietzsche's call for a "supra-German" music that "no longer knows anything of good and evil," Busoni noted: "It may be that we must leave Earth to find that music."[9] That not being physically possible in 1906, the next best thing was to leave behind the traditional laws of tonality. Indeed, Busoni himself described the *Sonatina secondo* of 1912 as being without tonality. Combined with the marking of "Lento occulto," Busoni succeeded in simultaneously looking forward into new harmonic vistas and backwards into a mysterious atmosphere of medieval occultism. The *Nocturne symphonique*, begun in the same year, started life as a piano piece, evolving rapidly into an orchestral work which was originally to have included a part for glass harmonica, the instrument that E. T. A. Hoffmann believed to be the closest earthly approximation to the music of the spheres. Although the finished score does not include a part for this instrument, the "other-worldly" inspiration that informed the origin of the piece remains.

Busoni was not alone in his harmonic explorations, and, significantly, it was the evocation of other-worldly atmospheres that first inspired that rather more well-known pioneer of atonality, Arnold Schoenberg. Busoni had first met Schoenberg in 1903 and they continued to correspond for many years. In his private diary, Schoenberg confessed that until he heard Busoni's much more experimental *Berceuse élégiaque* he had not cared much for Busoni's music; but this experience changed all that. However, even before his musical conversion, he had found much to praise in Busoni's *New Esthetic of Music*. In a letter to Busoni on August 24, 1909, just a few days before Schoenberg started work on his monodrama *Erwartung*, Schoenberg wrote: "Your 'Outline of a New Aesthetic of Music' gave me uncommon pleasure, above all on account of its audacity. Particularly at the beginning, there are a few powerful sentences, of compulsive logic and superlative acuteness of observation. I have also thought a lot about your idea of thirds in tones, though in a different way. But I had been thinking of quarter-tones.... I have long been occupied with the removal of all shackles of tonality."[10]

Busoni's opinion of Schoenberg was even more generous. In 1913, he was delighted to receive the ensemble who had performed Schoenberg's *Pierrot lunaire* (1912), amid the dancing Buddha and praying figures of his apartment in Viktoria-Luise Platz in Berlin. He was full of praise for *Pierrot lunaire* at a time when Schoenberg was derided by the critics ("a fifty-minute-long protracted wrong note,"[11] was how Ludwig Karpath described his *Pelleas und Melisande)*, so Busoni's support was extremely valuable:

> On 17th June, a Tuesday, I enjoyed the great privilege of receiving the *Pierrot lunaire* ensemble in my house and of hearing a complete and well nigh perfect performance of the cycle.
>
> It was an ideal musical afternoon; a highly ingenious new work, a perfect ensemble, afterwards stimulating change of ideas, tea and cigarettes and charming, intelligent women. This is the way in which art should be presented—and no other.—Schoenberg's Pierrot lunaire cycle is a work that stands alone and one hopes it will remain so.[12]

Schoenberg left Berlin and returned to Vienna in 1903 where, over the next few years, he wrote his *Harmonielehrer* (Theory of Harmony) in which, having demonstrated an overpowering command of the established rules of composition, he threw down the gauntlet to tradition: "To hell with all these theories, if they always serve only to block the evolution of art and if their positive achievement consists in nothing more than helping those who will compose badly anyway to learn it quickly."[13] It was also during this period that Schoenberg first "officially" suspended tonality in his Second String Quartet of 1908, in which a soprano sings the mystical words of Stefan George's poem "Entreuckung" ("Transport"), with its famous opening line, "Ich fühle luft von anderem planeten." Like Busoni, the urge to express a new world, an "air from other planets," led to the abandonment of tonality. Unlike Schoenberg, however, Busoni remained skeptical about the supernatural and left no doubt about his feelings with regard to orthodox Christianity, which he lumped together with Wagner, as having no meaning for him.

Schoenberg remained faithful to Judaism all his life, and indeed took on something of the authority of Moses in his pronouncements about the future of music after his development of serialism, which, he prophesied, would assure the supremacy of German music for the next hundred years. Ironically, this does rather foreshadow Hitler's dreams of a thousand year Third Reich. Schoenberg saw himself almost as the founder of a new musical religion, the cosmic implications of which Pierre Boulez (1925–2016) was in no doubt about. For Boulez, "no other language was possible." With twelve tone music, "music moved out of the world of Newton and into the world of Einstein. The tonal idea was based on a universe defined by gravity and attraction. The serial idea is based on a universe that finds itself in perpetual expansion"[14]—and it is perhaps more than mere coincidence that the year in which Einstein published his special theory of relativity (1906) was the same year in which Busoni completed the *Outline of a New Esthetic of Music*. In this work, Busoni had suggested the possibility of expanding the available instruments and urged pioneers at the frontier of tonality to press on, anticipating Schoenberg's prophecy that what used to be considered discords would eventually be regarded as "higher consonances." It would therefore be appropriate to regard Busoni in the role of the dancing Buddha and Schoenberg as one of the two youths at either side.

Schoenberg returned to Berlin in 1911; but even the founder of a new religion needs money, and being short of that, Schoenberg asked Busoni to put his name to an announcement of the impending series of lectures at the Stern Conservatorium in Berlin, appropriately on the subject of "Esthetics and the teaching of composition." 1909 had been the year of Schoenberg's *Five Orchestral Pieces*, the third of which contains his first experiment with the technique known as "Klangfarbenmelodie" (Tone-Color-Melody), which he explained in the closing pages of the *Harmonielehrer*:

> Pitch is nothing else but tone color measured in one direction. Now, if it is possible to create patterns out of tone colors that are differentiated according to pitch, patterns we call "melodies," progressions, whose coherence (*Zusammenhang*) evokes an effect analogous to thought processes, then it must also be possible to make such progressions out of tone colors of the other dimension, out of what we call simply "tone color," progressions whose relations with one another work with a kind of logic entirely equivalent to that logic which satisfies us in their melody of pitches.
>
> Tone color melodies! How acute the senses that would be able to perceive them! How high the development of spirit that could find pleasure in such subtle things![15]

This mystical and somewhat synesthetic evocation brings me to Edgard Varèse (1883–1965), whose piece *Arcana* is surrounded by images of color and an occult dream world. Varèse might be said to have played the role of the other praying youth beside the central figure of Busoni's Buddha. Busoni's kindness to young musicians was legendary. He liked nothing better than to be surrounded by the young, particularly as he grew older, and Varèse was just such a youth in 1907, the year he first became acquainted with the great man. He too had read Busoni's *New Esthetic of Music* and much admired the sentence, "Music is born free;

and to win freedom is its destiny." It was like hearing the echo of his own thought. Schoenberg had felt the same, and said as much in a letter to Busoni in 1909:

> I strive for: complete liberation from all forms
> from all symbols
> of cohesion and
> of logic.
>   Thus:
> away with "motivic working out."
> Away with harmony as
> cement or bricks of a building.
> Harmony is *expression*
> and nothing else.
>   Then:
> Away with Pathos!
> Away with protracted ten-ton scores, erected or constructed towers, rocks and other massive claptrap.
> My music must be
> *brief*.[16]

Such sentiments are fully in accord with Nietzsche's own esthetic of "supra-European music." Schoenberg spoke of "the illusory stuff of our dreams" in connection with "Klangfarbenmelodie," and Busoni's *Nocturne symphonique* inhabits the unsettling landscape of the sleeping mind. Varèse's *Arcana* was actually inspired by a dream, and though he was always keen to clarify that his music was about nothing but itself, he nonetheless left us an account of that strange and synesthetic dream vision in a letter to his wife Louise, which included a few bars of two trumpet fanfares that were also part of the experience:

> I was on a boat that was turning around and around—in the middle of the ocean—spinning around in great circles. In the distance I could see a lighthouse, very high—and on top an angel—and the angel was you—a trumpet in each hand. Alternating projectors of different colors: red, green, yellow, blue—and you were playing Fanfare no. 1, trumpet in right hand. Then suddenly the sky became incandescent—blinding—you raised your left hand to your mouth and the Fanfare 2 blared. And the boat kept turning and spinning—and the alternation of projectors and incandescence became more frequent—intensified—and the fanfares more nervous—impatient ... and then—Merde—I woke up.[17]

Varèse, the lover of freedom, was bound to enjoy the ultimate freedom of dreaming. For him, Busoni's plea for musical freedom overruled Schoenberg and his obsessive theorizing: "Schoenberg liberated music from tonality but it was as though frightened by so much freedom, he retreated to the refuge of a system.... Beware of codification of systems and, in spite of all the revolutionary slogans, their latest academicism. There is nothing more deplorable than traditionalists of the left."[18]

In a dream, the imagination knows no bounds, and it was perhaps to this that he was alluding by his quotation from Paracelsus at the head of the score of *Arcana*: "One star exists, higher than all the rest. This is the apocalyptic star. The second star is that of the ascendent. The third is that of the elements—of these there are four, so that six stars are established. Besides these there is still another star, *imagination*, which begets a new star and a new heaven."[19] The text comes form Paracelsus' *Hermetic Astronomy*. The great physician, alchemist, occultist and astrologer Theophrastus Baumbast von Hohenheim (1493–1541), chose the name Paracelsus because he thought himself superior to the first-century Roman physician Celsus. A mystic leading a sexless life, one of his greatest achievements was in persuading experimenters that the object of alchemy should be the cure of the sick rather than the fruitless search for gold. In our own times, Jung has drawn attention to alchemy as more a psychological than chemical process, concerned with the process of individuation. For Varèse, Paracelsus' placement of imagination as the highest star in the universe, agreed with his belief that our greatest mental health lies in the pursuit of imaginative freedom; but in order to prevent the listener from thinking that *Arcana* was "about" Paracelsus, Varèse later insisted that the work was more in the form of a "tribute" rather than a commentary upon the quotation itself.

Busoni's temple figures are now all dancing to Nietzsche's original melody:

> At my feet, my dancing-mad feet, you threw a glance, a laughing, questioning, melting tossing glance:
>
> Twice only did you raise your castanets in your little hands—then my feet were already tossing in a mad dance.
>
> My heels raised themselves, my toes listened for what you should propose: for the dancer wears his ears—in his toes![20]

But Busoni also responded to a darker side of Nietzsche's dangerous game. His opera, *Doktor Faust*, which he left incomplete on his death in 1924, explores the less desirable consequences of total freedom. In Busoni's version of the famous legend, Faust realizes that his (very Nietzschean) purpose is to deny both God and the Devil and to assert the "human, all-too-human" responsibility for our actions. As David Pountney, the director of English National Opera's 1986 production explained:

> Once again it is the Duchess and her baby who point the way. The dead child which she gives him [Faust] inspires him to the understanding that it is not in God that redemp-

tion lies, nor is it in the Devil that Hell is found. For Busoni the Faust story signifies that human beings are solely responsible for their own actions, and may not ascribe either their crimes or achievements to God or the Devil. The child who emerges at the end of the opera is as naked and vulnerable as any human child but he strides into the world with no evil or holy purpose: only the inherited residue of life experience of Faust—"an infinite will."[21]

Busoni wrote the libretto of *Doktor Faust* during the First World War, fully aware of the Faustian pact Germany had made with its destiny. His Mephistopheles offers Faust the complete freedom to live "as fast as he can think," with no restraint from society, conventional morality or even physical limitations. This necessarily takes no account of compassion or human weakness. In the twentieth century, such compete freedom was indeed achieved by Adolf Hitler. (Busoni eerily has students goose-stepping in the tavern scene of his opera.) In the twenty-first century, a celebrity such as the British DJ, television presenter and serial pedophile Jimmy Savile (1926–2011) attained a similar freedom to do anything he liked with official sanction from the highest circles of society. The pact he made was to raise money for charity: a devil masquerading as a saint. There are even rumors that he was a practicing occultist as well. Like Savile, Hitler and the renegade student Raskolnikov in Dostoyevsky's *Crime and Punishment*, Faust regards himself as a special person set apart from the normal rules and obligations of other people. His demand for limitless genius looks forward to the pact made by Adrian Leverkühn, the composer of Thomas Mann's identically named novel *Doctor Faustus*, which is the subject of the next chapter.

15

Thomas Mann

Mann (1875–1955) was not a composer, but music was absolutely central to his world view. Indeed, he often referred to his novels as "scores." The three most formative influences in his life were Schopenhauer, Wagner and Nietzsche; so, when the time came, it was inevitable that he should combine music and philosophy in a novel concerned with the underlying cultural causes of Nazism. This novel was *Doctor Faustus*, by which time Mann was an exile from Nazi Germany, living in America.

For Mann, the Nazis were "German Romanticism gone wrong."[1] Similarly, he felt that Schoenberg's atonal and later serial music was also German Romanticism gone wrong (despite the fact that Schoenberg saw himself as the inevitable and logical successor of Wagner). Mann was convinced that the Third Reich could not be explained in merely political terms: It was a movement rooted in and feeding off esthetics, which legitimized itself in the context of the Romantic movement as a whole, and promoted itself as the fulfilment of Nietzsche's dream of a state "founded on music." The Nazis offered a transfiguration of society into artistic terms, celebrating instinct (what Mann called "the daemonic") in a society "beyond good and evil," which would make possible (but of course did not deliver) numinous ecstasy in everyday life. Mann has his narrator, Zeitblom, speak of the Nazi's "world-rejuvinating barbarism"[2] at one point, and he was right: Hitler, as "Der Führer," was far more than a mere Chancellor; he presided over the Reich as the ultimate Artist-Savior, who promised to redeem the prosaic and transmute it into the poetic, transforming Volkswagens into Wagnerian chariots, politics into Wagnerian poetry, Nuremberg rallies into *Rienzi*.... (Unfortunately, it worked in reverse as well, when Wagnerian antisemitism was put into practice at Auschwitz, and Berlin became a real-life *Götterdämmerung*.) Hitler's new religion promised to replenish worn-out Christianity and cast its spell over every hour of the week, not just on Sundays, elevating everyone into a god.

15. Thomas Mann

Thomas Mann (1875–1955). Photograph by Carl Van Vechten, 1937 (Wikimedia Commons).

Mann knew how dangerous all this was because he could see the problem in himself. His admiration, indeed worship of Wagner's music, his identification with Nietzsche's liberating ideas, and his emotional recognition of Schopenhauer's luxurious pessimism acted upon him as they would upon all those misguided Germans who were beguiled by the counterfeit kingdom of Nazism; but Mann was perceptive enough to be wary of his enthusiasms. He saw the dangers in them, as Nietzsche had seen the dangers in Wagner and Schopenhauer—and even in himself. Nietzsche kept asking, "Have I been understood?" realizing, perhaps, that his ideas would be misinterpreted. He also suspected that Schopenhauer's nihilism would make anything possible, for in a world without God, humanity can do what it likes; and he also knew that Wagner's music was so emotionally overwhelming it had the power to make us all believe we were Siegfrieds slaying the Fafners of "the other," "the uninspired," "the inferior," and "the ugly." Though not inevitable, it is no accident that Wagner provided the soundtrack of the Third Reich. Hitler was a Wagnerian, of course, but Mann knew that there was much of Hitler in Wagner; and Nietzsche before him had identified Wagner as an obsession, a sickness, a magician, and a drug. Mann knew all too well that unchecked estheticism is the herald of uncontrollable barbarism.[3] In *Doctor Faustus* he allows himself an eloquent attack on all the Nazi's stood for, describing them as "liars, and lickspittles" who "mixed us a poison draught and took away our senses."[4] Nietzsche had described what he called the "ultimate men" who have "a little poison"—by which he means the drugs and stimulants in which the all-too-human indulge to produce "pleasant dreams. And a lot of poison at last, for a pleasant death."[5] Hagen, in *Götterdämmerung*, offers Siegfried a magic potion that makes him forget about his true love, Brünnhilde, in favor of a marriage of convenience with Gutrune: All this to attain ultimate power for an unscrupulous dwarf. It seems as though German culture predicted its own political destiny.

Music was therefore the root cause of the problem for Mann, and in *Doctor Faustus* he aimed to dig it up. Early on in the proceedings, he noted "it cannot be denied (and has never been) that the daemonic and irrational have a disquieting share in this radiant sphere"[6] (by which he means the radiant sphere of music). Music is ambiguous, and as for Mann's narrator, Serenus Zeitblom, despite "all its supposedly logical and moral austerity," it belongs "to a world of the spirit for whose absolute reliability in the things of reason and human dignity I would not just care to put my hand in the fire."[7] He adds that in Germany, music enjoys a respect among the people, which the French give to literature. Music is the common cultural currency of everyone in Germany, where "nobody is put off or embarrassed" by the fact that someone is a musician.[8] Music is described as "a magic marriage" between theology and mathematics,[9] and musical composition is likened to alchemy: "What a glorious mystery. I know none higher, deeper, better; none more thrilling, or occult."[10] Significantly, Wagner himself constantly resorts to occult metaphors throughout his essay on Beethoven.

Mann's hero, the composer Adrian Leverkühn, who speaks these words, is brought up on a farm where grows a noble linden tree—an image that echoes Schubert's famous song "Der Lindenbaum," one of the cornerstones of German Romanticism. Beneath its boughs, Adrian learns folk-songs from a stable-girl called Hanna. Her lessons are a sinister version of *The Sound of Music's* "Doh, Ray, Me," instructing him in the intervals of music and the basics of counterpoint. This linden tree also suggests the World-Ash of Wagner's *Ring*: Before the cycle even begins, Wotan has crucified himself on this tree to gain knowledge, and Adrian, soaked in knowledge as he becomes, is also crucified by music. Even as a child he too quickly grasps the tricks and arcane complexities of music; indeed, too much knowledge, too much facility does indeed *kill* one. Adrian absorbs knowledge with the frightening facility of the alien children in John Wyndham's science fiction novel, *The Midwich Cuckoos*.

His father enjoys amateur scientific investigations, which Zeitblom considers somewhat "occult." This probing and laughing at nature's oddities seems somehow indecent and dangerous, foreshadowing, indeed, the obscene medical experiments of Dr. Mengele at Auschwitz. The uncanny "devouring drop," which Adrian's father delights in demonstrating to the children, suggests a daemonic impulse in inanimate nature (it was foreshadowed in the "polyp" experiment that Murnau included in *Nosferatu*, which it would seem likely that Mann knew: He certainly much enjoyed watching Boris Karloff in that later Hollywood horror film *The Mummy*[11]). Among his father's butterfly collection, Adrian is drawn to a specimen called "Hetaera Esmerelda." Like the prostitute who later infects him with the syphilis that gives him his genius (thus, his Faustian bargain), the clear-wing butterfly has a "transparent nudity," and Adrian accordingly calls the prostitute "Esmerelda." ("Hetaera" means "courtesan.")Even at this young age he is therefore marked out for sacrifice.

Ambivalence (ice in the shape of ferns, chemicals that imitate vegetable forms, etc.) is seen by Mann as daemonic and unnerving, just as enharmonic relationships in music are thus regarded by Adrian later on. Everything depends on context. There is no absolute: C-sharp—at least on the magically "tempered" piano, that black box of musical illusions—can become D-flat depending on the tonal context in which it appears. The chemical "plants" are dead matter—they have never even been alive, but they nonetheless yearn for light and move towards the sun. They are like the undead (even though the undead are said to shun the light). Adrian finds all this amusing, just as he finds the "tricks" of music amusing, because, like the Devil who corrupts him later, he is himself ambivalence personified, and the Devil laughs at everything. Laughter is ultimately destructive. Indeed, Nietzsche aimed to destroy ideals with laughter. (Mann observes that Ham, son of Noah was the only man who laughed when he was born, and that could only have happened with the Devil's aid.[12]) As music is the most ambivalent of all the arts, Adrian is predestined to become a composer, even though he starts his studies as a theologian.

Adrian expresses very Nietzschean views regarding nineteenth-century Romantic culture. He argues, with bitter irony, that nineteenth-century Europe must have been "an uncommonly pleasant epoch"[13] as its culture still holds such an appeal for contemporary audiences. Also like Nietzsche, Adrian professes to be opposed to the post–Romantic "monster orchestra," and works for its reduction; but like Schoenberg, he also feels that one must have "command over what has been achieved even though one no longer finds it essential."[14] Instead of Romanticism, Adrian will aim for "irony, mockery; which, clearing the air, made an opposing party against the romantic, against pathos and prophecy, sound-intoxication ... that is with the rediscovery of music itself as an organization of time."[15] These words not only reflect Nietzsche's move away from Wagnerian Romanticism but also describe the esthetic of the Les Six, who, as we have seen, were comparably responding to Nietzsche's new esthetic. This desire for "intellectually winged simplicity"[16] and an "art without anguish" that is "psychologically healthy"[17] are all terms Nietzsche could have coined himself. Adrian, following Nietzsche's plea for the "Mediterraneanization" of music, writes his own "Mediterranean anthology" of Provençal and Catalan lyrics, along with "Spanish and Portuguese things"[18]—even though the music itself reflects Mahler's influence.

Mann, like Zeitblom, was a Romantic himself, and he mourns Adrian's modern approach, while simultaneously understanding the causes of it. Such a view emphasizes the underlying implication of the novel: that twentieth-century music (via Schoenberg) sold its soul to the devil. The reasons for this, previously identified by Nietzsche, are that we lost the guiding morality of religion (overlooking the fact that Schoenberg was a believing Jew); we also lost respect for nature due to the Industrial revolution, and we lost the restraint of reason when we recognized our fundamentally irrational reality, thus proving reason to be really only a fool's paradise. (One could, however, argue that Schoenberg's serial system is the apotheosis of reasoning.)

Like Mann, Adrian too mourns these losses, and in later years reproduces his childhood environment, yearning as he does for its *innocence* and the harmony of its natural order. But all around him, Germany was embracing the godless, industrial and irrational reality of Nazism, which sometimes cynically, sometimes sincerely, exploited such yearnings for innocence and natural harmony to further its cause. Zeitblom, who never fully condones the regime, while obviously disagreeing with it, nonetheless fears a German victory more than a German defeat,[19] for while in the realm of esthetics, Romanticism was a beautiful dream, in the realm of politics it rapidly became a terrible nightmare.

Alongside the spurious "modernity" and cult of youth promoted by the Nazis lay more atavistic forces. Adrian's home town of Kaisersaschen is presented as a metaphor for the whole of Germany. It is a cultured town, but with a museum that contains instruments of torture alongside 25,000 books, some of which are on occult subjects. Mann suggests that this "past" is merely overlaid, not swept aside by the "present," and that this irrational, occult past had been revived by the Nazis. Such atrocities as book burning were a revival of medievalism in a modern setting. Nietzsche, who praised the irrational freedom of instincts "beyond good and evil," understood that only a Superman would be strong enough to temper that instinct with moderation. As we have seen, the term "Dionysian," for Nietzsche, implied an individual who had *mastered* his instincts and contained them with Apollonian forms. The Nazis, for all their Superman imagery, were human, all too human, and they smashed the statues of Apollo on the altar of Dionysus.

Mann discusses the very masculine play-throughs of chamber music enjoyed by Adrian's father and his friends, "with the beer-glass on the floor beside the chair, a cigar in the mouth and frequent bursts of talk."[20] This very German mingling of the prosaic and the numinous was captured very nicely in episode nine ("Why We Fight") of the television series *Band of Brothers* in which American G.I.s observe a group of male musicians playing Beethoven's Quartet in C-sharp minor amid the shattered ruins of a bombed out German town. (We have seen how Wagner in particular identified this particular quartet as one of Beethoven's most significant works, the lengthy opening Adagio of which he described as "surely the saddest thing ever said in notes ... alike a penitential prayer, a communing with God in firm belief of the Eternal Goodness...."[21]) The spiritual ideal evoked and enshrined in this music—an ideal unshaken by war—is at odds with American modernity. Mann has one of his characters, the musician Wendell Kretschmar, describe music as "pure mind, pure spirit. But bound as she is to the world of sense, music must ever strive after the strongest, yes the most seductive sensuous realization: she is a Kundry, who wills not what she does, and flings soft arms of lust round the neck of the fool."[22] This reference to Wagner's last opera again roots the problem as a specifically German one, the idealism of which paved the way for its terrible distortion in the 1930s and '40s. Kretschmar teaches Adrian, much as Wagner "taught" Nietzsche. (Significantly, both Kretschmar and Wagner idolized Beethoven and Shakespeare.) Kretschmar illustrates his lectures with his own renditions at the piano—an instrument that represents music's "intellectuality" as opposed to the more sensuous impact of the orchestra.[23]

And this returns us to the dichotomy of "Kultur" versus "Zivilization" (culture versus civilization), which had been an important issue during the First World War and returned in the arena of the Second. In *Doctor Faustus*, Mann argued that truly cultured societies aren't aware of being cultured:

> Naïveté, unconsciousness, taken-for-grantedness, seem to me to be the first criterion of the constitution to which we give this name. What we are losing is just this naïveté,

and this lack, if one may so speak of it, protects us from many a colourful barbarism, which altogether perfectly agreed with culture, even with a very high culture—I mean: our stage is that of civilization—a very promiscuous state no doubt, but also neither was there any doubt that we should have to become very much more barbaric to be capable of culture again. Technique and comfort—in that state one talks about culture but one has not got it.[24]

These views recapitulate Nietzsche's ideas about ancient Greek culture, and also reflect Mann's argument in his earlier *Reflections of a Nonpolitical Man*. Like Nietzsche's ideas themselves, the Kultur versus Zivilization debate is dangerously prone to misuse in ruthless power politics:

The difference between intellect and politics includes that of culture and civilization, of soul and society, of freedom and voting rights, of art and literature; and German tradition is culture, soul, freedom, art and *not* civilization, society, voting rights, and literature. The difference between intellect and politics, as a further example, is the difference between cosmopolitan and international. The former concept comes from the cultural sphere and is German; the latter comes from the sphere of civilization and democracy and is—something quite different.[25]

Later in *Doctor Faustus*, Mann introduced a university professor called Helmut Institoris who is directly based on Nietzsche—along with a dash of Nietzsche's friend and admirer, Jacob Burckhardt (1818–1897). Like Burckhardt, Institoris is a professor of Italian Renaissance history. Burckhardt's famous *Civilization of the Renaissance in Italy* (1860) is full of blood-thirsty "Kultur." (While pointing out that Italy's despots such as Giovanni Maria Visconti used dogs to tear human bodies, and that Emperor Valentinian I set his mercenaries upon the starving populace, killing 200 people, Burckhardt also points out that "Florence was then the scene of the richest development of human individuality."[26]) Mann similarly has Institoris describe the Renaissance as a time that "reeked of blood and beauty," but Institoris is himself (also, like Nietzsche) a *sickly* admirer of strength who raves about "beautiful ruthlessness and Italian poisoners," glorying in a life of "splendid unthinkingness" in which "only human beings with strong and brutal instincts could create great works."[27] Of course, these are simplifications and partly misrepresentations of Nietzsche's ideas, but that is Mann's point: Nietzsche lays himself open to these distortions, and that is exactly what happened to him during the Third Reich. Mann makes clear that even during the First World War, Nietzsche was frequently employed to justify atrocity. Taking Nietzsche's observation that there are only necessities not laws in Nature, the German Chancellor claimed in 1914 that "Necessity knows no law" when it came to invading Belgium.[28]

But for Adrian Leverkühn all that lay in the future. He must first sell his soul to the devil, and he does this by visiting the prostitute who infects

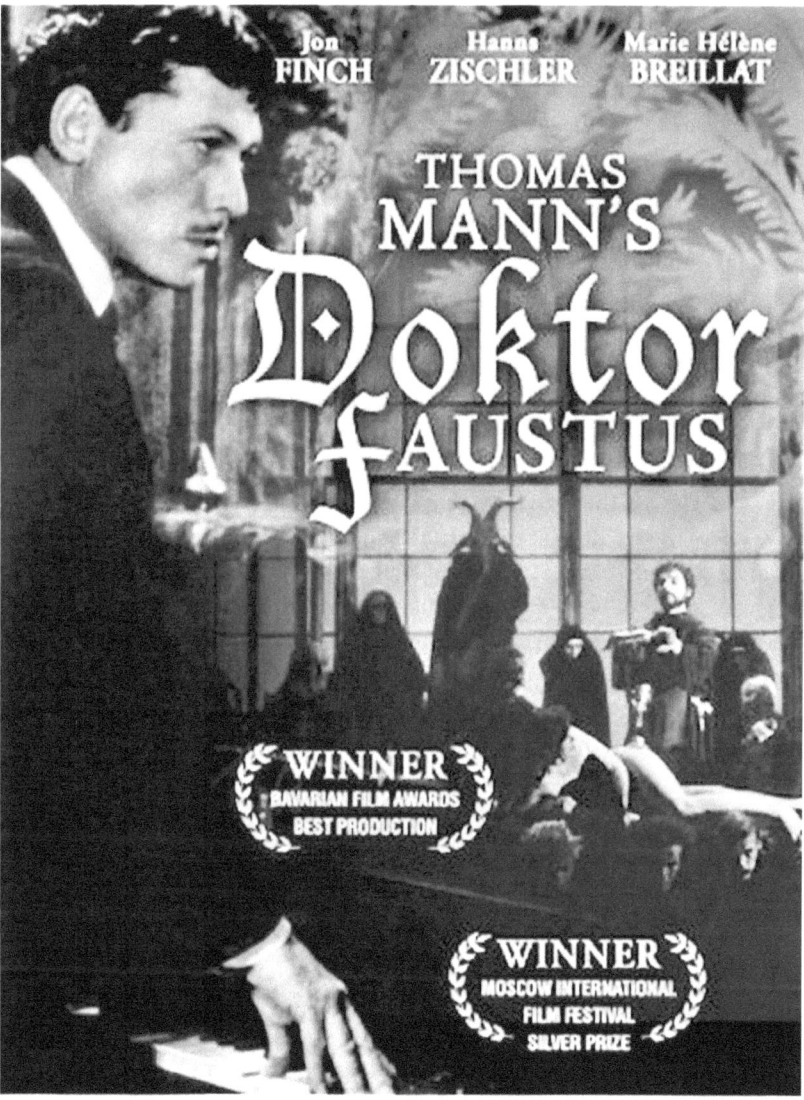

Poster for the film adaptation of *Doctor Faustus* (dir. Franz Seitz, 1982), starring Jon Finch.

him with syphilis. Sex, which is allied to Nietzsche's Will to Power, is also, like music, an ambivalent force, and consequently a gateway to the pit. Mann points out that "instinct does not spare the loftiest intellectual pride,"[29] suggesting the "mortal insult" that finally destroyed Nietzsche's relationship with Wagner. Adrian's visit to Esmerelda is closely modeled on Nietzsche's own visit to a prostitute (who may or may not have infected him). Adrian plays chords from Weber's singspiel *Der Freischütz* (1821) on Esmeralda's upright piano, just as Nietzsche had played the Hermit's Prayer from that same cornerstone of German Romanticism when he visited his own anonymous sex-worker.[30]

Visconti reproduced this scene in great detail when he incorporated it into *Death in Venice*. We see the girl "in a little Spanish jacket, with a big gam, snub nose, almond eyes, an Esmeralda, she brushed my cheek with her arm."[31] Apart from having the prostitute play Beethoven's "Für Elise" all this is meticulously recreated in *Death in Venice* by the master realist of Italian cinema, who also named the steamer that brings Aschenbach to the ambivalent, cholera infected city of Venice, "Esmeralda." Visconti even interpolates the scene from *Doctor Faustus* in which Adrian contemplates an hour-glass: "so fine, the little neck, through which the red sand runs, a threadlike trickle," which seems to last forever until the very end; "then it does seem to speed and to have gone fast. But that is so far away, the narrow part, it is not worth talking or thinking about."[32] Dirk Bogarde's Aschenbach draws on his cigarette and shudders, realizing the nearness of his own mortality. Similarly, the discussion between Bogarde and Mark Burns, who plays Aschenbach's friend (not present in the novella), is also derived from *Doctor Faustus*. The friend argues that inspiration has nothing to do with morality. "Wisdom? Human dignity?

Björn Andrésen as Tadzio in *Death in Venice* (dir. Luchino Visconti, 1971).

What use are they?" he asks. "Evil is a necessity. It is the *food* of genius." Similarly, the Devil in *Doctor Faustus* argues that "a genuine inspiration, immediate, absolute, unquestioned, ravishing ... is not possible with God.... It comes from the divil, the true master and giver of such rapture."³³

Adrian, who had not stayed with the prostitute on the first occasion, later seeks her out in Dresden, and it is there that she infects him. (Significantly, Dresden was much associated with Wagner and Richard Strauss.) He later uses the notes H (the German designation for B-natural), E. A, E and S (E-flat) as a musical cipher for Haetera Esmerelda. The disease, therefore, is not only in his blood—it is also in music.³⁴ There is a possibility that he might be cured, but the Devil saves him from this fate by having the first doctor he visits die, and the second one arrested. As the Devil, who appears to Adrian in an hallucination later on, explains: he did away with the doctors to preserve the syphilis, so that they did not botch "the beautiful case." Syphilis works slowly to allow, as the Devil puts it, again using hour-glass imagery, "a whole houre-glassful of divil-time, genius time."³⁵ Disease, which "rides on a high horse over all hindrances, and springs with drunken daring from peak to peak, is a thousand times dearer to life than plodding healthiness."³⁶

Thus does fate press inexorably around Adrian, for he knows that syphilis will grant him unique powers of musical invention. He will "dare to be barbaric."³⁷ Delius might not have agreed with him, but the parallel is striking. Sickness "puts a man in a mood rebellious and ironic against the bourgeois order,"³⁸ the Devil explains. And "irony" accordingly becomes Adrian's principal stylistic characteristic. Significantly, he composes his "ironic" operatic adaptation of Shakespeare's *Love's Labours Lost* in Italy—a suitably Nietzschean location, and ideal for the Superman. Just as Nietzsche tended toward the "barbaric" because he aimed to destroy the values on which past civilization was built, Adrian does the same in musical terms, by destroying tonality; but whereas Nietzsche aimed to create a freer, better world of joy and creative ecstasy after smashing convention with his philosopher's hammer, the consequences of Adrian's experiment lead to horror. And it is here that we really see Mann's complex and contradictory relationship with Nietzsche at its clearest. Just as Nietzsche loved and simultaneously loathed Wagner's music, Mann here wrestles with his joint admiration and suspicion of Nietzsche's program. Ultimately, the bourgeois humanist and Wagnerian Romantic in Mann triumphs over the Nietzschean Superman.

Another condition imposed by the Devil is that Adrian will never enjoy the love of another human being. This surely echoes the predicament of Alberich in Wagner's *Ring* cycle, as well as the pact made between Faust and Mephistopheles in Goethe's *Faust*:

> Werd ich zum Augenblicke sagen:
> Verweile doch! du bist so schön!
> Dann magst du mich in Fesseln schlagen,
> Dann will ich gern zugrunde gehn!
>
> (When, to the Moment then, I say:
> "Ah, stay a while! You are so lovely!"
> Then you can grasp me: then you may,
> Then, to my ruin, I'll go gladly!)

Goethe's Faust cannot imagine that life will ever be so beautiful for this to occur, and so feels safe. Adrian, like Alberich, forswears love to attain sinister power, and like Faust, cannot believe that he will ever be tempted by real love for any other human being. Indeed, echoing another real-life event in Nietzsche's biography, Adrian's friend Rudi Schwerdtfeger "steals" his fiancée, Marie Godeau. Exactly the same thing happened to Nietzsche, when he sent his own friend Paul Rée, with whom he had visited Wagner at Tribschen, to propose to Lou Salomé on his behalf. Rée fell in love with Salomé and they eloped. Nietzsche was devastated. Adrian understands his bargain, and even worse consequences occur towards the end of the novel when he begins to have fatherly affections for his nephew, who promptly dies of meningitis.

Adrian now revels in the freedom from morality and convention his disease provides him. He choses an "almost intolerable passage"[39] from Dante's *Inferno*, involving cruelty and martyrdom, which reflects Nietzsche's experience in the mountain hut, where cruelty is pure instinct, and pure instinct is the ultimate freedom. When Zeitblom expresses concern at this turn of events, Adrian's aloof distain suggests that of SS officers at Auschwitz. Adrian's expression is "mute, veiled, musing, aloof to the point of offensiveness, full of chilling melancholy."[40] Mann uses this episode to attack the esthetics of the avant grade, which makes humanism itself "a subject for mirth."[41]

To Schoenberg's dismay, Mann borrowed his serial technique and claimed it as Adrian's own invention. Worse, Mann suggested that Schoenberg's new style was the music of the Devil. Putting his own beliefs into the mouth of Zeitblom, Mann argued that serialism ("the complete integration of all musical dimensions, their neutrality towards each other due to complete organization"[42]) would result in "impoverishment and stagnation,"[43] and Zeitblom feels that the whole has a "vaguely daemonic" quality about it, like games of chance, fortune-telling or "magic."[44] Mann in fact regarded serialism as the musical equivalent of the Nazi's organized chaos, which one might epitomize by the neatly typed lists of names of those who were killed in death camps. (Mann's censure of serialism in this manner is, of course, unintentionally ironic, given that Schoenberg was not only a fellow exile in America but also a Jew.) Taking his cue from Schoenberg's *Harmonielehre*, but in fact misrepresenting Schoenberg's belief in musical *evolution* rather than *revolution* (Schoenberg was really quite conservative in his respect of the past), Mann has the Devil argue that tonality is no longer possible. "Impossible the diminished seventh, impossible certain chromatic passing notes."[45] These are now to be regarded as mere clichés; but Mann's main aim was to expose what he saw as the lie in the theory of serialism itself. In serialism, every note is said to be democratically *equal*. As there is no tonality, no one note is more significant than the other. This might be said to equate to the idea that under a socialist government everyone is free and equal too; but under National Socialism, while the lie was that everyone was equal, the truth was that no one had any freedom. When the *total* serialism of Pierre Boulez followed in the wake of the Second World War, in which not only notes, but every other form of expression: dynamics, phrasing, rhythm, etc., was "serialized," contemporary music truly became more totalitarian than the governments against whose pseudo-Romantic esthetics it claimed to be at odds.

Adrian's pact with the Devil is regarded by Mann as a microcosm of Germany's pact with Hitler—the promise of power and pseudo-creativity and the regeneration of what was seen by many as the degenerate culture of the Weimar Republic, at the price of ultimate catastrophe. "What uplifts you, what increases your feeling of power and might and domination, damn it," the Devil insists, "that is the truth—and whether ten times a lie when looked at from the moral angle."[46] Such words derive almost word for word from Nietzsche's *The Anti-Christ*:

> What is good?—All that heightens the feeling of power, the will to power, power itself in man.
> What is bad?—all that proceeds from weakness.
> What is happiness?—The feeling that power increases—*that a resistance is overcome*.[47]

It is in this context that Mann's belief that "the artist is the brother of the criminal and the madman" makes most sense, even though Mann's demonization of Nietzsche is colored by the context of the Second World War. It was, however, how Nietzsche was *interpreted* on a crude level by the

Nazis. Power, for Nietzsche, was about sublimation and what Jung called the "individuation of the psyche," rather than the jackboot and the gaschambers; but there is, unfortunately, a gateway to the Nazi Torture Garden through Nietzsche's ambivalently aphoristic prose.

So what of Adrian's music itself—this "barbaric," intellectualized, ironic serialism? Mann has several attempts at describing it. Adrian's *Apocalypse* is characterized by "barbaric"[48] glissandos, reverting to the savage time when individual pitches had not been rescued from chaos. The effect of these wailing glissandi might therefore resemble György Ligeti's use of them in his *Requiem* (1965), which was juxtaposed with Strauss' *Also Sprach Zarathustra* in the soundtrack of Kubrick's *2001—A Space Odyssey* (1968). Adrian's *Apocalypse* is also characterized by paradox: dissonance is used to express all that is lofty and pious; tonality is used to convey the horrors of hell, which, following Bernard Shaw's interpretation, is a place of banality and the commonplace: It is, indeed, the world of tonality-drenched commercial culture, which is being transmitted to millions of television screens while you are reading this book.

In his final composition, *The Lamentation of Dr. Faustus*, Adrian attempts to reverse the "calculated coldness" of his earlier works, even though it is indeed a serial work. Zeitblom, echoing the title of Nietzsche's autobiography, calls it an "Ecce Homo."[49] *Faustus* contains the Esmerelda cypher yet again: H, A, E, E, S, and also includes a mirror image of Beethoven's setting of Schiller's "Ode to Joy" at the end of the Ninth Symphony. Adrian's peon to despair concludes with an "Ode to Sorrow," but right at the end of the utter despair of this piece, Zeitblom can sense a glimmer of transfiguring hope, even though Adrian himself claims the piece to be "the devil's work." That hope was also Mann's hope that the Third Reich would be destroyed and German culture would be redeemed.

After playing through *The Lamentation of Dr. Faustus* to his friends on the piano Adrian collapses into insanity, echoing Nietzsche's own collapse. Significantly, both men were subsequently cared for by their mothers, until, in Nietzsche's case, his ghastly sister took over and delivered him into the hands of the Nazis.

As Mann provides such intriguing descriptions of Adrian's music, it is perhaps to be expected that later composers have been attracted to writing pieces based on these literary outlines. In 1997, Hans Werner Henze (1926–2012) wrote a violin concerto based on the one Leverkühn composes in chapter 38 of the novel. Zeitblom explains: "My readers are aware that Adrian in the end complied with Rudi Schwerdtfeger's long-cherished and expressed desire, and wrote him a violin concerto of his own. He dedicated to Rudi personally the brilliant composition, so extraordinarily suited to a violin technique, and even accompanied him to Vienna for the first performance."⁵⁰ Henze ignored the page of detailed "analysis" that Mann provided for this imaginary work, choosing instead to compose portraits, one for each of the three movements, of Esmerelda, Nepomuk Schneidewein (Adrian's ill-fated nephew), and Rudi himself. Henze used each movement to explore the emotional consequences of various psychological themes: sexual guilt, the death of children, and the problem of virtuosity, which can so often lead to musical "emptiness."

Henze's Concerto was followed, in 2001, by the completion of Dutch composer Alexander Comitas' Violin Concerto (Op. 34), also based the Leverkühn example, which at the time of this book's publication has still not been performed. (An electronic realization is, however, freely available online.) This one does follow some of Mann's analytical description. It has no key signature, and uses the titles Mann indicates: "Andante amoroso" for the first movement, which reflects Mann's description of "dulcet tenderness bordering on mockery."⁵¹ Comitas also makes sure that there is a "high F on the violin" and in general attempts the capture Mann's indications of key and pitch. The second movement is a Scherzo, reflecting Leverkühn's "extremely abandoned and virtuoso middle movement," with its quotation from Tartini's *Devil's Trill* Sonata. The third movement is also a "Theme and Variations" as indicated by Mann with an "intoxicating cantilena of great breadth, which decidedly has something showy about it."⁵² Everything then comes to an end in the required C major.

Geoffrey Gordon also composed a more general musical response to the novel as a whole in his *Doktor Faustus* Cello Concerto in 2014, which was commissioned by the Copenhagen Philharmonic for its principle cellist, Toke Møldrup, and premièred on January 31, 2014, at the Royal Danish Academy of Music, under Rory Macdonald. One review described the overall effect as "a mysterious, shiny backdrop through which the woodwinds rose up like bubbles in a chaotic, creative, primordial soup, before dramatic percussion eruptions and brass-crested waves stole the show."⁵³

However, the twentieth-century composer who perhaps most successfully evoked the serial style of Leverkühn is the American Lukas Foss (1922–2009), whose setting of the "O Mensch, gib acht" forms part of his 1960 *Time Cycle* for soprano and instrumental ensemble consisting of piano, celesta, cello, clarinet and percussion. The other-worldly timbre of the vibraphone aptly suggests the timelessness of Nietzsche's hymn to eternal recurrence. The text is at first meant to be whispered by the male voices of the orchestral players in classic Schoenbergian Sprechstimme style, though sometimes the soprano performs this duty before taking over with Foss' somnambulistic setting of "Ich schlief, ich schlief." At the end of the text, the note row very much in evidence, Foss creates a mood of hushed avant-garde mysticism with a chiming finger-cymbal.

Finale: Nietzsche and Popular Music

Great composers are not, of course, confined to the art-music tradition, and Nietzsche has not failed to influence the arena of popular music. So-called "classical" music is often very dark and melancholy in a way that runs counter to Nietzsche's own demands for joy from music. As we have seen, his writings have often inspired somewhat sombre music. The popularity of Bizet's *Carmen*, with its eminently whistleable melodies and infectious rhythms has far more in common with popular music than with Wagner, Mahler and many of the other composers we have been discussing. Indeed, Nietzsche's entire philosophy, which preaches optimism, joy, ecstasy and the revaluation of all values, anticipated the whole counterculture movement of the 1960s.

Before that, Jean-Paul Sartre (1905–1980) had combined the idea of popular music as a cure for the existential dilemma that Nietzsche's revolution created. In Sartre's novel *Nausea* (1938), the existential hero, Antoine Roquentin, suffers from a spiritual and often even physical nausea caused by his awareness of the futility of existence. (Another character is described as suffering from "the unbearable reality: that he is alone, without any attainments, without any past, with a mind which is growing duller, a body which is disintegrating."[1]) Roquentin escapes from this nausea by listening to a record of Shelton Brooks' song "Some of These Days," played in a café: "What has just happened is that the Nausea has disappeared. When the voice sounded in the silence, I felt my body harden and the Nausea vanished. All of a sudden: it was almost painful to become so hard, so bright."[2] Roquentin feels he lives *in* the music, and his perception of "wretched time" is crushed by it—crushed by the internal time structure of the music: "At the same time the duration of the music dilated, swelled like a water spout. It filled the room with its metallic transparency, crushing our wretched time against the walls. I am *in* the music."[3] Music, which has been usefully described as sound organized in time, ironically has the ability to remove us from our perception of time. Music therefore helps us to live more easily in the moment. These are very Nietzschean concepts: the need to live in the here-and-now rather than projecting ourselves into the future (not to mention the life to come, which religion promises us after death). Sartre's use of the term "hard" also relates to Nietzsche's plea for us to become "hard"—music, through its beauty, allows us to gain the strength to negotiate reality. Significantly, Sartre chooses popular rather than classical music to effect this remedy, and was one of the first European intellectuals to do so, paving the way for those Nietzschean aspects of 1960s counter-culture.

The most enthusiastic Nietzschean rockers were probably Jim Morrison of The Doors and Robert Plant of Led Zeppelin were also enthusiastic Nietzscheans. Morrison (1943–1971) famously improvised an "Ode" to Nietzsche on a backstage grand piano in New York in 1968, for the documentary *A Feast of Friends* (dir. Paul Ferrara, 1968). The "lyrics," accompanied by a succession of thrashed-out, some might say "Dionysian" tone-clusters, were inspired by Nietzsche's final moments of sanity in Turin when he intervened to protect a horse that was being beaten in the street, soon thereafter collapsing:

> He threw his arms around the horse's neck and kissed him everywhere. I love my horse. A crowd gathered, his landlord appeared and took Frederick back up to his room on the second floor, where he began to play the piano madly and sing madly like ... ooooooh.... I'm crucified and inspected and resurrected and if you don't believe that I'll give you my latest philanthropic sonata; and the landlord's family was amazed, so they sent for his friend Overbeck, and he got there in three days by coach, and they took Frederick to the asylum, and his mother joined him, and for the next fifteen years, they cried and cried and laughed and looked at the sun and everyone.

This is hardly great music (or great poetry), but is certainly a testament to Morrison's devotion to Nietzsche, who apparently inspired his "Dionysian" persona on stage, raising the consciousness of his audiences through music, and inducing, as it were, the Birth of Psychedelia out of the Spirit of Music.

Robert Plant, born in 1948, also read Nietzsche, and felt suitably influenced, though just how much is open to question. Erin E. Flynn is certainly in no doubt that he was, though rock music when combined with philosophy can often sound as incoherent as Nazi Nietzscheanism:

> Our individuation, though it appears so real, is a temporary and excruciating manifestation of forces that outstrip us. Such is the Dionysian wisdom Nietzsche finds expressed in all art. Good Dionysian art redeems this lamentable fate by celebrating our struggle

against and ultimate release into the very forces that undo us. Rather than a flight into hedonism, Dionysian art is steeped in the awareness of our painful, contradictory condition. Led Zeppelin gives ecstatic expression to this wisdom and so something like Nietzsche's Dionysian metaphysics of the self: that we are temporary manifestations of nature's endlessly transformative power.[4]

In this psychedelic climate, it is not at all surprising that a cardboard cut-out of Nietzsche was considered as one of the "people we like" on Peter Brook's cover for The Beatles' *Sgt. Pepper* album. Though the magician Aleister Crowley made it into the finished artwork, Nietzsche was rejected. Rather more worryingly, Hitler was indeed made into a cardboard cut-out but was either omitted or obscured at the last minute, depending on whose account one reads: John Lennon's mordant sense of humor obviously wasn't shared by EMI company executives. Having claimed that The Beatles were bigger than Christ, Lennon presumably wanted to make the quite legitimate case for Hitler as one of the most significant men in twentieth-century history.

The fact that Nietzsche didn't make it onto the cover does not mean he was not significant enough to be included. Nietzsche's short-lived academic career and his subsequent very early retirement on a modest pension, allowed him to become the world's first "drop-out"—resembling, indeed, The Beatles' "Nowhere Man." (Nietzsche, after all, described *Zarathustra* as "A Book for Everyone and No One.") He wintered in Italy and summered in Switzerland like a homeless hippy. His absurd mustache, eccentric even at a time of lavish facial hair, made him even more eccentric. Isolated from the mainstream by his radical ideas, he anticipated the existential concept of alienation, and though his use of drugs was medicinal rather than recreational, his pursuit of joy, his revaluation of all values, his emphasis on the human body as our only reality, and sexual freedom as our most important goal ("The degree and kind of a man's sexuality reaches up into the topmost summit of his spirit"[5]), made him very attractive to hippy culture in general.

However, Sgt. Pepper's "Lucy in the Sky with Diamonds" (a coded tribute to the mind-bending powers of LSD) is not the kind of ecstasy of which Nietzsche would have approved. Alcohol and the use of drugs to retreat from reality were not what Nietzsche meant by joy, for joy depended on the strength to contemplate reality as it is, as "My Roses," one of the poems with which introduces his tribute to joy, *The Gay Science*, makes clear:

> Yes! My joy—it wants to gladden,
> every joy wants so to gladden!
> Would you pluck my rose and sadden?

> You must crouch on narrow ledges,
> prop yourself on ropes and wedges,
> prick yourself on thorny hedges!
> For my joy—it loves to madden!
> For my joy—is malice laden!
> Would you pluck my rose and sadden?[6]

The Beatles' immediately post–Pepper anthem, "All You Need Is Love," also promotes rather too simplistic a message to have gained Nietzsche's intellectual approval, though love was exactly what Nietzsche was most in need of, and he certainly believed everything was "entwined together, everything in love" (see below). Paul McCartney's "Eleanor Rigby" is the existentialism of Sartre's *Nausea* propelled into the popular arena: "the alienation of the personality and the mystery of being," as the blurb on the Penguin edition of Sartre's novel puts it. "Eleanor Rigby" is about loneliness, an empty church, death without salvation—the very world Nietzsche contemplated and worried about—the existentialism he inaugurated before he found salvation in his theory of Eternal Recurrence, and the total affirmation of everything: pain, suffering, ecstasy and joy.

> Did you ever say Yes to one joy? O my friends, then you said Yes to *all* woe as well. All things are chained and entwined together, all things are in love; if you ever wanted one moment twice, if you ever said: "You please me, happiness, instant, moment!" then you wanted *everything* to return! you wanted everything anew, everything eternal, everything chained, entwined together, everything in love.[7]

The power of "Eleanor Rigby" was, of course, immeasurably enhanced by producer George Martin's string accompaniment, which consciously echoed the cold, staccato, non-vibrato style of Bernard Herrmann's string-only score for Alfred Hitchcock's *Psycho* (1960). Martin's inspired musical arrangement brilliantly accentuates the bleakness of the lyrics and again echoes Nietzsche's famous statement in *Zarathustra* urging us to "*become hard!*"[8]—for hardness is not only strength but also beauty, like a diamond. Softness to others—mere "pity"—achieves little that really helps the afflicted. Softness to oneself—self-pity—is also counter-productive. Practical help is always of more benefit than pity, while stoicism helps one cope with suffering and make something beautiful out of it. Truth, in other words, is always better than a lie. In these significant ways, "Eleanor Rigby" is a truly Nietzschean song. It is bleak, but realistic, and not without compassion, unlike Father Mackenzie in his empty church, who is powerless to do anything about it. Only truth can teach us; only truth can ultimately comfort us and help us.

Finale: Nietzsche and Popular Music

After the break-up of The Beatles, Lennon went on to write one of the most Nietzschean of all pop songs with "Imagine" (1970). Nietzsche, an accomplished composer of songs himself, was not as melodically inventive as Lennon (still less than McCartney), but from a purely musical point of view "Imagine" has much in common with Nietzsche's setting of Freidrich Rückert's poem "Aus der Jugendzeit." To begin with, the range of pitches used is comparable. Lennon moves up from G to B and then down to A in his opening measures, encompassing very nearly the same range of pitches as Nietzsche's melody, which in its different key moves down from G to F and then E. There is really only a semitone difference between them. Nietzsche repeats his material just as much as Lennon, and the accompaniment in Nietzsche is even more straightforward than Lennon's gently rocking piano figurations, for Nietzsche's piano merely harmonizes the melody. Both songs are simple and direct, uncomplicated and memorable; but "Auf der Jugendzeit" has nothing of Nietzsche's later philosophy in it being merely a memory of the poet's youth. One finds a rather more comparable sentiment to Lennon's song in Nietzsche's setting of Sandor Petöfi's "Postlude" as translated into German by Karl Maria Kertbeny (and translated into English here by Stewart Spencer):

> I'd like to quit this garish world,
> in which joy and anguish hold me in thrall,
> and, leaving my fellow man far behind me,
> seek out the woodland's wild and beauteous solitude.
> There I would heed the whispering leaves
> and listen to the bright brook's purling
> and woodbirds' singing,
> and watch the sun as it sets—
> and sink with it betimes.

Here we have elements of which Lennon would surely have approved: a retreat from conventional society into nature (the "sky" of "Imagine"). Nietzsche's setting of this poem is even more restrained than that of "Auf der Jugendzeit," being almost like a hymn, which, of course, "Imagine" is too in its secular way; and it is the text of "Imagine" that is its most significant element. Like Nietzsche, Lennon hopes for a world without established religion (though in favor of what Jesus actually taught); he hopes for a society without concepts of heaven or hell, and an approach to existence that lives in the here and now. Nietzsche, the good European, who was nervous of nationalism and all it stood for, would surely have approved of Lennon's dream of a world without national boundaries; for nationalism, like religion, causes wars, just as capitalism causes poverty on the one hand and encourages greed on the other. Lennon's hope for the brotherhood of man might have raised one of Nietzsche's famously bushy eyebrows, fully aware as he was of the Will to Power, but, as we have had occasion to observe before, Nietzsche made war with ideas, not with the sword. As Walter Kaufmann points out, when Nietzsche writes a line such as "You should love peace as a means to new war—and the short peace more than the long,"[9] he is using the word "war" metaphorically. "It is the quest for knowledge that he discusses, and he evidently believes that it need not be an entirely private affair: it can be a contest, as it was in Socrates' day; and the goal might be truth rather than winning an argument. Hence one may triumph even in defeat."[10] Fully in accord with Lennon's pacifist agenda, Nietzsche praises a nation that exclaims:

> "We will break the sword," and will smash its entire military establishment down to its lowest foundations. *Rendering oneself unarmed when one has been the best-armed*, out of a height of feeling—that is the means to real peace, which must always rest on a peace of mind; whereas the so-called armed peace, as it now exists in all countries, is the absence of peace of mind. One trusts neither oneself nor one's neighbor, and, half from hatred, half from fear, does not lay down arms. Rather perish than hate and fear, and *twice rather perish than make oneself hated and feared*—this must some day become the highest maxim for every single commonwealth, too.[11]

There is plenty here for Lennon to have approved of, if he had indeed read it. Nietzsche's attack on the life-denying consequences of Pauline Christian morality would also have appealed. Indeed, Lennon's famous remark that the Beatles were "bigger than Christ" is in the tradition of Nietzsche's half-ironic titles "Why I am So Wise," "Why I Am So Clever" and "Why I Write Such Excellent Books" in his own autobiography *Ecce Homo*. Nietzsche's irony was borne from his isolation, whereas Lennon's was merely a statement of fact; but calling a book *The Anti-Christ* is something Lennon might have done if he had written an autobiography himself. Famous Lennon quotes, now posted all over the internet, such as "Time you enjoy wasting was not wasted" and "Reality leaves a lot to the imagination" could have been written by Nietzsche himself, though, admittedly, the misogynist in Nietzsche would have baulked at Lennon's "As usual, there is a great woman behind every idiot." When it comes to Lennon's comment "You don't need anyone to tell you who you are and what you are. You are what you are," Nietzsche actually did express the same sentiment in aphorism 270 of *The Gay Science*: "What does your conscience say?—'You should become who you are,'" which itself is a shortened version of Pindar's fifth-century statement "Become who you are *through knowledge*."

It is not too simplistic, therefore, to equate Barry Mann and Cynthia Weil's 1968 song "Make Your Own Kind of Music," which became a hit for Mama Cass Elliot the following year, with distinctly Nietzschean sentiments. This song encourages defiance of convention, self-confidence, "being who you are," imperviousness to criticism, and not least the courage to keep on singing against a wall of indifference. Nietzsche would surely have sung along.

Having claimed Nietzsche for popular culture, drug-fuelled clubbers raving in a nightclub are not exactly what Nietzsche had in mind when Zarathustra, "came upon a green meadow quietly surrounded by trees and bushes: and in the meadow girls were dancing together."[12] His praise of their defiance of the "Spirit of Gravity," and their "feet with fair ankles" along with all his other uses of dance imagery is always metaphorical and goes beyond the merely literal; but it is certainly the case that dancing, lightness of foot, music and *ecstasy* belong together in the literal sense on a contemporary dance floor. As Sartre understood, music in general and popular music in particular seems to defeat our perception of time and permit us a glimpse of the eternal present through the logic of its structure.

We are absorbed by musical rhythm, absorbed *into it;* simultaneously, it expresses the internal rhythm of the *body:* the beating of the heart, the surge of the blood, the expansion and contraction of the internal organs—all those purely biological motions, which Sartre describes as the true nature of existence in *Nausea*. "My body of living flesh, the flesh which swarms and turns gently liqueuers, which turns cream, the flesh which turns, turns, turns, the sweet sugary water of my flesh, the blood of my hand…"[13] For Sartre, existence is problematic, if not quite literally nauseating; but for Nietzsche, who placed all his trust in the body, such an expression of its reality is both pure joy and pure pain united into a Dionysian whole. Indeed, it is not at all a *reductio ad absurdum* to suggest that the music of Abba expresses just such a Dionysian unity. Such optimistic, joyful music simultaneously acknowledges pain. The melancholy of Abba's lyrics ("Knowing Me, Knowing You," "S.O.S.," "Super Trouper," etc.) only enhances its ecstasy. Dancing to Abba might be just as, if not more Dionysian as listening to Scriabin's *Poem of Ecstasy* in a concert hall, where dancing is, after all, not encouraged. (The film director Ken Russell once told me that he often wanted to dance in the aisles during classical concerts, and sometimes did indeed leave his seat to do so.) At one performance of *The Poem of Ecstasy* I certainly felt *weightless*, as if Scriabin's music had given me the power to levitate—to *defeat the Spirit of Gravity* quite literally. It began to feel possible that I might float over the balcony of the Albert Hall where I was sitting and hover over the orchestra below. I have felt similarly weightless during the concluding bacchanal of Ravel's *Daphnis et Chloë*, with its infectious 5/4 rhythm, which so confused the dancers in the original Diaghilev production that Nijinsky had to shout out the syllables of "Ser-gei-Di-ag-liev" during rehearsals. And this is the point. Ravel intended this music to be danced to, and dancing to Abba would perhaps be closer to the spirit of Nietzsche than internalizing the physical excitement of, say, the coda of Glazunov's Sixth Symphony, or the end of Tchaikovsky's *Francesca da Rimini*, both of which are concerned with ramping up the excitement of the listener as they work to a climax in a manner which is, frankly, profoundly physiological.

Analysis in this arena is a mere scalpel, injuring the *feeling* to no purpose, and this is to some extent what Nietzsche meant by his praise of the dancing girls, along with his plea to them not to stop dancing on his account: "He who is not afraid of my darkness will find rose bowers too under my cypresses." (i.e. intellect shelters physical ecstasy.) Nietzsche's mission was to encourage the ecstasy of the dance, the joy of life in the moment rather than a Christian denial of these things, along with the deadening hand of analysis and *academe* in general. But he did not mean the ecstasy of a tablet or alcohol. His ideal was the combination of joy with consciousness, of the *alertness* of the senses, not their dulling: not mere hedonism but rather a joy that acknowledges—indeed *absorbs* suffering into itself, and thus becomes all the stronger. Applying the words of Walter Pater, Nietzsche seems to be urging a joyful state that burns "with a hard, gemlike flame"[14] rather than an artificially enhanced euphoria.

David Bowie, whose death in 2016 revealed his apparently God-like status, demonstrated the power of pop music and tonality over the elite total serialism of Pierre Boulez, whose death only five days earlier received somewhat less sensational coverage. Both Boulez and Bowie had things to say about Nietzsche. Boulez, who probably knew more about the subject than Bowie, interestingly compared Nietzsche with E. T. A. Hoffmann, whose "best musical compositions are certainly not the ones he actually wrote but the ones of which he gives 'ideal' descriptions in his books; and the same is true of Nietzsche."[15] He also compared himself to the philosopher:

> I always think of the subtitle of Nietzsche's *Also Sprach Zarathustra*—"A book for everyone and for no one." I can say the same of my own role as I see it: the advice I give is

for everyone and for no one. You are at liberty, like Hamlet, to see a cloud as a camel, a weasel or a whale, and, whatever you say, I shall not contradict you. It always comes back to the same thing, which means everything and nothing: freedom. I will be neither a paternalist nor a dictator of ideas but I will—if I am allowed to—organise your dissatisfaction. You are free to hold it against me or to refuse.[16]

In 1974, Boulez composed incidental music for Jean-Louis Barrault's "scenic version" of *Thus Spoke Zarathustra*, translated as *Ainsi parla Zarathustra*. The work, first performed at the Renaud-Barrault theater in Paris, remains unpublished and, consequently, much more obscure than David Bowie's Nietzschean pronouncements, which are slightly more tenuous, though no less intriguing.

The title of Bowie's song "Supermen" (1970) is enough to suggest the influence of Nietzsche, while the use of timpani in it might also suggest a futile echo of Strauss' *Also Sprach Zarathustra*. "Oh, You Pretty Things" (1971) considers Nietzsche's creative evolutionism, positing the emergence of "homo superior" out of homo sapiens. Along with references to Aleister Crowley and The Golden Dawn, "Quicksand" (1971) insists that Bowie is not a prophet but a mortal "with the potential of a superman," but he rather undermines the seriousness of these references by confessing: "I was still going through the thing when I was pretending that I understood Nietzsche.... And I had tried to translate it into my own terms to understand it so 'Supermen' came out of that."[17] This kind of thing might suggest adolescent cherry-picking for superficial effect rather than a considered response to Nietzsche's ideas, but Bowie's fascination with the philosopher continued into his maturity. In "Seven" (1999) Bowie forgets the gods who also have forgotten they made him; and Bowie's desire to be kind of Superman was genuine. Indeed, as his death proved, in commercial terms at least, he achieved this iconic status, which Boulez could never have achieved, even if he'd wanted to, which is very unlikely.

While Schopenhauer's name only appeared in the lyrics of "Zip" from Rogers and Hart's musical *Pal Joey*, Nietzsche actually put in an appearance as one of the philosophers who turn up in the prologue ("The Tower of Babble") in the original productions of Stephen Schwartz and John-Michael Tebelak's *Godspell* (1971). Mel Brooks also referenced Nietzsche in *The Producers* (2007), when, during the auditions for "Springtime for Hitler," Jason Green, the man who eventually tries his luck for the part of Hitler with "Have you ever heard the German band?" is proud to reveal that he has been in a 16-year run of a musical called *No, No, Nietzsche*. Recently, Nietzsche has indeed inspired the genuine article—a

Broadway musical called *Nietzsche—The Musical*, with book and lyrics by Jeremy Richards, and music by Rob Scherzer, which received its première in Seattle in 2010. As Richards pointed out "Nietzsche was obsessed with music and poetry. I thought he'd make an ideal candidate for a musical."[18] And we have already considered *The Sound of Music* as a Nietzschean entertainment.

Whether Nietzsche would have recognized his Übermensch in the Superman of Marvel Comics is also debatable. After all, Superman is an alien from the planet Krypton, and therefore, hardly a superior kind of human; but there is no denying that Superman is the most popular manifestation of Nietzsche's term, and so John Williams' theme for the *Superman* films starring Christopher Reeve should really be classified as another of Nietzsche's influences on popular music. Composed in Williams' usual Americana style, it begins somewhat ironically by echoing Aaron Copland's *Fanfare for the Common Man*, surely the last thing Superman is intended to be, but nonetheless providing the appropriately patriotic connotations. Then, elements of William Walton's coronation march, *Crown Imperial* lend a suitably majestic swagger to the piece, before Williams briefly quotes the "Idealism" motif from Richard Strauss' tone poem *Tod und Verklärung*, adding a dash of German Romanticism to the mix. Alas, in the grandest of ironies, Christopher Reeve was thrown from his horse while off-duty from his

Christopher Reeve in *Superman* (dir. Richard Donner, 1978).

Finale: Nietzsche and Popular Music

role and ended his life as a paraplegic. As for myself, I once wrote a poem, so far not set to music:

> Am I *really* with you, Nietzsche?
> Have I *really* reached
> a level of such affirmation
> that I want to do it all again?
>
> I find myself upon a train.
> It's full of schoolboys munching chips.
> With genuine horror
> I remember my own past.
>
> It seems I'm now no more than I have ever been,
> And I have no wish to repeat the pain,
> the doubt;
> but I still want to dance
> when after months of drought—
> the rain.

Chapter Notes

Overture

1. Friedrich Nietzsche (trans. R. J. Hollingdale), *Ecce Homo*, Harmondsworth: Penguin, 1982, p. 61.
2. Eero Tarasti, *Myth and Music*, Helsinki: Suomen Musiikkitieteellinen Seura, 1978, p. 78.
3. P. G. Wodehouse, "Jeeves Takes Charge," http://lib.ru/INPROZ/WUDHAUS/jeeves01 engl.txt.
4. A. N. Wilson, *God's Funeral*, London: John Murray, 1999, p. 281.
5. *Ibid.*, p. 29.
6. David Eden and Reinhard Saremba (eds.), *The Cambridge Companion to Gilbert and Sullivan*, Cambridge: Cambridge University Press, 2009, p. 219 (Jana Polianovskaia, "'See how the Fates their gifts allot': the reception of productions and translations in continental Europe").
7. "Dr Hanslick on Music in England" *Musical Times* (Sept. 1, 1886), p. 518.
8. Ferruccio Busoni (trans. Antony Beaumont), *Selected Letters*, London: Faber and Faber, 1987, p 183 (Diary entry, Sept. 10, 1914).
9. Peter J. Pirie, *The English Musical Renaissance*, London: Victor Gollancz, 1979, pp. 18–22.
10. *Ibid.*, p. 19.
11. Arthur Schopenhauer (trans. E. F. J. Payne), *The World as Will and Representation*, Vol. 1, New York: Dover, 1969, p. 264.
12. Oliver Strunk (ed.), *Source Readings in Music History–Vol. 5, The Romantic Era*, London: Faber and Faber, 1981, pp. 108–128 (Franz Liszt, "*From* Berlioz and His "Harold" Symphony").
13. Hans Penner (ed.), *Teaching Lévi-Strauss*, Atlanta: Scholars Press, 1998, p. 294 (Claude Lévi-Strauss, "Finale").
14. Eero Tarasti, *Myth and Music*, p. 27, note 2.
15. *Ibid.*, p. 32.
16. Arthur Schopenhauer (trans. E. F. J. Payne), *The World as Will and Representation*, Vol. 1, p. 264, note 11.
17. E. T. A. Hoffmann (ed. Christopher Lazare), *Tales of Hoffmann*, New York: A. A. Wyn, 1946, p. 104 ("Don Juan").
18. Oliver Strunk (ed.), *Source Readings in Music History—Vol. 5, The Romantic Era*, pp. 70–71, note 12 (Hector Berlioz, "Rossini's "William Tell").
19. *Ibid.*, p. 263.
20. *Ibid.*, p. 262.
21. Joan Chissell, *Schumann*, London: J. M. Dent, 1977, p. 89.
22. Oliver Strunk (ed.), *Source Readings in Music History—Vol. 5, The Romantic Era*, p. 27, note 12 (Jean Paul, "*From the* Hesperus").
23. *Ibid.*, p. 104 (Robert Schumann, "Davidsbündlerblätter).
24. *Ibid.*, p. 11 (Franz Liszt, "*From* Berlioz and His 'Harold' Symphony").
25. Richard Wagner (ed. Charles Osborne), *Stories and Essays*, London: Peter Owen, 1973, p. 58 ("A Pilgrimage to Beethoven").
26. *Ibid.*, p. 111 ("An End in Paris").
27. Richard Wagner, *Götterdämmerung, Complete Vocal Score by Otto Singer*, Leipzig: Breitkopf and Härtel, 1914, p. viii (Introduction by Carl Waack).
28. Thomas Mann (trans. Walter D. Morris), *Reflections of a Nonpolitical Man*, New York: Frederick Ungar, 1983, p. 55.
29. *Ibid.*, p. 126.
30. Modris Eksteins, *Rites of Spring*, London: Papermac, 2000, p. 92.
31. Thomas Mann (trans. Walter D. Morris), *Reflections of a Nonpolitical Man*, p. 147 (note 28).
32. Friedrich Nietzsche (trans. R. J. Hollingdale), *Untimely Meditations*, Cambridge: Cam-

bridge University Press, 1983 ("Richard Wagner in Bayreuth"), p. 217.

33. Jacques Barzun, *Pleasures of Music*, London: Michael Joseph, 1954, p. 486 (Friedrich Nietzsche's marginal note to the "Habanera" in *Carmen*, 1881).

Chapter 1

1. Oscar Wilde (ed. Vyvyan Holland), *Complete Works of Oscar Wilde*, London: Collins, 1977, p. 164 ("The Picture of Dorian Gray").
2. Friedrich Nietzsche (trans. A. M. Ludovici), *Selected Letters of Friedrich Nietzsche*, London: Soho, 1985, p. 18 (Letter to Freiherr Karl von Gersdorff, May 25 1865).
3. Friedrich Nietzsche (trans. R. J. Hollingdale), *Ecce Homo*, Harmondsworth: Penguin, 1982, p. 58).
4. Richard Wagner (trans. W. Ashton Ellis), *Religion and Art*, Lincoln: University of Nebraska Press, 1994, p. 130 ("Shall We Hope?").
5. Friedrich Nietzsche, *Ecce Homo*, pp. 123–125, note 3.
6. Ronald Hayman, *Nietzsche: A Critical Life*, London: Phoenix, 1995, p. 63.
7. Cosima Wagner (ed. Erhart Thierbach), Vol. 12 of *Jahresgabe der Gesellschaft der Freunde des Nietzsche-Archivs: Die Briefe Cosima Wagners an Friedrich Nietzsche 1869–1871* (Vol. 1), Weimar: Nietzsche-Archiv, 1938, p. 16 (Letter to Friedrich Nietzsche, Dec. 30 1871).
8. Friedrich Nietzsche (trans. Josefine Nauckhoff), *The Gay Science*, Cambridge: Cambridge University Press, 2001, p. 194.
9. Friedrich Nietzsche (trans. A. M. Ludovici), *Selected Letters of Friedrich Nietzsche*, p. 335, note 2 (Letter to Georg Brandes, March 27, 1888).
10. *Ibid.* pp. 263–264 (Letter from Hans von Bülow to Nietzsche, July 24, 1872).
11. *Ibid.* p. 265 (Letter from Hans von Bülow to Nietzsche, July 24, 1872).
12. A. Phillips Griffiths (ed.), *Philosophy, Psychology and Psychiatry* (Anthony Storr, "Nietzsche and Music"), Cambridge: Cambridge University Press, 1994, p. 220.
13. Norman Lebrecht (ed.), *Mahler Remembered*, London: Faber and Faber, 1987, p. 210 (extracted from *Neue Freie Presse*, May 25, 1911).
14. Ronald Hayman, *Nietzsche: A Critical Life*, p. 155, note 6.
15. Thomas Mann (trans. H. T. Lowe-Porter), *Essays of Three Decades*, London: Secker & Warburg, 1947, p. 392 ("Schopenhauer").
16. Norman Lebrecht (ed.), *Mahler Remembered*, p. 210, note 13.
17. Friedrich Nietzsche (trans. A. M. Ludovici), *Selected Letters of Friedrich Nietzsche*, p. 173, note 2 (Letter to Erwin Rohde, Feb. 22, 1884.
18. Friedrich Nietzsche (trans. R. J. Hollingdale), *Ecce Homo*, p. 61, note 3.
19. Gabrielle D'Annunzio (trans. Georgina Harding), *The Triumph of Death*, Sawtry: Dedalus, 1990, pp. 278–279.
20. *Ibid.*, p. 253.
21. Gabrielle D'Annunzio (trans. Susan Bassnett), *The Flame*, London: Quartet Books, 1991, p. 101.
22. George Moore, *Evelyn Innes*, London: T. Fisher Unwin, 1898, p. 193.
23. Romain Rolland (trans. Gilbert Cannan) *Jean Christophe*, New York: Random House, no date, Book 1, pp. 373–374.
24. Bo Carpelan (trans. David McDuff), *Axel*, Manchester: Carcanet, 1989, p. 139.
25. Édouard Dujardin (trans. Anthony Suter), *The Bays Are Sere and Interior Monologue*, London: Librium, 1991, p. 111 ("Interior Monologue").
26. Friedrich Nietzsche (trans. A. M. Ludovici), *Selected Letters of Friedrich Nietzsche*, p. 43, note 2 (Letter to Frau Ritschl, Beginning of July, 1868).
27. Friedrich Nietzsche, *Ecce Homo*, p. 99, note 3.
28. *Ibid.*, p. 100
29. Robert E. Norton, *Nietzsche: Attempt at a Mythology*, Champaign: University of Illinois Press, 2009, p. 91.
30. Friedrich Nietzsche (trans. A. M. Ludovici), *Selected Letters of Friedrich Nietzsche*, pp. 318–319, note 2 (Letter to Georg Brandes, Dec. 2, 1887).
31. *Ibid.* p. 344–345 (Letter to Georg Brandes, May 4, 1888).
32. Friedrich Nietzsche (trans. R. J. Hollingdale), *Ecce Homo*, p. 100, note 3.
33. Friedrich Nietzsche (trans. R. J. Hollingdale), *Twilight of the Idols/The Anti-Christ*, Harmondsworth: Penguin, 1981, p. 23 ("Twilight of the Idols").

Chapter 2

1. Friedrich Nietzsche (trans. R. J. Hollingdale), *Ecce Homo*, Harmondsworth: Penguin, 1982, p. 90.

2. Cosima Wagner (trans. Geoffrey Skelton), *Diaries, Vol. 1 1869-1877*, London: Collins, 1978, p. 96 (Monday, May 17, 1869).
3. *Ibid.*, p. 317 (Sunday, Dec. 25, 1870).
4. Friedrich Nietzsche (trans. A. M. Ludovici), *Selected Letters of Friedrich Nietzsche*, London: Soho, 1985, p. 73 (Letter to Erwin Rohde, Dec. 15, 1870).
5. Richard Wagner (trans. William Ashton Ellis), *Actors and Singers*, Lincoln: University of Nebraska Press, 1995, p. 123 ("Beethoven").
6. Friedrich Nietzsche (trans. R. J. Hollingdale), *Ecce Homo*, pp. 59-60, note 1.
7. Joachim Köhler (trans. Ronald Taylor), *Nietzsche and Wagner: A Lesson in Subjugation*, New Haven: Yale University Press, 1998, p. 101.
8. Marc A. Weiner, *Richard Wagner and the Anti-Semitic Imagination*, Lincoln: University of Nebraska Press, 1995, p. 338 (Wagner's letter to Otto Eisner quoted).
9. Friedrich Nietzsche (trans. A. M. Ludovici), *Selected Letters of Friedrich Nietzsche*, p. 233, note 4 (Letter to Karl Knortz, June 21, 1888).
10. Cosima Wagner (trans. Geoffrey Skelton), *Diaries, Vol. 1, 1869-1877*, p. 555 (Nov. 9, 1872), note 2.
11. Arthur Schopenhauer (trans. E. F. J. Payne), *The World as Will and Representation*, Vol. 1, New York: Dover, 1969, p. 257.
12. Immanuel Kant (trans. James Creed Meredith), *Critique of Judgement*, Oxford: Oxford University Press, 2007, p. 158.
13. Arthur Schopenhauer (trans. E. F. J. Payne), *The World as Will and Representation*, Vol. 1, p. 262, note 11.
14. *Ibid.*, p. 260.
15. Friedrich Nietzsche (trans. Walter Kaufmann), *The Birth of Tragedy and The Case of Wagner*, New York: Random House (Vintage), 1967, p. 131 ("The Birth of Tragedy").
16. *Ibid.*, p. 137 ("The Birth of Tragedy").
17. *Ibid.*, pp. 104-105 ("The Birth of Tragedy").
18. Friedrich Nietzsche (trans. R. J. Hollingdale), *Untimely Meditations*, Cambridge: Cambridge University Press, 1983, p. 217.
19. *Ibid.*, p. 223.
20. *Ibid.*, p. 242.
21. Friedrich Nietzsche (trans. R. J. Hollingdale), *Thus Spoke Zarathustra*, Harmondsworth: Penguin, 1969, p. 41.
22. Friedrich Nietzsche (trans. Walter Kaufmann), *The Birth of Tragedy and The Case of Wagner*, p. 157 ("The Case of Wagner"), note 14.
23. Cosima Wagner (trans. Geoffrey Skelton), *Diaries, Vol. 1, 1869-1877*, p. 399 (Aug. 3, 1872), note 2.
24. *Ibid.*, p. 451 (Jan. 20, 1872).
25. Joachim Köhler (trans. Ronald Taylor), *Nietzsche and Wagner: A Lesson in Subjugation*, p. 103, note 7.
26. Cosima Wagner (trans. Geoffrey Skelton), *Diaries, Vol. 1, 1869-1877*, p. 622 (April 11, 1873), note 2.
27. Joachim Köhler (trans. Ronald Taylor), *Nietzsche and Wagner: A Lesson in Subjugation*, p. 56, note 7.
28. Ronald Hayman, *Nietzsche: A Critical Life*, London: Phoenix, 1995, p. 49.
29. Cosima Wagner (trans. Geoffrey Skelton), *Diaries, Vol. 1, 1869-1877*, p. 472 (April 1, 1872), note 2.
30. Ronald Hayman, *Nietzsche: A Critical Life*, London: Phoenix, 1995, p. 335.
31. Cosima Wagner (trans. Geoffrey Skelton), *Diaries, Vol. 1, 1869-1877*, p. 480 (April 26, 1872), note 2.
32. *Ibid.*, p. 491 (May 29, 1872).
33. *Ibid.*, p. 232 (June 12, 1870).
34. Friedrich Nietzsche (trans. Walter Kaufmann), *The Birth of Tragedy and The Case of Wagner*, p. 180 ("The Case of Wagner"), note 15.
35. Cosima Wagner (trans. Geoffrey Skelton), *Diaries, Vol. 1, 1869-1877*, p. 148 (Sept. 19, 1869), note 2.
36. *Ibid.*, p. 75 (April 9, 1874).
37. *Ibid.*, p. 780 (Aug. 9-18, 1874).
38. Joachim Köhler (trans. Ronald Taylor), *Nietzsche and Wagner: A Lesson in Subjugation*, p. 60, note 7.
39. Friedrich Nietzsche (trans. A. M. Ludovici), *Selected Letters of Friedrich Nietzsche*, p. 61 (Letter to his mother, Aug. 30, 1869), note 4.
40. *Ibid.*, p. 62 (Letter to Erwin Rohde, Feb. 15, 1870).
41. *Ibid.*, p. 77 (Letter to Erwin Rhode, Jan. 28, 1872).
42. *Ibid.*, p. 75 (Letter to Erwin Rhode, Dec. 15, 1870).
43. Richard Wagner (trans. Stewart Spencer), *Selected Letters of Richard Wagner*, London: Dent, 1987, p. 306 (Letter to August Röckel, Jan. 25/26, 1854).
44. *Ibid.*, p. 301 (Letter to August Röckel, Jan. 25/26, 1854).
45. Friedrich Nietzsche (trans. R. J.

Hollingdale), *Beyond Good and Evil*, Harmondsworth: Penguin, 1973, p. 73.
46. Friedrich Nietzsche (trans. Josefine Nauckhoff), *The Gay Science*, Cambridge: Cambridge University Press, 2001, p. 110.
47. Friedrich Nietzsche (trans. R. J. Hollingdale), *Twilight of the Idols and the Anti-Christ*, Harmondsworth: Penguin, 1968, p. 115.
48. Friedrich Nietzsche (trans. R. J. Hollingdale), *Ecce Homo*, p. 71, note 1.
49. Walter Kaufmann, *Nietzsche: Philosopher, Psychologist, Antichrist*, Princeton: Princeton University Press, 1974, p. 252. (Nietzsche quoted).
50. Friedrich Nietzsche (trans. Walter Kaufmann), *The Birth of Tragedy and The Case of Wagner*, p. 164 ("The Case of Wagner"), note 15.
51. Friedrich Nietzsche (trans. R. J. Hollingdale), *Ecce Homo*, p. 126, note 1.
52. Friedrich Nietzsche (trans. A. M. Ludovici), *Selected Letters of Friedrich Nietzsche*, p. 145 (Letter to his sister, Feb. 3, 1882), note 4.
53. *Ibid.*, p. 130 (Letter to Peter Gast, Aug. 20, 1880).
54. *Ibid.*, p. 145 (Letter to his sister, Feb. 3, 1882).
55. *Ibid.*, p. 151 (Letter to Peter Gast, Feb. 19, 1883).
56. *Ibid.*, p. 153 (Letter to Peter Gast, Feb. 19, 1883).
57. Cosima Wagner (trans. Geoffrey Skelton), *Diaries, Vol. 2 1878–1883*, London: Collins, 1980, p. 222 (Monday, Dec. 9, 1878).
58. *Ibid.*, p. 128 (Friday, Aug. 2, 1878).
59. *Ibid.*, p. 308 (Thursday, May 15, 1879).
60. *Ibid.*, p. 362 (Thursday, Sept. 9, 1879).
61. *Ibid.*, p. 946 (Thursday, Nov. 7, 1882).
62. *Ibid.*, p. 706 (Sunday, Aug. 14, 1881).
63. *Ibid.*, p. 878 (Saturday, June 24, 1882).
64. *Ibid.*, p. 66 (Saturday, April 27, 1878).
65. *Ibid.*, p. 261 (Tuesday, Jan. 28, 1879).
66. *Ibid.*, p. 778 (Wednesday, Dec. 28, 1881).

Chapter 3

1. Friedrich Nietzsche (trans. Ladislaus Löb), *Writings from the Early Notebooks*, Cambridge, Cambridge University Press, 2009, p. 89.
2. Elliot Forbes (ed.) *Thayer's Life of Beethoven*, Princeton: Princeton University Press, 1970, p. 896.
3. Friedrich Nietzsche (trans. Ladislaus Löb), *Writings from the Early Notebooks*, p. 192, note 1.
4. Richard Wagner (trans. W. Ashton Ellis), *Actors and Singers*, Lincoln: University of Nebraska Press, 1995, pp. 92–93 ("Beethoven").
5. *Ibid.*, p. 121("Beethoven").
6. Friedrich Nietzsche (trans. Walter Kaufmann), *The Birth of Tragedy and The Case of Wagner*, New York: Random House (Vintage), 1967, p. 65 ("The Birth of Tragedy").
7. *Ibid.*, p. 137 ("The Birth of Tragedy").
8. *Ibid.*, p. 143 ("The Birth of Tragedy").
9. Richard Wagner (trans. W. Ashton Ellis), *Actors and Singers*, p. 89 ("Beethoven"), note 4.
10. *Ibid.*, p. 97 ("Beethoven").
11. *Ibid.*, pp. 97–98 ("Beethoven").
12. Friedrich Nietzsche (trans. Walter Kaufmann), *The Birth of Tragedy and The Case of Wagner*, pp. 4–5 ("The Birth of Tragedy"), note 6.
13. Richard Wagner (trans. W. Ashton Ellis), *Actors and Singers*, pp. 92–93 ("Beethoven"), note 4.
14. Elliot Forbes (ed.) *Thayer's Life of Beethoven*, p. 481, note 2.
15. Richard Wagner (trans. W. Ashton Ellis), *Actors and Singers*, p. 92 ("Beethoven"), note 4.
16. Friedrich Nietzsche (trans. Ladislaus Löb), *Writings from the Early Notebooks*, p. 46, note 1.
17. Friedrich Nietzsche (trans. Walter Kaufmann), *The Birth of Tragedy and The Case of Wagner*, p. 55 ("The Birth of Tragedy"), note 6.
18. Richard Wagner (trans. W. Ashton Ellis), *Actors and Singers*, p. 303 ("On the Name Musikdrama"), note 4.
19. Friedrich Nietzsche (trans. Walter Kaufmann), *The Birth of Tragedy and The Case of Wagner*, pp. 37–38 ("The Birth of Tragedy"), note 6.
20. *Ibid.*, p. 59 ("The Birth of Tragedy"), note 6.
21. Richard Wagner (trans. W. Ashton Ellis), *Actors and Singers*, p. 92 ("Beethoven"), note 4.
22. Fredrick Nietzsche (trans. R. J. Hollingdale), *Twilight of the Idols/The Anti-Christ*, Harmondsworth: Penguin, 1968, p. 26 ("Twilight of the Idols").
23. Friedrich Nietzsche (trans. R. J. Hollingdale), *Untimely Meditations*, Cambridge: Cambridge University Press, 1983, p. 241 ("Richard Wagner in Bayreuth").

24. *Ibid.*, p. 240 ("Richard Wagner in Bayreuth").
25. *Ibid.*, p. 22 ("David Strauss, the confessor and the writer").
26. Friedrich Nietzsche (trans. Marion Faber and Stephen Lehmann), *Human, All Too Human*, London: Penguin, 1984, p. 106.
27. *Ibid.*, p. 107.
28. Friedrich Nietzsche (trans. R. J. Hollingdale), *Beyond Good and Evil*, Harmondsworth: Penguin, 1973, p. 157.
29. *Ibid.*, p. 159.
30. Friedrich Nietzsche (trans. Josefine Nauckhoff), *The Gay Science*, Cambridge: Cambridge University Press, 2001, p. 100.
31. Fredrick Nietzsche (trans. R. J. Hollingdale), *Twilight of the Idols/The Anti-Christ*, p. 104, note 22.
32. William Murdoch, *Brahms*, London: Rich & Cowan, p. 70.
33. Friedrich Nietzsche (trans. Walter Kaufmann), *The Birth of Tragedy and The Case of Wagner*, p. 187 ("The Case of Wagner"), note 6.
34. *Ibid.*, p. 188 ("The Case of Wagner").
35. *Ibid.*, p. 37 ("The Birth of Tragedy").
36. *Ibid.*, p. 37 ("The Birth of Tragedy").
37. *Ibid.*, p. 46 ("The Birth of Tragedy")
38. Richard Wagner (trans. W. Ashton Ellis), *Pilgrimage to Beethoven and Other Essays*, Lincoln: University of Nebraska Press, 1994, p. 247 ("Beethoven's Choral Symphony at Dresden").
39. *Ibid.*, p. 249.
40. Richard Wagner (trans. W. Ashton Ellis), *Jesus of Nazareth and Other Writings*, Lincoln: University of Nebraska Press, 1995, p. 312.

Chapter 4

1. Friedrich Nietzsche (trans. R. J. Hollingdale), *Ecce Homo*, Harmondsworth: Penguin, 1982, p. 119.
2. Arnold Schoenberg (trans. Leo Black), *Style and Idea*, New York: St. Martin's Press, 1975, p. 33 ("How One Becomes Lonely").
3. Robin Holloway, *Debussy and Wagner*, London: Eulenburg, 1979, p. 13.
4. Josiah Fisk and Jeff William Nichols (eds.), *Composers on Music: Eight Centuries of Writings*, Boston: Northeastern University Press, 1997, p. 204.
5. Rollo Myers (ed.), *Richard Strauss & Romain Rolland: Correspondence*, London: Calder and Boyars, 1968, p. 152.

6. Arthur Schopenhauer (trans. E. F. J. Payne), *The World as Will and Representation*, Vol. 1 New York: Dover, 1969, p. 321.
7. *Ibid.*, p. 257.
8. Friedrich Nietzsche (trans. Marion Faber and Stephen Lehmann), *Human, All Too Human*, London: Penguin, 1984, p. 128.
9. Friedrich Nietzsche (trans. Douglas Smith), *On the Genealogy of Morals*, Oxford: Oxford University Press, 1996, p. 83.
10. Friedrich Nietzsche (trans. Walter Kaufmann), *The Birth of Tragedy and The Case of Wagner*, New York: Random House (Vintage), 1967, pp. 163–164 ("The Case of Wagner").
11. Friedrich Nietzsche (trans. Josefine Nauckhoff), *The Gay Science*, Cambridge: Cambridge University Press, 2001, pp. 87–88.
12. Friedrich Nietzsche (trans. A. M. Ludovici), *Selected Letters of Friedrich Nietzsche*, London: Soho, 1985, pp. 186–187 (Letter to Peter Gast, Jan. 21, 1887).
13. Friedrich Nietzsche (trans. R. J. Hollingdale), *Ecce Homo*, p. 61, note 1.
14. *Ibid.*, p. 40.
15. Friedrich Nietzsche (trans. Josefine Nauckhoff), *The Gay Science*, p. 232, note 11.
16. Friedrich Nietzsche (trans. A. M. Ludovici), *Selected Letters of Friedrich Nietzsche*, p. 210 (Letter to Karl Fuchs, Dec. 14, 1887), note 12.
17. Friedrich Nietzsche (trans. Josefine Nauckhoff), *The Gay Science*, p. 234, note 11.
18. Friedrich Nietzsche (trans. R. J. Hollingdale), *Beyond Good and Evil*, Harmondsworth: Penguin, 1973, p. 151.
19. Friedrich Nietzsche (trans. A. M. Ludovici), *Selected Letters of Friedrich Nietzsche*, p. 193 (Letter to his sister, March 23, 1887), note 12.
20. Friedrich Nietzsche (trans. R. J. Hollingdale), *Ecce Homo*, p. 62, note 1.
21. *Ibid.*, p. 82.
22. Friedrich Nietzsche (trans. A. M. Ludovici), *Selected Letters of Friedrich Nietzsche*, p. 72 (Letter to his mother and sister, Dec. 12, 1870), note 12.
23. *Ibid.*, p. 64 (Letter to his mother, Aug. 28, 1870).
24. *Ibid.*, p. 188 (Letter to Reinhart von Seydlitz, Feb. 24, 1887).
25. Friedrich Nietzsche (trans. Walter Kaufmann), *The Birth of Tragedy and The Case of Wagner*, p. 164 ("The Case of Wagner"), note 10.
26. Friedrich Nietzsche (trans. A. M. Lu-

dovici), *Selected Letters of Friedrich Nietzsche*, p. 116 (Letter to Reinhart von Seydlitz, Jan. 5, 1878), note 12.

27. Bram Stoker, *Dracula*, London: Constable, 1904, p. 39.

28. Richard Wagner, *Parsifal* (ENO Opera Guide), London: John Calder, 1986, p. 114.

29. Friedrich Nietzsche (trans. A. M. Ludovici), *Selected Letters of Friedrich Nietzsche*, p. 116 (Letter to Reinhart von Seydlitz, Jan. 5, 1878), note 12.

30. Friedrich Nietzsche (trans. R. J. Hollingdale), *Thus Spoke Zarathustra*, Harmondsworth: Penguin, 1969, pp. 28-29 (Hollingdale's introduction).

31. Richard Wagner (trans. Stewart Spencer), *Selected Letters of Richard Wagner*, London: Dent, 1987, p. 873 (Letter to Otto Eisner, Oct. 23, 1877).

32. Bram Stoker, *Dracula*, p. 52, note 27.

33. Marc A. Weiner, *Richard Wagner and the Anti-Semitic Imagination*, Lincoln: University of Nebraska Press, 1995, p. 327.

34. *Ibid.*, pp. 312-313.

35. Bram Stoker, *Dracula*, p. 16, note 27.

36. *Ibid.*, p. 18.

37. Bram Stoker (ed. Leonard Wolf), *The Annotated Dracula*, London: New English Library, 1976, p. 22.

38. *Ibid.*, p. 23.

39. Friedrich Nietzsche (trans. Walter Kaufmann), *The Birth of Tragedy and the Case of Wagner*, p. 176 ("The Case of Wagner"), note 10.

40. Friedrich Nietzsche (trans. Anthony M. Ludovici, *I: The Case of Wagner, II: Nietzsche Contra Wagner, III: Selected Aphorisms*, Edinburgh: T. N. Foulis, 1911, p. 73 ("Nietzsche Contra Wagner").

41. Bram Stoker, *Dracula*, p. 291, note 27.

42. Richard Wagner, *Parsifal* (ENO Opera Guide), p. 98, note 28.

43. Christopher Frayling (ed.), *Vampyres: Lord Byron to Count Dracula*, London: Faber and Faber, 1983, p. 180.

44. Thomas Mann (trans. Allan Blunden), *Thomas Mann: Pro and Contra Wagner*, London: Faber and Faber, 1985, p. 129 ("The Sorrows and Grandeur of Richard Wagner").

45. Christopher Frayling (ed.), *Vampyres: Lord Byron to Count Dracula*, p. 50, note 43.

46. Robert W. Gutman, *Richard Wagner: The Man, His Mind, and His Music*, New York: Time-Life Records Special Edition, 1972, p. 432.

47. Friedrich Nietzsche (trans. Walter Kaufmann), *The Birth of Tragedy and The Case of Wagner*, p. 166 ("The Case of Wagner"), note 10.

Chapter 5

1. Friedrich Nietzsche (trans. Christopher Middleton), *Selected Letters of Friedrich Nietzsche*, Indianapolis: Hackett/University of Chicago, 1996, p. 149 (Letter to his mother and sister, Oct. 28, 1876).

2. Friedrich Nietzsche (trans. Josefine Nauckhoff), *The Gay Science*, Cambridge: Cambridge University Press, 2001, p.161.

3. Friedrich Nietzsche (trans. R. J. Hollingdale), *Ecce Homo*, Harmondsworth: Penguin, 1982, p. 90.

4. Cosima Wagner (trans. Geoffrey Skelton), *Diaries, Vol. 1, 1869-1877*, London: Collins, 1978, p. 930 (Friday, Oct. 27, 1876).

5. *Ibid.*, p. 931 (Wednesday, Nov. 1, 1876).

6. Robert W. Gutman, *Richard Wagner: The Man, His Mind, and His Music*, New York: Time-Life Records Special Edition, 1972, pp. 394-395.

7. Richard Wagner (trans. William Ashton Ellis), *Religion and Art*, Lincoln: University of Nebraska Press, 1994, p. 213 ("Religion and Art").

8. Friedrich Nietzsche (trans. R. J. Hollingdale), *Ecce Homo*, Harmondsworth: Penguin, 1982, p. 93.

9. Stanley Sadie (ed.), *The New Grove Dictionary of Music and Musicians*, vol. 2, London: Macmillan, 1980, p. 754 (entry for Bizet by Winton Dean).

10. *Ibid.*, p. 758 (entry for Bizet by Winton Dean).

11. *Ibid.*, p. 760 (entry for Bizet by Winton Dean).

12. Friedrich Nietzsche (trans. Josefine Nauckhoff), *The Gay Science*, p. 84, note 2.

13. *Ibid.*, p. 86.

14. *Ibid.*, p. 248.

15. *Ibid.*, p. 78.

16. Friedrich Nietzsche (trans. R. J. Hollingdale), *Thus Spoke Zarathustra*, Harmondsworth: Penguin, 1969, p. 131.

17. *Ibid.*, p. 215.

18. Joachim Köhler (trans. Ronald Taylor), *Zarathustra's Secret*, New Haven: Yale University Press, 2002, p. 193.

19. Friedrich Nietzsche (trans. Walter Kaufmann), *The Birth of Tragedy and The Case of Wagner*, New York: Random House (Vintage), 1967, p. 170 ("The Case of Wagner").

20. *Ibid.*, p. 171 ("The Case of Wagner").
21. *Ibid.*, p. 157 ("The Case of Wagner").
22. Friedrich Nietzsche (trans. Josefine Nauckhoff), *The Gay Science*, p. 90, note 2.
23. Friedrich Nietzsche (trans. A. M. Ludovici), *Selected Letters of Friedrich Nietzsche*, London: Soho, 1985, p. 142 (Letter to Peter Gast, Nov. 28, 1881).
24. *Ibid.*, p. 152 (Letter to Peter Gast, March 22, 1883).
25. *Ibid.*, p. 254 (Letter to Peter Gast, Dec. 2, 1888).
26. *Ibid.*, p. 255 (Letter to Peter Gast, Dec. 2, 1888).
27. Vladimir Volkoff, *Tchaikovsky: A Self-Portrait*, London: Robert Hale, 1975, p. 280.
28. *Ibid.*, p. 257.
29. Friedrich Nietzsche (trans. A. M. Ludovici), *Selected Letters of Friedrich Nietzsche*, p. 239 (Letter to Peter Gast, Sept. 27, 1888), note 23.
30. Cosima Wagner (trans. Geoffrey Skelton), *Diaries, Vol. 2 1878-1883*, London: Collins, 1980, p. 447 (Sunday, March 7, 1880).
31. Friedrich Nietzsche (trans. A. M. Ludovici), *Selected Letters of Friedrich Nietzsche*, p. 353 (Letter from Georg Brandes to Nietzsche, Oct. 6, 1888), note 23.
32. Martin Cooper, *French Music: From the death of Berlioz to the Death of Fauré*, London: Oxford University Press, 1951, p. 56.
33. Friedrich Nietzsche (trans. Walter Kaufmann), *The Birth of Tragedy and The Case of Wagner*, p. 157 ("The Case of Wagner"), note 19.
34. Friedrich Nietzsche (trans. Ladislaus Löb), *Writings from the Early Notebooks*, Cambridge: Cambridge University Press, 2009, pp. 46-47.
35. *Ibid.*, p. 17.
36. *Ibid.*, p. 21.
37. Eduard Hanslick, *On the Beautiful in Music*, http://www.cengage.com/music/book_content/049557273X_wrightSimms/assets/ITOW/7273X_58_ITOW.pdf.
38. Friedrich Nietzsche (trans. Ladislaus Löb), *Writings from the Early Notebooks*, p. 10, note 34.
39. *Ibid.*, p. 11.
40. *Ibid.*, p. 47.
41. Friedrich Nietzsche (trans. Josefine Nauckhoff), *The Gay Science*, p. 81, note 2.
42. Friedrich Nietzsche (trans. R. J. Hollingdale), *Beyond Good and Evil*, Harmondsworth: Penguin, 1973, p. 41.
43. *Ibid.*, p. 169.

Chapter 6

1. Rollo Myers (ed.), *Richard Strauss & Romain Rolland: Correspondence*, London: Calder and Boyars, 1968, p. 177 (Rolland's essay, "Richard Strauss").
2. Kurt Wilhelm, *Richard Strauss: An Intimate Portrait*, London: Thames and Hudson, 1989, p. 39.
3. E. J. Dent, *Ferruccio Busoni*, London: Eulenberg, 1974, p. 135.
4. Norman del Mar, *Richard Strauss: A Critical Commentary on His Life and Works*, Vol. 1, London: Barrie and Jenkins, 1962, p. 134.
5. Friedrich Nietzsche (trans. R. J. Hollingdale), *Thus Spoke Zarathustra*, Harmondsworth: Penguin, 1969, p. 39.
6. *Ibid.*, p. 59.
7. *Ibid.*, p. 61.
8. Kurt Wilhelm, *Richard Strauss: An Intimate Portrait*, p. 213, note 2.
9. *Ibid.*, p. 135.
10. Friedrich Nietzsche (trans. R. J. Hollingdale), *Thus Spoke Zarathustra*, p. 311, note 5.
11. *Ibid.*, p. 313.
12. Friedrich Nietzsche (trans. Josefine Nauckhoff), *The Gay Science*, Cambridge: Cambridge University Press, 2001, p. 78.
13. Thomas Mann (trans. H. T. Lowe-Porter), *Doctor Faustus*, London: Secker & Warburg, 1949, p. 156.
14. Rollo Myers (ed.) *Richard Strauss & Romain Rolland: Correspondence*, p. 191 (Rolland's essay, "Richard Strauss"), note 1.
15. *Ibid.*, p. 183 (Rolland's essay, "Richard Strauss").
16. Kurt Wilhelm, *Richard Strauss: An Intimate Portrait*, p. 230, note 2.
17. Rollo Myers (ed.), *Richard Strauss & Romain Rolland: Correspondence*, p. 194 (Rolland's essay, "Richard Strauss"), note 1.
18. *Ibid.*, p. 195.
19. Modris Eksteins, *Rites of Spring*, London: Papermac (Macmillan), 2000, p. 93.
20. Michael Kennedy, *Richard Strauss: Man, Musician, Enigma*, Cambridge: Cambridge University Press, 1999, p. 177.
21. Gerald Abraham, *The Concise Oxford History of Music*, Newton Abbot: Readers Union, 1979, p. 809.
22. Kurt Wilhelm, *Richard Strauss: An Intimate Portrait*, p. 19, note 2.
23. Friedrich Nietzsche (trans. A. M. Ludovici), *Selected Letters of Friedrich Nietzsche*, London: Soho, 1985, p. 23 (Letter to Freiherr Karl von Gersdorff, April 7, 1866).

24. Walter Kaufmann, *Nietzsche: Philosopher, Psychologist, Antichrist*, Princeton: Princeton University Press, 1974, p. 323 (Nietzsche quoted).
25. Friedrich Nietzsche (trans. R. J. Hollingdale), *Ecce Homo*, Harmondsworth: Penguin, 1982, p. 34.
26. Kurt Wilhelm, *Richard Strauss: An Intimate Portrait*, p. 106, note 2.
27. *Ibid.*, 106.
28. Thomas Mann (trans. Allan Blunden), *Thomas Mann: Pro and Contra Wagner*, London: Faber and Faber, 1985, p. 108 ("The Sorrows and Grandeur of Richard Wagner").
29. Timothy Jackson in conversation for the BBC Radio 3 documentary *Richard Strauss: A Musical Ostrich?*, written and presented by David Huckvale, produced by Andrew Lyle, broadcast Dec. 30, 1999.
30. Friedrich Nietzsche (trans. R. J. Hollingdale), *Untimely Meditations*, Cambridge: Cambridge University Press, 1983, p. 217.
31. http://www.vonhausegger.com/files/Pan%20German%20Symphonist.pdf, p. 12.
32. Friedrich Nietzsche (trans. Walter Kaufmann), *The Birth of Tragedy and the Case of Wagner*, New York: Random House (Vintage), 1967, p. 42 ("The Birth of Tragedy").
33. Friedrich Nietzsche (trans. R. J. Hollingdale), *Ecce Homo*, p. 34, note 25.
34. Friedrich Nietzsche (trans. Walter Kaufmann), *The Birth of Tragedy and the Case of Wagner*, New York: Vintage, 1967, p. 52.

Chapter 7

1. Friedrich Nietzsche (trans. A. M. Ludovici), *Selected Letters of Friedrich Nietzsche*, London: Soho, 1985, p. 160 (Letter to his mother, Aug. 1883).
2. Friedrich Nietzsche (trans. Marion Faber and Stephen Lehmann), *Human, All Too Human*, London: Penguin, 1984, p. 229.
3. Norman Lebrecht (ed.), *Mahler Remembered*, London: Faber and Faber, 1998, p. 207 (from "Klemperer on Music: Shavings from a Musician's Workbench," ed. Martin Anderson, London: Toccata Press, 1986).
4. *Ibid.*, p, 164 (from *Die Bildnisse von Gustav Mahler* (ed. Alfred Roller), Leipzig: E. P. Tal, 1922).
5. Friedrich Nietzsche (trans. Josefine Nauckhoff), *The Gay Science*, Cambridge: Cambridge University Press, 2001, p. 104.
6. *Ibid.*, p. 79.

7. Alma Mahler (trans. Basil Creighton), *Gustav Mahler: Memories and Letters*, London: Cardinal (Macdonald) 1990, pp. 140–141.
8. Alma Mahler-Werfel (trans. Anthony Beaumont), *Diaries 1898–1902*, London: Faber and Faber, 1998, p. 67 (Friday, Oct. 28, 1898).
9. *Ibid.*, p. 360 (Monday, Dec. 24, 1900).
10. Alma Mahler (trans. Basil Creighton), *Gustav Mahler: Memories and Letters*, p. 19, note 7.
11. Edward Seckerson, *Mahler: His Life and Times*, Tunbridge Wells: Midas Books, 1982, p. 93.
12. Knut Hamsun (trans. James W. McFarlane), *Pan*, London: Alkin Books, 1994, p. 34.
13. Alma Mahler (trans. Basil Creighton), *Gustav Mahler: Memories and Letters*, London: Cardinal, 1990, p. 38n.
14. Donald Mitchell, *Gustav Mahler: The Early Years*, Berkeley: University of California Press, 1980, p. 99 (from *Briefe Gustav Mahler* (ed. Alma Mahler), Berlin, 1924, pp. 214–215).
15. Friedrich Nietzsche (trans. Josefine Nauckhoff), *The Gay Science*, p. 3, note 5.
16. Knut Hamsun (trans. James W. McFarlane), *Pan*, p. 16, note 12.
17. *Ibid.*, p. 43.
18. *Ibid.*, p. 27.
19. Norman Lebrecht (ed.), *Mahler Remembered*, p. 210, note 3.
20. Friedrich Nietzsche (trans. R. J. Hollingdale), *Thus Spoke Zarathustra*, Harmondsworth: Penguin, 1969, pp. 243–244.
21. Friedrich Nietzsche (trans. Ladislaus Löb), *Writings from the Early Notebooks*, Cambridge: Cambridge University Press, 2009, p. 11.
22. Gustav Mahler, *Symphonie VII*, Budapest: Edito Muisca, no date (introduction by Ferenc Skodnitz).
23. Friedrich Nietzsche (trans. R. J. Hollingdale), *Thus Spoke Zarathustra*, Harmondsworth: Penguin, 1969, p. 129.
24. Thomas Mann, *Stories of Three Decades*, London: Martin Secker & Warburg, 1946, p. 414 ("Death in Venice").
25. *Ibid.*, p. 413 ("Death in Venice").
26. *Ibid.*, p. 387 ("Death in Venice").
27. Dirk Bogarde, *Snakes and Ladders*, London: Chatto & Windus, 1978, p. 311.

Chapter 8

1. Richard Wagner (trans. Stewart Spencer), *Selected Letters of Richard Wagner*,

London: Dent, 1987, p. 991 (Letter to Judith Gautier, Feb. 6, 1878).
2. *Ibid.*, p. 879 (Letter to Judith, Dec. 18, 1877).
3. Hugh Macdonald, *Skryabin* (Oxford Studies of Composers), London: Oxford University Press, 1978, p. 68.
4. G. W. F. Hegel (trans. W. Wallace and A. V. Miller, rev. Michael Inwood), *Philosophy of Mind*, Oxford: Oxford University Press, 2007, p. 165.
5. Faubion Bowers, *Scriabin: A Biography*, New York: Dover, 1996, p. 135 (Scriabin's "Poem of Ecstasy").
6. *Ibid.*, p. 256.
7. *Ibid.*, pp. 254–255.
8. *Ibid.*, p. 256 (Boris Schloezer quoted).
9. *Ibid.*, p. 255.
10. *Ibid.*, p. 306.
11. *Ibid.*, pp. 311–312.
12. *Ibid.*, p. 307.
13. Quoted in Boston Symphony Orchestra program for a performance of *The Divine Poem* by the BSO under Serge Koussevitsky, April 19, 1940.
14. Friedrich Nietzsche (trans. R. J. Hollingdale), *Thus Spoke Zarathustra*, Harmondsworth: Penguin, 1969, pp. 119–120.
15. Faubion Bowers, *Scriabin: A Biography*, p. 135, note 5.
16. Hugh Macdonald, *Skryabin* (Oxford Studies of Composers), p. 10, note 3.
17. *Ibid.*, p. 68.
18. Walter Kaufmann, *Nietzsche: Philosopher, Psychologist, Antichrist*, Princeton: Princeton University Press, 1974, p. 250.
19. Friedrich Nietzsche (trans. R. J. Hollingdale), *Thus Spoke Zarathustra*, p. 297, note 14.
20. *Ibid.*, p. 297, note 14.
21. *Ibid.*, p. 298.
22. Simon Morrison, *Russian Opera and the Symbolist Movement*, Berkeley: University of California Press, 2002, p. 346. (The Libretto of the *Preparatory Act*).
23. Friedrich Nietzsche (trans. John McFarland Kennedy), *The Dawn of Day*, New York: Macmillan, 1911, p. 395 (http://www.gutenberg.org/files/39955/39955-h/39955-h.html).
24. Friedrich Nietzsche (trans. R. J. Hollingdale),*Thus Spoke Zarathustra*, p. 211, note 14.
25. *Ibid.*, p. 305.
26. Alexander Pasternak (trans. Ann Pasternak Slater), *A Vanished Present*, Oxford: Oxford University Press, 1984, p. 73.

27. *Ibid.*, pp. 79–80.
28. H. P. Blavatsky *Studies in Occultism* (The Dennis Wheatley Library of the Occult), London: Sphere, 1974, p. 157 ("The Esoteric Character of the Gospels").
29. Friedrich Nietzsche (trans. R. J. Hollingdale), *Thus Spoke Zarathustra*, p. 29 (Hollingdale's introduction), note 14.
30. Colin Wilson, *Rudolf Steiner: The Man and His Vision*, Wellingborough: The Aquarian Press, 1985, p. 89.
31. Rudolf Steiner, *Friedrich Nietzsche: Fighter for Freedom*, http://wn.rsarchive.org/Books/GA005/English/RSPI1960/GA005_c01_2.html.
32. Israel Regardi, *The Tree of Life: An Illustrated Study in Magic* (ed. Chic Cicero and Sandra Tabatha Cicero, St. Paul: Llewellyn Publications, 2003, p. 17.
33. *Ibid.*, p. 101.
34. *Ibid.*, p. 110.
35. Percy Bysshe Shelley (ed. Thomas Hutchinson), *The Complete Poetical Works of Percy Bysshe Shelley*, London: Oxford University Press, 1934, p. 208 ("Prometheus Unbound").
36. Faubion Bowers, *Scriabin: A Biography*, p. 135, note 5.
37. Percy Bysshe Shelley, *Essays and Letters by Percy Bysshe Shelley*, London: Walter Scott Ltd. (no date), pp. 26–27 ("A Defence of Poetry").
38. Ronald Hayman, *Nietzsche: A Critical Life*, London: Phoenix, 1995, p. 34.
39. Hugh Macdonald, *Skryabin* (Oxford Studies of Composers), p. 44, note 3 (Scriabin quoted).
40. H. P. Blavatsky *Studies in Occultism* (The Dennis Wheatley Library of the Occult), p. 8 (Dennis Wheatley's introduction), note 28.
41. Friedrich Nietzsche (trans. R. J. Hollingdale),*Thus Spoke Zarathustra*, p. 104, note 14.
42. Hugh Macdonald, *Skryabin* (Oxford Studies of Composers), p. 9, note 3 (Scriabin quoted).
43. Lucy Hughes-Hallett, *The Pike: Gabrielle D'Annunzio, Poet, Seducer and Preacher of War*, London: Fourth Estate, 2013, p. 450.
44. Hugh Macdonald, *Skryabin* (Oxford Studies of Composers), p. 10, note 3 (Scriabin quoted).
45. Faubion Bowers, *The New Scriabin*, Newton Abbot: David & Charles, 1974, p. 193.
46. Faubion Bowers, *Scriabin: A Biography*, p. 71, note 5.

47. Percy Bysshe Shelley (ed. Thomas Hutchinson), *The Complete Poetical Works of Percy Bysshe Shelley*, London: Oxford University Press, p. 268 ("Prometheus Unbound").

Chapter 9

1. A. L. Bacharach, *British Music of Our Time*, Harmondsworth: Pelican, 1946, p. 32 (R. L. Stevenson's *Essay of Travel* quoted).
2. Rudolf Steiner, *Autobiography: Chapter in the Course of My Life 1861–1907*, SteinerBooks, 2006, p. 130.
3. Eric Fenby, *Delius as I Knew Him*, London: Quality Press, 1948, p. 15.
4. Arthur Hutchings, *Delius*, London: Macmillan, 1948, pp. 61–62.
5. Ibid., p. 63.
6. Ibid.
7. Ibid., p. 64.
8. Ibid., p. 66.
9. Thomas Beecham, *A Mingled Chime: Leaves from an Autobiography*, London: White Lion Publishers, 1973, p. 73.
10. Arthur Hutchings, *Delius*, London: Macmillan, pp. 73–74, note 4.
11. Ibid., p. 66.
12. Eric Fenby, *Delius as I Knew Him*, p. 176, note 3.
13. Jonathan Harvey, *Music and Inspiration*, London: Faber and Faber, 1999, pp. 121–122.
14. Eric Fenby, *Delius as I Knew Him*, p. 179, note 3.
15. Ibid., pp. 182–183.
16. Ibid., pp. 74–75.
17. Ibid., p. 178.
18. Cosima Wagner (trans. Geoffrey Skelton), *Diaries, Vol. 2 1878–1883*, London: Collins, 1980, p. 265 (Monday, Feb. 3, 1879.
19. Ibid., p. 265 (Monday, Feb. 3, 1879).
20. Peter J. Pirie, *The English Musical Renaissance*, London: Victor Gollancz, 1979, pp. 44–45.
21. Hugo Daffner, *Friedrich Nietzsche's Randglossen zu Bizet's Carmen*, Regensburg, 1938, p. 50.

Chapter 10

1. George Bernard Shaw, *Complete Plays of Bernard Shaw*, London: Odhams (no date), p. 379.
2. Michael Hurd, *Rutland Boughton and the Glastonbury Festivals*, Oxford: Clarendon Press, 1993, p. 137.
3. Friedrich Nietzsche (trans. R. J. Hollingdale), *Thus Spoke Zarathustra*, Harmondsworth: Penguin, 1969, p. 61.
4. Ibid., p. 64.
5. Ibid., p. 131.
6. Stephen Lloyd, *H. Balfour Gardiner*, Cambridge: Cambridge University Press, 1984, p. 23.
7. Mervyn Cooke (ed.), *The Cambridge Companion to Benjamin Britten*, Cambridge: Cambridge University Press, 1999, p. 263.
8. Friedrich Nietzsche (trans. R. J. Hollingdale), *Thus Spoke Zarathustra*, p. 131, note 3.
9. Judith LeGrove, *Toward a World Unknown: Exhibition Catalogue*, Aldeburgh: The Britten-Pears Library, 1999, p. 11.
10. Friedrich Nietzsche (trans. R. J. Hollingdale), *Ecce Homo*, Harmondsworth: Penguin, 1982, p. 62.
11. Gabrielle D'Annunzio (trans. Susan Bassnett), *The Flame*, London: Quartet Books, 1991, p. 154.
12. Raymond Furness, *Wagner and Literature*, Manchester: Manchester University Press, 1982, p. 45.
13. Friedrich Nietzsche (trans. Walter Kaufmann), *The Birth of Tragedy and The Case of Wagner*, New York: Random House (Vintage), 1967, p. 35 ("The Birth of Tragedy").
14. Myfanwy Piper, *Death in Venice: An Opera in Two Acts*, London: Faber Music, 1973, p. 11.
15. Ibid., p. 13.
16. Friedrich Nietzsche (trans. Walter Kaufmann), *The Birth of Tragedy and The Case of Wagner*, p. 72 ("The Birth of Tragedy"), note 13.
17. Myfanwy Piper, *Death in Venice: An Opera in Two Acts*, p. 22, note 14.
18. Ibid., p. 2.
19. Friedrich Nietzsche (trans. Walter Kaufmann), *The Birth of Tragedy and The Case of Wagner*, pp. 124–125 ("The Birth of Tragedy"), note 13.
20. Richard Noll, *The Aryan Christ: The Secret Life of Carl Gustav Jung*, London: Macmillan, 1997, p. 126.
21. Thomas Mann (trans. H. T. Lowe-Porter), *The Magic Mountain*, London: Secker & Warburg, 1979, p. 493.
22. Michael Tippett (ed. Meirion Bowen), *Tippet on Music*, Oxford: Oxford University Press, 2001, p. 195.

23. Michael Kennedy, *Britten (The Dent Master Musicians)*, London: Dent, 1993, p. 239.
24. Myfanwy Piper, *Death in Venice: An Opera in Two Acts*, p. 36, note 14.
25. Michael Kennedy, *Britten (The Dent Master Musicians)*, p. 242, note 23.
26. Friedrich Nietzsche (trans. R. J. Hollingdale), *Beyond Good and Evil*, Harmondsworth: Penguin, 1973, p. 169.
27. Joachim Köhler (trans. Ronald Taylor), *Zarathustra's Secret*, New Haven: Yale University Press, 2002, p. 193.
28. *Ibid.*, p. 131. The line "Lips made for kissing" is also a quotation from E. T. A. Hoffmann's story "Der Artushof" (1815): "Her skin is snow white, her hair red but not too red—lips made for kissing—a mouth perhaps a little too wide which she also makes mouths with, though when she does so the teeth she reveals are like pearls" (eee E. T. A. Hoffmann (trans. R. J. Hollingdale), *Tales of Hoffmann*, London: Penguin, 2004, p. 133).

Chapter 11

1. Béla Bartók (trans. Peter Balabán and István Farkas, trans. rev. Elisabeth West and Colin Mason), *Béla Bartók: Letters*, London: Faber and Faber, 1971, pp. 49–50.
2. Nicholas Payne (ed.), Opera North program for 1990/91 Autumn Season, vol. ON37, Leeds: Opera North, p. 14 (Hugh Macdonald, "Dukas's Ariane and Bluebeard").
3. Béla Bartók (trans. Peter Balabán and István Farkas, trans. rev. Elisabeth West and Colin Mason), *Béla Bartók: Letters*, p. 30, note 1.
4. *Ibid.*, p. 52.
5. *Ibid.*, p. 53.
6. Kenneth Chalmers, *Béla Bartók*, London: Phaidon, 1995, p. 38.
7. Béla Bartók (trans. Peter Balabán and István Farkas, trans. rev. by Elisabeth West and Colin Mason), *Béla Bartók: Letters*, p. 53, note 1.
8. *Ibid.*, p. 50.
9. Friedrich Nietzsche (trans. R. J. Hollingdale), *Ecce Homo*, Harmondsworth: Penguin, 1982, p. 34.
10. Béla Bartók (trans. Peter Balabán and István Farkas, trans. rev. by Elisabeth West and Colin Mason), *Béla Bartók: Letters*, p. 76, note 1.
11. Friedrich Nietzsche (trans. R. J. Hollingdale), *Beyond Good and Evil*, Harmondsworth: Penguin, 1983, p. 85.
12. David Cooper, *Béla Bartók*, New Haven: Yale University Press, 2015, p. 81.
13. *Ibid.*, p. 74.
14. Kenneth Chalmers, *Béla Bartók*, p. 110, note 6.
15. David Cooper, *Béla Bartók*, New Haven: Yale University Press, 2015, p. 188.
16. George Bernard Shaw, *Complete Plays of Bernard Shaw*, London: Odhams (no date), p. 790 ("Heartbeak House").

Chapter 12

1. Alistair Wightman (ed.), *Szymanowski on Music*, London: Toccata Press, 1999, p. 85 ("On Contemporary Musical Opinion in Poland").
2. *Ibid.*, p. 126 ("The Ethnic Question in relation to Contemporary Music").
3. *Ibid.*, p. 49.
4. Friedrich Nietzsche (trans. R. J. Hollingdale), *Beyond Good and Evil*, Harmondsworth: Penguin, 1973, p. 173.
5. Teresa Chyli´nska (trans. A. T. Jordan), *Szymanowski*, New York: Twayne, 1973, p. 42. (Letter to Z. Jachimecki, Dec. 4, 1910.)
6. Alistair Wightman (ed.), *Szymanowski on Music*, pp. 75–76, note 1.
7. *Ibid.*, p. 98 ("My Splendid Isolation.").
8. Teresa Chyli'nska (trans. A. T. Jordan), *Szymanowski*, p. 89, note 5.
9. Alistair Wightman (ed.), *Szymanowski on Music*, pp. 37–38, note 1.
10. *Ibid.*, p. 39.
11. Program for Royal Opera House production of *Król Roger*, May 2015, London: Royal Opera House, 2015, p. 15 (John Lloyd Davies, "The Will to Power and the Will to Live").
12. Jarosław Iwaszkiewicz and Karol Szymanowski (trans. Andrzej Duszenko), *King Roger* libretto, Act I, http://duszenko.northern.edu/szymanowski/act1.html.
13. *Ibid.*, Act I.
14. Program for Royal Opera House *Król Roger*, May 2015, p. 32 (Stephen Downes, "Between Synthesis and Disintegration."), note 11.
15. Jarosław Iwaszkiewicz and Karol Szymanowski (trans. Andrzej Duszenko), *King Roger* libretto, Act II, http://duszenko.northern.edu/szymanowski/act2.html.
16. Thomas Mann (trans. Allan Blunden), *Pro and Contra Wagner*, London: Faber and

Faber, 1985), p. 100 ("The Sorrows and Grandeur of Richard Wagner").
17. Friedrich Nietzsche (trans. Walter Kaufmann), *The Birth of Tragedy and The Case of Wagner*, New York: Random House (Vintage),1967, p. 176 ("The Case of Wagner").
18. Robin Holloway, *Debussy and Wagner*, London: Eulenburg Books, 1979, p. 15.
19. *Ibid.*, p. 17.
20. *Ibid.*, p. 18.
21. Ferruccio Busoni (trans. Antony Beaumont), *Selected Letters*, London: Faber and Faber, 1987, p. 301 (Letter to Philipp Jarnach, Dec. 2, 1919).
22. *Ibid.*, p. 139 (Letter to Egon Petri, Dec. 20, 1911).
23. Martin Cooper, *French Music: From the Death of Berlioz to the Death of Fauré*, London: Oxford University Press, 1951, p. 185.
24. *Ibid.*, p. 186.
25. *Ibid.*, p. 196.
26. Jarosław Iwaszkiewicz and Karol Szymanowski (trans. Andrzej Duszenko), *King Roger* libretto, Act II, note 15.
27. *Ibid.*, Act III, http://duszenko.northern.edu/szymanowski/act3.html.

Chapter 13

1. Ernest Newman, *Hugo Wolf*, London: Methuen, 1907, p. 224.
2. Friedrich Nietzsche (trans. R. J. Hollingdale), *Thus Spoke Zarathustra*, Harmondsworth: Penguin, 1969, p. 311.
3. Friedrich Nietzsche (trans. Marion Faber and Stephen Lehmann), *Human, All Too Human*, London: Penguin, 1984, p. 260.
4. Friedrich Nietzsche (trans. R. J. Hollingdale), *Ecco Homo*, Harmondsworth: Penguin, 1979, p. 34.
5. Friedrich Nietzsche (ed. Christopher Middleton), *Selected Letters of Friedrich Nietzsche*, Chicago: Hackett, 1996, p. 149 (Letter to Franziska and Elisabeth Nietzsche, Oct. 22, 1876).
6. Plato (trans. Benjamin Jowett), *Plato's Republic*, New York: Airmont, 1968, p. 390.
7. Alma Mahler (trans. Basil Creighton), *Gustav Mahler: Memories and Letters*, London: Cardinal/Sphere, 1990, p. 309.
8. *Musicology Journal*, No. 11, 201, Serbian Academy of Sciences and Arts, Belgrade, pp. 164–165 (Gerard van der Leeuw, "Alphons Diepenbrock and the European World of Composers at the Fin-de-Siècle"). http://www.doiserbia.nb.rs/img/doi/1450-9814/2002/1450-98140202157v.pdf.
9. Friedrich Nietzsche (trans. J. M. Kebbedy), *Dawn of Day*, London: George Allen & Unwin, 1924. www.archive.org/stream/dawnofday029675mbp/dawnofday029675mbp_djvu.txt.
10. Malcolm Pasley (ed.), *Nietzsche: Imagery and Thought: A Collection of Essays*, Berkeley: University of California Press, 1978, p. 97 (W. D. Williams, "Nietzsche's Masks").
11. Friedrich Nietzsche (trans. John McFarland Kennedy), *The Dawn of Day*, New York: Macmillan, 1911, pp. 151–152. http://www.gutenberg.org/files/39955/39955-h/39955-h.html.
12. *Ibid.*, p. 243.
13. Richard Wagner (trans. W. Ashton Ellis), *Actors and Singers*, Lincoln: University of Nebraska Press, 1995, pp. 73–74 ("Beethoven").
14. Friedrich Nietzsche (trans. John McFarland Kennedy), *The Dawn of Day*, pp. 117–119, note 11.

Chapter 14

1. Ferruccio Busoni (trans. Antony Beaumont), *Selected Letters*, London: Faber and Faber, 1987, p. 131 (Letter to Egon Petri, July 16, 1911).
2. Edward J. Dent, *Ferruccio Busoni*, London: Eulenburg Books, 1974, p. 172.
3. *Ibid.*, p. 143 (Letter to Egon Petri, April 6, 1912).
4. *Ibid.* p. 153 (Letter to Egon Petri, Sept, 7, 1912).
5. Bernard Shaw, *Prefaces by Bernard Shaw*, London: Odhams Press, 1938, pp. 378–382 ("Heartbreak House").
6. Ferruccio Busoni (trans. Antony Beaumont), *Selected Letters*, p. 86 (Letter to Egon Petri, Aug. 9, 1907).
7. *Ibid.*, p. 166 (Letter to Egon Petri, May 22, 1913).
8. *Ibid.*, pp. 250–251 (Letter to José Vianna da Motta, Oct. 20, 1916).
9. Ferruccio Busoni (trans. Theodore Baker), *Sketch of a New Aesthetic of Music*, New York: Schirmer, 1907, p. 37.
10. *Ibid.*, p. 395 (Schoenberg's letter to Busoni, August 24, 1909).
11. Ludwig Karpath, *Signale für die musikalische Welt*, Berlin, March 1, 1905 (Review of Schoenberg's *Pelleas und Melisande*).

12. Ferruccio Busoni (trans. Antony Beaumont), *Selected Letters*, p. 169, note 1 (Letter to Egon Petri, June 19, 1913).
13. Arnold Schoenberg (trans. Roy E. Carter), *Theory of Harmony*, London: Faber and Faber, 1983, p. 9.
14. Joan Peyser, *Boulez: Composer, Conductor, Enigma*, London: Cassell, 1976, p. 26.
15. Arnold Schoenberg (trans. Roy E. Carter), *Theory of Harmony*, pp. 421–422, note 13.
16. Ferruccio Busoni (trans. Antony Beaumont), *Selected Letters*, p. 389, note 1 (Schoenberg's letter to Busoni, undated, 1909).
17. Louise Varèse, *Varèse: A Looking-Glass Diary, Vol. 1*, London, 1972, p. 238.
18. *Ibid.*, p. 240.
19. Edgard Varèse, Preface to *Arcana*, quoted from *The Hermetic and Alchemical Writings of Paracelsus, Vol. 2* (ed. Arthur Waite), London, 1894, p. 310.
20. Friedrich Nietzsche (trans. R. J. Hollingdale), *Thus Spoke Zarathustra*, Harmondsworth: Penguin, 1969, p. 241.
21. Nicholas John (ed.), *ENO Doctor Faustus Program*, London: Cabbell Publishing, 1986 (David Pountney "On *Doctor Faust*").

Chapter 15

1. Thomas Mann (trans. H. T. Lowe-Porter, Agnes E. Meyer and Eric Sutton), *Order for the Day*, New York: Alfred A. Knopf, 1942 ("Culture and Politics"), pp. 223–237.
2. Thomas Mann (trans. H. T. Lowe-Porter), *Doctor Faustus*, London: Secker & Warburg, 1949, p. 173.
3. *Ibid.*, p. 373.
4. *Ibid.*, p. 175.
5. Friedrich Nietzsche (trans. R. J. Hollingdale), *Thus Spoke Zarathustra*, Harmondsworth: Penguin, 1969, p. 46.
6. Thomas Mann (trans. H. T. Lowe-Porter), *Doctor Faustus*, p. 4, note 2.
7. *Ibid.*, p. 9.
8. *Ibid.*, p. 125.
9. *Ibid.*, p. 131.
10. *Ibid.*, p. 132.
11. Thomas Mann (trans. Richard and Clara Winston), *Diaries 1918–1939*, London: Robin Clark, 1984, p. 248 (Tuesday, November 12 1935).
12. Thomas Mann (trans. H. T. Lowe-Porter), *Doctor Faustus*, p. 85, note 2.
13. *Ibid.*, p. 25.
14. *Ibid.*, p. 151.
15. *Ibid.*, p. 321.
16. *Ibid.*,
17. *Ibid.*, p. 322.
18. *Ibid.*, p. 161.
19. *Ibid.*, p. 30.
20. *Ibid.*, p. 44.
21. Richard Wagner (trans. W. Ashton Ellis), *Actors and Singers*, Lincoln: University of Nebraska Press, 1995, p. 97 ("Beethoven").
22. Thomas Mann (trans. H. T. Lowe-Porter), *Doctor Faustus*, p. 61, note 2.
23. *Ibid.*, p. 62.
24. *Ibid.*, p. 60.
25. Thomas Mann (trans. Walter D. Morris), *Reflections of a Nonpolitical Man*, New York: Frederick Ungar, 1983, p. 17.
26. Jacob Burckhardt (trans. S. G. Middlemore), *The Civilisation of the Renaissance in Italy*, London: The Folio Society, 2004, p. 11.
27. Thomas Mann (trans. H. T. Lowe-Porter), *Doctor Faustus*, p. 287, note 2.
28. *Ibid.*, p. 302.
29. *Ibid.*, p. 147.
30. *Ibid.*, p. 142.
31. *Ibid.*
32. *Ibid.*, p. 227.
33. *Ibid.*, p. 237.
34. *Ibid.*, p. 156.
35. *Ibid.*, p. 234.
36. *Ibid.*, p. 242.
37. *Ibid.*, p. 243.
38. *Ibid.*, p. 233.
39. *Ibid.*, p. 162.
40. *Ibid.*, p. 163.
41. *Ibid.*, p. 164.
42. *Ibid.*, p. 191.
43. *Ibid.*, p. 192.
44. *Ibid.*, p. 193–193.
45. *Ibid.*, p. 239.
46. *Ibid.*, p. 242.
47. Friedrich Nietzsche (trans. R. J. Hollingdale), *Twilight of the Idols/The Anti-Christ*, Harmondsworth: Penguin, 1981, p. 115 ("The Anti-Christ").
48. Thomas Mann (trans. H. T. Lowe-Porter), *Doctor Faustus*, p. 374, note 2.
49. *Ibid.*, p. 485.
50. *Ibid.*, p. 409.
51. *Ibid.*, p. 407.
52. *Ibid.*, p. 410.
53. *Politiken* (ed. Tøger Seidenfaden), Copenhagen: JP/Politikens, 2 Feb, 2014.

Finale

1. Jean-Paul Sartre (trans. Robert Baldick), *Nausea*, Harmondsworth: Penguin, 1987, p. 103.
2. *Ibid.*, 38.
3. *Ibid.*
4. Scott Calef (ed.), *Led Zeppelin and Philosophy: All Will Be Revealed*, Chicago: Open Court, 2013 (Erol E. Flynn "Celebrating the Agony of Life"). https://books.google.co.uk/books?id=Ozfg785V0E4C&pg=PT181&lpg=PT181&dq=Nietzsche+and+Robert+Plant&source=bl&ots=5r9C4ooZ7a&sig=grLH6jHQvIwVmUa05x_x4WfkmII&hl=en&sa=X&ved=0CCYQ6AEwAWoVChMI-4yKgI2VyAIVCb0aCh2PYQQd#v=onepage&q=Nietzsche%20and%20Robert%20Plant&f=false.
5. Friedrich Nietzsche (trans. R. J. Hollingdale), *Beyond Good and Evil*, Harmondsworth: Penguin, 1973, aphorism 75, p. 73.
6. Friedrich Nietzsche (trans. Josefine Nauckhoff), *The Gay Science*, Cambridge: Cambridge University Press, 2001, p. 13.
7. Friedrich Nietzsche (trans. R. J. Hollingdale), *Thus Spoke Zarathustra*, Harmondsworth: Penguin, 1969, pp. 331–332.
8. *Ibid.*, p. 231.
9. *Ibid.*, p. 74.
10. Walter Kaufmann, *Nietzsche: Philosopher, Psychologist, Antichrist*, Princeton: Princeton University Press, 1974, p. 386.
11. *Ibid.*, p. 187 (*The Wanderer and His Shadow*, quoted).
12. Friedrich Nietzsche (trans. R. J. Hollingdale), *Thus Spoke Zarathustra*, pp. 130–131, note 7.
13. Jean-Paul Sartre (trans. Robert Baldick), *Nausea*, p. 148, note 1.
14. Walter Pater, *The Renaissance: Studies in Art and Poetry*, London: Macmillan, 1915, p. 250.
15. Pierre Boulez (trans. Martin Cooper), *Orientations*, London: Faber and Faber, 1986, p. 81.
16. *Ibid.*, p. 128.
17. David Buckley, *Strange Fascination-David Bowie: The Definitive Story*: London: Virgin, 1999, p. 267.
18. https://nietzschethemusical.wordpress.com.

Bibliography

Abraham, Gerald. *The Concise Oxford History of Music*. Newton Abbot: Readers Union, 1979.

Bacharach, A. L. *British Music of Our Time*. Harmondsworth: Pelican, 1946.

Bartók, Béla (trans. Peter Balabán and István Farkas, trans., rev. Elisabeth West and Colin Mason). *Béla Bartók: Letters*. London: Faber and Faber, 1971.

Barzun, Jacques. *Pleasures of Music*. London: Michael Joseph, 1954.

Beecham, Thomas. *A Mingled Chime: Leaves from An Autobiography*. London: White Lion Publishers, 1973.

Blavatsky, H. P. *Studies in Occultism* (The Dennis Wheatley Library of the Occult). London: Sphere, 1974.

Boulez, Pierre (trans. Martin Cooper). *Orientations*. London: Faber and Faber, 1986.

Bowers, Faubion. *The New Scriabin*. Newton Abbot: David & Charles, 1974.

Bowers, Faubion. *Scriabin: A Biography*. New York: Dover, 1996.

Buckley, David. *Strange Fascination—David Bowie: The Definitive Story*. London: Virgin, 1999.

Burckhardt, Jacob (trans. S. G. Middlemore). *The Civilisation of the Renaissance in Italy*. London: The Folio Society, 2004.

Busoni, Ferruccio (trans. Antony Beaumont). *Selected Letters*. London: Faber and Faber, 1987.

Busoni, Ferruccio (trans. Theodore Baker). *Sketch of a New Esthetic of Music*. New York: Schirmer, 1911.

Calef, Scott (ed.). *Led Zeppelin and Philosophy: All Will Be Revealed*. Chicago: Open Court, 2013.

Carpelan, Bo (trans. David McDuff). *Axel*. Manchester: Carcanet, 1989.

Chalmers, Kenneth. *Béla Bartók*. London: Phaidon, 1995.

Chissell, Joan. *Schumann*. London: J. M. Dent, 1977.

Chyli´nska, Teresa (trans. A. T. Jordan). *Szymanowski*. New York: Twayne, 1973.

Cooke, Mervyn (ed.). *The Cambridge Companion to Benjamin Britten*. Cambridge: Cambridge University Press, 1999.

Cooper, David. *Béla Bartók*. New Haven: Yale University Press, 2015.

Cooper, Martin. *French Music: From the Death of Berlioz to the Death of Fauré*. London: Oxford University Press, 1951.

Daffner, Hugo. *Friedrich Nietzsche's Randglossen zu Bizet's Carmen*. Regensburg, 1938.

D'Annunzio, Gabrielle (trans. Susan Bassnett). *The Flame*. London: Quartet Books, 1991.

D'Annunzio, Gabrielle (trans. Georgina Harding). *The Triumph of Death*. Sawtry: Dedalus, 1990.

Davies, John Lloyd. "The Will to Power and the Will to Live" in program for Royal Opera House production of *Król Roger*, May 2015.

Dent, E. J. *Ferruccio Busoni*. London: Eulenberg, 1974.

Eden, David, and Reinhard Saremba (eds.). *The Cambridge Companion to Gilbert and Sullivan*. Cambridge: Cambridge University Press, 2009.

Eksteins, Modris. *Rites of Spring*. London: Papermac (Macmillan), 2000.

Erb, J. Laurence. *Brahms*. London: Dent, 1934.

Fenby, Eric. *Delius as I Knew Him*. London: Quality Press, 1948.

Fisk, Josiah, and Jeff William Nichols (eds.). *Composers on Music: Eight Centuries of Writings*. Boston: Northeastern University Press, 1997.

Frayling, Christopher (ed.). *Vampyres: Lord Byron to Count Dracula*, London: Faber and Faber, 1983.
Furness, Raymond. *Wagner and Literature*. Manchester: Manchester University Press, 1982.
Gutman, Robert W. *Richard Wagner: The Man, His Mind, and His Music*. New York: Time-Life Records Special Edition, 1972.
Hanslick, Eduard. *On the Beautiful in Music*. http://www.cengage.com/music/book_content/049557273X_wrightSimms/assets/ITOW/7273X_58_ITOW.pdf
Hamsun, Knut (trans. James W. McFarlane). *Pan*. London: Alkin Books, 1994.
Harvey, Jonathan. *Music and Inspiration*. London: Faber and Faber, 1999.
Hayman, Ronald. *Nietzsche: A Critical Life*. London: Phoenix, 1995;
Hegel, G. W. F. (trans. W. Wallace and A. V. Miller, rev. Michael Inwood). *Philosophy of Mind*. Oxford: Oxford University Press, 2007.
Hoffmann, E. T. A. (ed. Christopher Lazare). *Tales of Hoffmann*. New York: A. A. Wyn, 1946.
Holloway, Robin. *Debussy and Wagner*. London: Eulenburg, 1979.
Hughes-Hallett, Lucy. *The Pike: Gabrielle D'Annunzio, Poet, Seducer and Preacher of War*. London: Fourth Estate, 2013.
Hurd, Michael. *Rutland Boughton and the Glastonbury Festivals*. Oxford: Clarendon Press, 1993.
Hutchings, Arthur. *Delius*. London: Macmillan, 1948.
Iwaszkiewicz, Jarosław, and Karol Szymanowski (trans. Andrzej Duszenko). *King Roger* libretto, Act I. http://duszenko.northern.edu/szymanowski/act1.html.
John, Nicholas (ed.). *ENO Doctor Faustus Program*. London: Cabbell Publishing, 1986.
Kant, Immanuel (trans. James Creed Meredith). *Critique of Judgement*. Oxford: Oxford University Press, 2007.
Kaufmann, Walter. *Nietzsche: Philosopher, Psychologist, Antichrist*. Princeton: Princeton University Press, 1974.
Kennedy, Michael. *Britten (The Dent Master Musicians)*. London: Dent, 1993.
Kennedy, Michael. *Richard Strauss: Man, Musician, Enigma*. Cambridge: Cambridge University Press, 1999.
Köhler, Joachim (trans. Ronald Taylor). *Nietzsche and Wagner: A Lesson in Subjugation*. New Haven and London: Yale University Press, 1998.

Köhler, Joachim (trans. Ronald Taylor). *Zarathustra's Secret*. New Haven: Yale University Press, 2002.
Lebrecht, Norman (ed.). *Mahler Remembered*. London: Faber and Faber, 1987.
Leeuw, Gerard van der. "Alphons Diepenbrock and the European World of Composers at the Fin-de-Siècle" *Musicology Journal* 11, 201.
LeGrove, Judith. *Toward a World Unknown: Exhibition Catalogue*. Aldeburgh: The Britten-Pears Library, 1999.
Liébert, Georges. *Nietzsche and Music*. Chicago: University of Chicago Press, 2004.
Lloyd, Stephen. *H. Balfour Gardiner*. Cambridge: Cambridge University Press, 1984.
Macdonald, Hugh. *Skryabin* (Oxford Studies of Composers). London: Oxford University Press, 1978.
Mahler, Alma (trans. Basil Creighton). *Gustav Mahler: Memories and Letters*. London: Cardinal/Sphere, 1990.
Mahler-Werfel, Alma (trans. Anthony Beaumont). *Diaries 1898–1902*. London: Faber and Faber, 1998.
Mann, Thomas (trans. H. T. Lowe-Porter, Agnes E. Meyer and Eric Sutton). *Order for the Day*. New York: Alfred A. Knopf, 1942.
Mann, Thomas (trans. H. T. Lowe-Porter). *Doctor Faustus*. London: Secker & Warburg, 1949.
Mann, Thomas (trans. H. T. Lowe-Porter). *The Magic Mountain*. London: Secker & Warburg, 1979.
Mann, Thomas (trans. Walter D. Morris). *Reflections of a Nonpolitical Man*. New York: Frederick Ungar, 1983.
Mann, Thomas. *Stories of Three Decades*. London: Martin Secker & Warburg, 1946.
Mann, Thomas (trans. Allan Blunden). *Thomas Mann: Pro and Contra Wagner*. London: Faber and Faber, 1985.
Mar, Norman del. *Richard Strauss: A Critical Commentary on His Life and Works*. London: Barrie and Jenkins, 1962.
Mitchell, Donald. *Gustav Mahler: The Early Years*. Berkeley: University of California Press, 1980.
Moore, George. *Evelyn Innes*. London: T. Fisher Unwin, 1898.
Morrison, Simon. *Russian Opera and the Symbolist Movement*. Berkeley: University of California Press, 2002.
Myers, Rollo (ed.) *Richard Strauss & Romain Rolland: Correspondence*. London: Calder and Boyars, 1968.
Nietzsche, Friedrich (trans. R. J. Hollingdale).

Beyond Good and Evil. Harmondsworth: Penguin, 1973.
Nietzsche, Friedrich (trans. Walter Kaufmann). *The Birth of Tragedy and The Case of Wagner*. New York: Random House (Vintage), 1967.
Nietzsche, Friedrich (trans. Anthony M. Ludovici). *I: The Case of Wagner, II: Nietzsche Contra Wagner, III: Selected Aphorisms*. Edinburgh: T. N. Foulis, 1911.
Nietzsche, Friedrich (trans. John McFarland Kennedy). *The Dawn of Day*. New York: Macmillan, 1911.
Nietzsche, Friedrich (trans. R. J. Hollingdale). *Ecce Homo*. Harmondsworth: Penguin, 1982.
Nietzsche, Friedrich (trans. Josefine Nauckhoff). *The Gay Science*. Cambridge: Cambridge University Press, 2001.
Nietzsche, Friedrich (trans. Marion Faber and Stephen Lehmann). *Human, All Too Human*. London: Penguin, 1984.
Nietzsche, Friedrich (trans. Douglas Smith). *On the Genealogy of Morals*. Oxford: Oxford University Press, 1996.
Nietzsche, Friedrich (trans. A. M. Ludovici). *Selected Letters of Friedrich Nietzsche*. London: Soho, 1985.
Nietzsche, Friedrich (trans. Christopher Middleton). *Selected Letters of Friedrich Nietzsche*. Indianapolis: Hackett/University of Chicago, 1996.
Nietzsche, Friedrich (trans. R. J. Hollingdale). *Thus Spoke Zarathustra*. Harmondsworth: Penguin, 1969.
Nietzsche, Friedrich (trans. R. J. Hollingdale). *Twilight of the Idols/The Anti-Christ*. Harmondsworth: Penguin, 1981.
Nietzsche, Friedrich (trans. R. J. Hollingdale). *Untimely Meditations*. Cambridge: Cambridge University Press, 1983.
Nietzsche, Friedrich (trans. Ladislaus Löb). *Writings from the Early Notebooks*. Cambridge: Cambridge University Press, 2009.
Newman, Ernest. *Hugo Wolf*. London: Methuen, 1907.
Noll, Richard. *The Aryan Christ: The Secret Life of Carl Gustav Jung*. London: Macmillan, 1997.
Norton, Robert E. *Nietzsche: Attempt at a Mythology*. Champaign: University of Illinois Press, 2009.
Pasley, Malcolm (ed.). *Nietzsche: Imagery and Thought: A Collection of Essays*. Berkeley: University of California Press, 1978.
Pasternak, Alexander (trans. Ann Pasternak Slater). *A Vanished Present*. Oxford: Oxford University Press, 1984.
Pater, Walter. *The Renaissance: Studies in Art and Poetry*, London: Macmillan, 1915.
Payne, Nicholas (ed.). Opera North program for 1990/91 Autumn Season, vol. ON37. Leeds, Opera North.
Peyser, Joan. *Boulez: Composer, Conductor, Enigma*, London: Cassell, 1976.
Piper, Myfanwy. *Death in Venice: An Opera in Two Acts*. London: Faber Music, 1973.
Pirie, Peter J. *The English Musical Renaissance*. London: Victor Gollancz, 1979.
Phillips Griffiths, A. (ed.). *Philosophy, Psychology and Psychiatry*. Cambridge: Cambridge University Press, 1994.
Plato (trans. Benjamin Jowett). *Plato's Republic*. New York: Airmont, 1968.
Regardi, Israel (ed. Chic Cicero and Sandra Tabatha Cicero). *The Tree of Life: An Illustrated Study in Magic*. St. Paul: Llewellyn Publications, 2003.
Rolland, Romain (trans. Gilbert Cannan). *Jean Christophe*. New York: Random House, no date.
Sartre, Jean-Paul (trans. Robert Baldick). *Nausea*. Harmondsworth: Penguin, 1987.
Schoenberg, Arnold (trans. Leo Black). *Style and Idea*. New York: St Martin's Press, 1975.
Schoenberg, Arnold (trans. Roy E. Carter). *Theory of Harmony*. London: Faber and Faber, 1983.
Schopenhauer, Arthur (trans. E. F. J. Payne). *The World as Will and Representation*, Vol. 1. New York: Dover, 1969.
Seckerson, Edward. *Mahler: His Life and Times*. Tunbridge Wells: Midas Books, 1982.
Shaw, George Bernard. *Complete Plays of Bernard Shaw*. London: Odhams, no date.
Shaw, Bernard. *Prefaces by Bernard Shaw*. London: Odhams Press, 1938.
Shelley, Percy Bysshe (ed. Thomas Hutchinson). *The Complete Poetical Works of Percy Bysshe Shelley*. London: Oxford University Press, 1934.
Shelley, Percy Bysshe. *Essays and Letters by Percy Bysshe Shelley*. London: Walter Scott Ltd., no date.
Steiner, Rudolf. *Autobiography: Chapter in the Course of My Life 1861–1907*. SteinerBooks, 2006.
Steiner, Rudolf, *Friedrich Nietzsche—Fighter for Freedom*.http://wn.rsarchive.org/Books/GA005/English/RSPI1960/GA005_c01_2.html.
Stoker, Bram (ed. Leonard Wolf). *The Anno-*

tated Dracula. London: New English Library, 1976.

Stoker, Bram. Dracula. London: Constable, 1904.

Strunk, Oliver (ed.), Source Readings in Music History–Vol. 5, The Romantic Era. London: Faber & Faber, 1981.

Tarasti, Eero. Myth and Music. Helsinki: Suomen Musiikkitieteellinen Seura, 1978.

Tippet, Michael (ed. Meirion Bowen). Tippet on Music. Oxford: Oxford University Press, 2001.

Varèse, Louise. Varèse: A Looking-Glass Diary. New York: W. W. Norton, 1972.

Volkoff, Vladimir, Tchaikovsky: A Self-Portrait, London: Robert Hale, 1975.

Wagner, Cosima (ed. Erhart Thierbach), Vol. 12 of Jahresgabe der Gesellschaft der Freunde des Nietzsche-Archivs: Die Briefe Cosima Wagners an Friedrich Nietzsche 1869–1871 (Vol. 1). Weimar: Nietzsche-Archiv, 1938.

Wagner, Richard (trans. William Ashton Ellis). Actors and Singers. Lincoln: University of Nebraska Press, 1995.

Wagner, Richard. Parsifal (ENO Opera Guide). London: John Calder, 1986.

Wagner, Richard (trans. William Ashton Ellis). Religion and Art. Lincoln: University of Nebraska Press, 1994.

Wagner, Richard (trans. Stewart Spencer). Selected Letters of Richard Wagner. London: Dent, 1987.

Wagner, Richard (ed. Charles Osborne). Stories and Essays. London: Peter Owen, 1973.

Weiner, Marc A. Richard Wagner and the Anti-Semitic Imagination. Lincoln: University of Nebraska Press, 1995.

Wightman, Alistair (ed.). Szymanowski on Music. London: Toccata Press, 1999.

Wilde, Oscar (ed. Vyvyan Holland). Complete Works of Oscar Wilde. London: Collins, 1977.

Wilhelm, Kurt. Richard Strauss: An Intimate Portrait. London: Thames and Hudson, 1989.

Wilson, A.N. God's Funeral. London: John Murray, 1999.

Wilson, Colin, Rudolf Steiner: The Man and His Vision. Wellingborough: The Aquarian Press, 1985.

Index

Numbers in **_bold italics_** refer to pages with photographs.

Abba 193, 194
Abraham, Gerald 85
Acton, William 62
Adrian, Max 123
Ahna, Pauline de 84
Albert Herring 137
Eine Alpensinfonie 85–89, 93, 97
Also Sprach Zarathustra 78–83, 84, 87, 89, 95, 111, 116, 140, 184, 195, 196
Andrésen, Björn **_180_**
Andrews, Julie 89
The Anti-Christ 183, 192
Arabella 47, 81
Arányi, Jelly d' 144
Arcana 168–170
Armin, Achim von 64
"The Artwork of the Future" 162
Ashby, Hal 79
Auric, Georges 154
Aus Italien 76–78, 157
Axel 17, 19

Bach, Johann Sebastian 81
"Das Bachlein" 90
Band of Brothers (prod. Steven Spielberg, 2001) 177
Barbarossa 92
Barrault, Jean-Louis 195
Bartók, Béla 138–146, **_139_**, 147, 150, 151; *Bluebeard's Castle* 138–139, 143, 144, 150, 151; 14 Bagatelles 142; *The Miraculous Mandarin* 144–145; Piano Concerto No. 3 144; *Sketches* 142; Sonata for Two Pianos and Percussion 144; Songs, Op. 15 143; String Quartet No. 1 142; Ten Easy Pieces for Piano 142; Two Romanian Dances 145; Violin Concerto 142
Batka, Richard 98
Baudelaire, Charles 64–65, 72, 157
The Beatles 189, 190, 191, 192
Beecham, Sir Thomas 121
"Beethoven" 25, 42, 43, 48, 161, 174
Beethoven, Ludwig van 7, 8, 9, 25, 32, 41–49, **_48_**, **_49_**, 71, 72, 73, 78, 88, 90, 113, 177, 184; "Für Elise" 180; Quartet in C-sharp minor 43, 177; Symphony No. 3 *Eroica* 43, 89, 90; Symphony No. 6 *Pastoral* 7–8, 43–44, 88; Symphony No. 7 70; Symphony No. 9 *Choral* 41–42, 44, 45, 49, 184
Beiber, Emil **16**
Being There (dir. Hal Ashby, 1979) 79
Benjamin, Walter 91
Berceuse élégiaque 166
Berlioz, Hector 7–8, 157
Bernard, James 137
Beyond Good and Evil 36, 76, 147, 149, 166
Billy Budd 137
The Birth of Tragedy 27, **27**, 42, 43, 44, 45, 48, 50, 92, 102, 107, 130, 132, 133, 149, 155, 156
Bizet, Georges 4, 5, 68, 70, 71, 73, 74, 127, 187; *Carmen* 4, 5, 68, 70, 71, 73, 74, 127, 149, 187
Blavatsky, Helena Petrovna 108, 111, 114–115
Bluebeard's Castle 138–139, 143, 144, 150, 151
Böcklin, Arnold 58, 76
Bogarde, Dirk 102, 180
Böhler, Otto **94**
Borgia, Cesare 37
Boughton, Rutland 128–129; *The Immortal Hour* 128, 129; *Mystic Dance of the Grail* 129; Violin Sonata 129
Boulez, Pierre 167–168, 183, 194, 195
Bowers, Faubion 107, 117
Bowie, David 194–195
Bradlaugh, Charles 120
Brahms, Johannes 8, 12, 21, 33, 46–47; Songs, Op. 3 12; Symphony No. 1 46; *Triumphlied* 33, 46
Brandes, Georg 16, 20, 71
Britten, Benjamin 126, 128, 130–137, **_136_**, 155; *Albert Herring* 137; *Billy Budd* 137; *Death in Venice* 130, 131–133, 135, 155; *Michelangelo Sonnets* 135; *The Prince of the Pagodas* 135; *Sechs Hölderlin Fragmente* 130–131; *Seven Sonnets of Michelangelo* 130; *The Turn of the Screw* 137; *Young Apollo* 130, 135

218　INDEX

Brook, Peter 189
Brooks, Mel 195
Brooks, Shelton 187
Bülow, Hans von 1, 16–17, *16*, 32, 46, 76
Burckhard, Max 95
Burckhardt, Jacob 178
Burns, Marc 180
Burton, Richard 23
Busoni Ferruccio 5, 78, 153, 164–*165*;
　Berceuse élégiaque 166; *Doktor Faust* 170–171; *Gesang vom Reigen der Geister* 165; *Der mächtige Zauberer* 165; *Nocturne symphonique* 165, 166, 169; *Outline of a New Esthetic of Music* 165, 166, 168; Piano Concerto 78; *Sonatina seconda* 165, 166
Byron, Lord George Gordon 12

Capriccio 90
Carjat Étienne **68**
Carmen 4, 5, 68, 70, 71, 73, 74, 127, 149, 187
Carpelan, Bo 17, 19; *Axel* 17, 19
The Case of Wagner 18, 33, 46, 68
Chamisso, Adalbert von 11, 13
Chausson, Ernest 72
Chipp, E.T. 21
Chopin, Frédéric 59, 104, 147
Cocteau, Jean 153–154
Comitas, Alexander 185
Cooper, David 142
Cooper, Martin 154
Copland, Aaron 196
Crighton, Charles 154
Crowley, Aleister 113, 189, 195
Czárdzás macabre 145

La damoiselle élue 51, 153
Dance Rhapsodies 123
D'Annunzio, Gabrielle 17, 18–19, 56, 116, 131;
　The Flame 19, 131; *The Triumph of Death* 17, 18
Dante 182
Darkens, Rodolphe 65
Darwin, Charles 115
Davis, Bette 81
Davis, Sir Colin 2
Davis, John Lloyd 150
Dawn of Day 123, 159, 160–161, *161*
Death in Venice 130, 131–133, 135, 155
"Death in Venice" 36, 101–102, 107, 131, 137
Death in Venice (dir. Luchino Visconti, 1971) 101–102, ***101***, 131, 134, 180, **180**
Debussy, Claude 14, 51–52, 56, 125, 149, 152–153, **152**, 157, 162; *La damoiselle élue* 51, 153; "Golliwog's Cakewalk" 152; *Ibéria* 149; *Jeux* 51, 153; *La Mer* 152; *Nocturnes* 149; *Pelléas et Mélisande* 52, 153
Dehring, Theodor 83
Delibes, Léo 71
Delius, Frederick 20, 52, 119–127, **120**, 128, 129; *Dance Rhapsodies* 123; *Life's Dance* 123; *A Mass of Life* 20, 121, 122–127, 129, 140, 152; *On Hearing the First Cuckoo in Spring* 127; *A Poem of Life and Love* 123; *Requiem* 123; "Sleigh-Ride" 127; *A Song Before Sunrise* 123; *A Song of Summer* 123; Songs 123; *A Village Romeo and Juliet* 124, 126, 127; "A Walk to the Paradise Garden" 124, 127
Delius, Jelka 123
Delville, Jean 117, ***117***
Dent, Edward 78
Deodata, Eumir 79
Diaghilev, Sergei 194
Dichterliebe 12
Diepenbrock, Alphons 156–163, ***157***; *Im grossen Schweigen* 158
Dionÿsische Fantasie 91
Doctor Faustus 17, 83, 171, 172–186
Doktor Faust 170–171
Doktor Faustus (dir. Franz Seitz, 1982) ***179***
Don Giovanni 7
Donner, Richard **196**
The Doors 188
Dósa, Lidi 141
Dostoyevsky, Fyodor 171
Downes, Stephen 151
Dracula 60, 61–62, 63–65
Dracula (dir. Terence Fisher, 1958) 61
The Dream of Gerontius 21, 124
Dujardin, Édouard 19–20
Dukas, Paul 72, 138

Ecce Homo 12, 13–14, 21, 25, 56, 87, 109,
Eckerman, Johann Peter 149
Efebos 149–150
Ehlert, Louis 20
Eichendorff, Joseph von 14
Einstein, Albert 168
Eiser, Otto 26
Eksteins, Modris 9
Elektra 83
Elgar, Sir Edward 4, 5, 21, 129; *The Dream of Gerontius* 21, 124
Eliot, T.S. 163
Elliot, Mama Cass 193
Ellis, W. Ashton 42, 44
Emerson, Ralph Waldo 70
"An End in Paris" 9
Erwartung 166
Eschenbach, Wolfram von 55
Evelyn Innes 17, 19

Fallersleben, August Hoffmann von 12, 13
Fanck, Albert 89
Fauré, Gabriel 72
Faust 182
Eine Faust-Symphonie 17, 82
A Feast of Friends (dir. Paul Ferrara, 1968) 188
Fenby, Eric 119–120, 122, 123

Index

Ferrara, Paul 188
Finch, Jon **179**
Fisher, Terence 61
Five Orchestral Pieces 168
Five Piano Pieces 82
The Flame 19, 131
Der fliegende Holländer 19
"Die Flüchtlinge" 14
Flynn, Erin E. 188
Flynn, Errol 86
Forster, Bernhard 93
Forward, Anthony 102
Foss, Lukas 185
14 Bagatelles 142
Die Frau ohne Schatten 85
Frauenliebe und -leben 11
Der Freischütz 180
"Für Elise" 180

Gagarin, Yuri 111
Gálffi, László 23
Gamley, Douglas 79
Ganz, Bruno **2**
Gardiner, H. Balfour 129
Gast, Peter 20, 39, 71
Gautier, Judith 104
The Gay Science 46, 54–55, 68, 69, 70, 74,
George, Stefan 167
Gersdorff, Freiherr Karl von 11, 32, 71, 85, 88
Gesang vom Reigen der Geister 165
Geyer, Ludwig 61
Geyer, Stefi 141–142, 144
Giehrl, Joseph 77
Gilbert, E. Ouseley 21
Gilbert, Sir W.S. 4, 126
Glazunov, Alexander 194
Gloeden, Wilhelm von 70, 137
Gobineau, Count Arthur 55
Godspell 195
Goebbels, Josef 90
Goethe, Johann Wolfgang von 46, 58, 76, 78, 81, 90, 92, 157, 182; *Faust* 182; *Proömium* 92
The Golden Legend 8
Goldmark, Karl 71
"Golliwog's Cakewalk" 152
Gombossy, Klára 143
Gordon, Geoffrey 185
Götterdämmerung 2, 9, 19, 38, 62, 99, 125, 172, 174
Gounod, Charles 81
Grainger, Percy 123
Groth, Klaus 12, 13
Gutman, Robert 65, 67

Hadden, J. Cuthbert **77**
Hale, Georgina 99
Hammerstein, Oscar, II 88
Hamsun, Knut 91, 97; *Pan* 97, 98

Handel, George Frideric 5, 8, 11, 34
Hanslick, Eduard 4, 73–74, 83
Hart, Lorenz 195
Harvey, Jonathan 122
Hauk, Minnie 71
Hausegger, Siegmund von 91–92, **91**; *Barbarossa* 92; *Dionÿsische Fantasie* 91; *Natursymphonie* 92
Haydn, Joseph 11, 45
Hayes, Pattison 21
Hayman, Ronald 114
Heap, Charles Swinnerton 21
Hebbel, Christian Friedrich 14
Hegel, Georg Wilhelm Friedrich 106
Heine, Heinrich 12
Ein Heldenleben 83–84, 89, 99
Hemmings, David 137
Henze, Hans Werner 184–185
Herrmann, Bernard 146, 190
Herzog, Werner 1, **2**, 26, 60, 145
Hickox, Richard 126, 127
Hindemith, Paul 157
Historical Portraits 11
Hitchcock, Alfred **146**, 154, 190
Hitler, Adolf 31–32, 89, 90–91, 92, 168, 171, 172, 183, 189, 195
Hoffmann, Ernst Theodor Amadeus 7, 164, 166, 194, 209*n*
Hoffmann, Joseph **72**
Hofmannsthal, Hugo von 81, 85
Holbein, Hans 137
Hölderlin, Friedrich 157
Hollingdale, R.J. 61, 111–112, 129
Holloway, Robin 153
Holst, Gustav 4, 84, 129; *The Planets* 84
Honegger, Arthur 154
Horace 157
Howard, Trevor 25
Hughes-Hallett, Lucy 116
Hülsen-Haeseler, Dietrich von 32
Human, All Too Human 40, 45, 67, 158
Hume, David 3
Hurd, Michael 129
Hutchings, Arthur 120–122, 124
Hymn to Life 17, 20–21

Ibéria 149
Im grossen Schweigen 158
The Immortal Hour 128, 129
Indy, Vincent, d' 72
Iwaszkiewicz, Jarosław 149, 150, 152

Jachimecki, Zdzisław 148
Jackson, Timothy 90
Jean Christophe 17, 19
Jeux 51, 153
Joukowsky, Paul 38
Joyce, James 19
Jung, Carl Gustav 133–134, 150, 170, 184
Jurkovics, Irmy 141

INDEX

Kant, Immanuel 27–28, 106
Karajan, Herbert von 2, 3
Karloff, Boris 175
Karpath, Ludwig 167
Kaufmann, Walter 45, 109, 192
Kennedy, Michael 135
Kertbeny, Karl Maria 191
Klemperer, Otto 94
Klimt, Gustav 49–50
Klinger, Max **48**, 49, 113, 156
Knortz, Karl 26
Köhler, Joachim 34, 36, 70, 137
Korngold, Erich Wolfgang 88
Köselitz, Heinrich *see* Gast, Peter
Król Roger 149–152, 154–155
Kubrick, Stanley 79, 116, **126**, 127, 184

Lämmel, Martin Moritz **54**
Landor, Walter Savage 70
La Rochefoucauld, François de 20
Leblanc, Georgette 138
Led Zeppelin 188, 189
The Legend of the Invisible City of Kitezh 52
Leibniz, Gottfried Wilhelm 5
Lenbach, Franz von 76
Lennon, John 9, 14, 189, 191–192
Leopardi, Giacomo 70
Lévi-Strauss, Claude 6
Liberace 47, 79
Life's Dance 123
Ligeti, György 184
"Der Lindenbaum" 174
Liszt, Franz 6, 7, 8, 11, 14, 17, 32, 46, 59, 71, 82, 83, 145, 165–166; *Czárdás macabre* 145; *Eine Faust-Symphonie* 17, 82; *Historical Portraits* 11; "Mazeppa" 165; "Der traurige Mönch" 14
Lohengrin 9, 17, 19, 67, 77, 125, 142
Long, Robin 137
Ludwig (dir. Luchino Visconti, 1972) 25
Ludwig II of Bavaria 1, 22, 106
Lux, Joseph August **48**

Macdonald, Hugh 105, 109
Macdonald, Rory 185
Machen, Arthur 97
Der mächtige Zauberer 165
Maeterlinck, Maurice 138
The Magic Mountain 92, 134
Mahler (dir. Ken Russell, 1974) 99, 103
Mahler, Alma 49, 50, 95–96, 97, 159
Mahler, Gustav 17, 49, 50, 62, 93–103, **94**, 125, 135, 135, 158, 159, 176, 187; Symphony No. 2, *Resurrection* 94; Symphony No. 3 96–100; Symphony No. 4 159; Symphony No. 7 100–101; Symphony No. 8 94
Manfred Overture 12
Mann, Barry 193
Mann, Thomas 9, 17, 35–36, 64, 82–83, 88, 92, 101, 102, 103, 107, 131, 132, 134, 135, 152, 172–186, **173**; "Death in Venice" 36, 101–102, 107, 131, 137; *Doctor Faustus* 17, 83, 171, 172–186; *The Magic Mountain* 92, 134; *Reflections of a Nonpolitical Man* 9, 178; "Sorrows and Grandeur of Richard Wagner" 64
Marschner, Heinrich 26; *Der Vampyr* 26
Martell, Philip 79
Martin, George 190
A Mass of Life 20, 121, 122–127, 129, 140, 152
"Mazeppa" 165
McCartney, Paul 190, 191
Die Meistersinger von Nürnberg 15, 18, 22, 23, 32, 34, 58, 70, 73, 80, 82, 83, 162
Mendelssohn, Felix 5, 34, 56
Mendès, Catulle 72
Mengele, Josef 175
La Mer 152
Mérimée, Prosper 70
Metamorphosen 89–90, 92
Metope 147, 148
Meyerbeer, Giacomo 55
Meysenbug, Malwida von 66
Michelangelo Sonnets 135
A Midsummer Marriage 133–134
The Midwich Cuckoos 174
The Mikado 4
Milhaud, Darius 154
Milton, John 114
The Miraculous Mandarin 144–145
Mitchell, Donald 97
Mity 147, 148
Møldrup, Toke 185
Moore, George 17, 19; *Evelyn Innes* 17, 19
Morrison, Jim 188
Mosley, Sir Oswald 29
Mottl, Felix 21
Mozart, Wolfgang Amadeus 4, 7, 8, 9, 46; *Don Giovanni* 7; Symphony No. 40 in G minor 4
Müller, Wilhelm 13
The Mummy (dir. Karl Freund, 1932) 175
Murnau, F.W. 1, 175
Mystery 118–119
Mystic Dance of the Grail 129

Nachfolger, C.F. Kant **91**
Napoleon Bonaparte 43, 90
Natursymphonie 92
Newman, Ernest 157
Newton, Sir Isaac 168
Nietzsche, Elisabeth 15, 39, 63, 66, 93, 96, 119, 128, 184
Nietzsche, Friedrich **86**, *passim*; *The Anti-Christ* 183, 192; *Beyond Good and Evil* 36, 76, 147, 149, 166; *The Birth of Tragedy* 27, **27**, 42, 43, 44, 45, 48, 50, 92, 102, 107, 130, 132, 133, 149, 155, 156; *The Case of Wagner* 18, 33, 46, 68; *Dawn of Day* 123, 159, 160–161, 161; *Ecce Homo* 12, 13–14, 21, 25, 56,

87, 109, 118, 131, 141, 184, 192; *The Gay Science* 46, 54–55, 68, 69, 70, 74, 78, 96, 98, 108, 189–190, 192; *Human, All Too Human* 40, 45, 67, 158; *Hymn to Life* 17, 20–21; Songs and Piano Pieces 12–17, 25, 32, 191; *Thus Spoke Zarathustra* (*Also Sprach Zarathustra*) 3, 15, 17, 20, 69, 78, 87, 92, 99, 101, 107, 109, 111, 112, 121, 123, 129, 130, 138, 155, 189, 190, 193, 194, 195; *Twilight of the Idols* 11, 16, 21; *Untimely Meditations* 29–30, 45, 59
Nietzsche—The Musical 196
Nijinsky, Vaslav 194
Nikisch, Arthur 97
Nocturne symphonique 165, 166, 169
Nocturnes 149
Noll, Richard 133
Nosferatu (dir. F.W. Murnau, 1922) 1, **2**, 175
Nosferatu: Phantom der Nacht (dir. Werner Herzog, 1979) 1, **2**, 26, 60, 145
Novalis 157
Now Voyager (dir. Irving Rapper, 1942) 81
Nunn, E. Cuthbert 21

Olbrich, Joseph Maria 49
On Hearing the First Cuckoo in Spring 127
Opera and Drama 23
Opitz, Theodor 14
Orff, Carl 157
Ormandy, Eugene 104
Outline of a New Esthetic of Music 165, 166, 168

Pal Joey (dir. George Sidney, 1957) 195
Palmer, Tony 23, 38
Pan 97, 98
Papillons 15
Paracelsus 170
Parerga and Paralipomena 159
Parry, Sir Hubert 4
Parsifal 12, 19, 44, 51–52, 54, 55–56, **57**, 60–61, 63–65, 67, 78, 82, 105, 124, 153, 163, 164, 177
Pasternak, Alexander 110–111
Pasternak, Boris 110
Pásztory, Ditta 143–144
Pater, Walter 194
Pears, Sir Peter 131, 137
Pelléas et Mélisande 52, 153
Pelleas und Melisande 159, 167
Penderecki, Kryzsztof 147
Perkins, Anthony **146**
Peterson-Berger, Wilhelm 156
Petit, Pierre **52**
Petöfi, Sándor 11, 12, 13, 191
Petri, Egon 164
Piano Concerto 78
Piano Concerto No. 3 144
Piano Sonata No. 3 in F-sharp minor 106–107

Piano Sonata, No. 4 148
Pickup, Ronald 23
Pierrot lunaire 167
"A Pilgrimage to Beethoven" 9
Pindar 192
Piper, Myfanwy 132, 135
Pirie, Peter J. 5, 126
Pitt, Percy 21
The Planets 84
Plant, Robert 188
Plato 106, 158, 159
Poe, Edgar Allan 164
The Poem of Ecstasy 104, 109, 111, 193
A Poem of Life and Love 123
Pogge, Hans 156
Porter, Andrew 2
Poulenc, Francis 154
Pountney, David 170
Powell, Robert 103
Preparatory Act 110
The Prince of the Pagodas 135
The Producers (dir. Mel Brooks, 2007) 195
Prometheus—The Poem of Fire 49, 104, 105, 113–117, **117**
Proömium 92
Proust, Marcel 56
Psycho (dir. Alfred Hitchcock, 1960) 146, **146**, 190
Purcell, Henry 5
Pushkin, Alexander 11, 14

Quartet in C-sharp minor 43, 177

Rapper, Irving 81
Radó, Aladár 156
Rasputin, Grigory 145
Ravel, Maurice 152, 194
Rée, Paul 66, 182
Reeve, Christopher 196–197, **196**
Reflections of a Nonpolitical Man 9, 178
Regardie, Israel 112–113
"Religion and Art" 67, 111
Requiem 123
Reznicek, Emil von 156
Das Rheingold 1, **2**, 80, 88
Richards, Jeremy 196
Richter, Jean Paul 8
"The Ride of the Valkyries" 60, 165, 166
Riefenstahl, Leni 89
Rienzi 172
Rimsky-Korsakoff, Nikolai 52; *The Legend of the Invisible City of Kitezh* 52
Der Ring des Nibelungen 2, 8, 18, 19, 30, 38, 54, 62, 66, 67, 68, 73, 106, 108, 154, 174, 182
Rischl, Friedrich Wilhelm 20
Röckel, August 35, 39
Rogers, Richard 88
Rohde, Erwin 25, 34
Rolland, Romain 17, 19, 76, 83, 84–85; *Jean Christophe* 17, 19

Roller, Alfred 94
Rope (dir. Alfred Hitchcock, 1948) 154
Rops, Félicien 65
Der Rosenkavalier 81
Rossini, Gioachino 8, 59; *William Tell* 8
Rubinstein, Josef 39
Rückert, Friedrich 14, 191
Russell, Ken 99, 103, 123, 193

Salomé 83
Salomé, Lou von 14, 21, 182
Sartre, Jean-Paul 187, 190, 193
Savile, Jimmy 171
Scenes from Goethe's Faust 11
Scharlitt, Bernard 99
Schauwecker, Franz 85
Scherzer, Rob 196
Schiller, Friedrich von 41, 44, 49, 50, 69, 184
Schiller, Rudolf 156
Schirach, Baldur von 89, 90
Schloezer, Boris 107
Schmitt, Florent 152
Schmitz, Oscar Adolf Hermann 4–5
Schoenberg, Arnold 14, 51, 82, 157, 159, 166–169, 172, 175, 176, 182–183, 185; *Erwartung* 166; *Five Orchestral Pieces* 168; *Five Piano Pieces* 82; *Pelleas und Melisande* 159, 167; *Pierrot lunaire* 167; String Quartet No. 2 167; *Theory of Harmony* (*Harmonielehrer*) 167, 168, 183; *Verklärte Nacht* 51
"Schön' Hedwig" 14
Die schöne Müllerin 13, 14
Schopenhauer, Arthur 5–6, 7, 8, 17, 27, 28, 37–38, 45, 52–53, **54**, 58, 67, 87, 106, 128, 159, 162, 172, 173, 196; *Parerga and Paralipomena* 159; *The World as Will and Representation* 5, 17
Schubert, Franz 13, 71, 174; "Der Lindenbaum" 174; *Die schöne Müllerin* 13, 14
Schumann, Robert 4, 8, 11, 12, 14, 15, 21, 34, 46, 157; *Dichterliebe* 12; "Die Flüchtlinge" 14; *Frauenliebe und -leben* 11; *Manfred Overture* 12; *Papillons* 15; *Scenes from Goethe's Faust* 11; "Schön' Hedwig" 14
Schwartz, Alexander 156
Schwartz, Stephen 195
Scott, Cyril 129
Scott, Sir Walter 13
Scriabin, Alexander 47–48, 104–118, **105**, 147, 148, 150, 157, 159, 193; *Mystery* 118–119; Piano Sonata No. 3 in F-sharp minor 106–107; Piano Sonata, No. 4 148; *The Poem of Ecstasy* 104, 109, 111, 193; *Preparatory Act* 110; *Prometheus—The Poem of Fire* 49, 104, 105, 113–117, **117**; Symphony No. 3, "The Divine Poem" 108–109
Scriabin, Tatyana 108
Sechs Hölderlin Fragmente 130–131
Seitz, Franz **179**

Sellers, Peter 79
Seven Sonnets of Michelangelo 130
Shakespeare, William 41, 177, 181
"Shall We Hope?" 12
Shaw, George Bernard 122, 128–129, 144, 164–165, 184
Shelley, Mary 87
Shelley, Percy Bysshe 14, 113–114, 118
Sibelius, Jean 52; *The Swan of Tuonela* 52
Siegfried 22, 34
Siegfried Idyll 15, 22, 24–25, 31, 59, 153
Simon, Heinrich 123
Sinding, Christian 91
Sketches 142
Skodnitz, Ferenc 100–101
"Sleigh-Ride" 127
Socrates 135
Soder, Alfred **86**
Sonata for Two Pianos and Percussion 144
Sonatina seconda 165, 166
A Song Before Sunrise 123
A Song of Summer 123
Song of Summer (dir. Ken Russell, 1968) 123
Songs 123
Songs and Piano Pieces 12–17, 25, 32, 191
Songs, Op. 3 12
Songs, Op. 15 143
Sophocles 157
"Sorrows and Grandeur of Richard Wagner" 64
The Sound of Music (dir. Robert Wise, 1965) 88–89, 174, 196
Spencer, David 137
Spencer, Stewart 191
Stanford, Sir Charles Villiers 4
Steiner, Max 81
Steiner, Rudolf 112, 119, 157
Sterndale Bennett, Sir William 4
Stoker, Bram 60, 61, 62; *Dracula*, 60, 61–62, 63–65
Stokowski, Leopold 1
Strauss, David 45
Strauss, Richard 47, 52, 76–92, **77**, 93, 99, 111, 140, 158, 181, 184, 195; *Eine Alpensinfonie* 85–89, 93, 97; *Also Sprach Zarathustra* 78–83, 84, 87, 89, 95, 111, 116, 140, 184, 195, 196; *Arabella* 47, 81; *Aus Italien* 76–78, 157; "Das Bächlein" 90; *Capriccio* 90; *Elektra* 83; *Die Frau ohne Schatten* 85; *Ein Heldenleben* 83–84, 89, 99; *Metamorphosen* 89–90, 92; *Der Rosenkavalier* 81; *Salomé* 83; *Tod und Verklärung* 196
Stravinsky, Igor 154
String Quartet No. 1 142
String Quartet No. 2 167
Sullivan, Sir Arthur 4, 8, 126; *The Golden Legend* 8; *The Mikado* 4
Superman (dir. Richard Donner, 1978) 196, **196**
Symphony No. 1 46

Symphony No. 2, *Resurrection* 94
Symphony No. 3 96–100
Symphony No. 3 *Eroica* 43, 89, 90
Symphony No. 3, "The Divine Poem" 108–109
Symphony No. 4 159
Symphony No. 6 *Pastoral* 7–8, 43–44, 88
Symphony No. 7 70, 100–101
Symphony No. 8 94
Symphony No. 9 *Choral* 41–42, 44, 45, 49, 184
Symphony No. 40 in G minor 4
The Swan of Tuonela 52
Syzmanowski, Karol 147–152, **148**, 154–155, 158; *Efebos* 149–150; *Król Roger* 149–152, 154–155; *Metope* 147, 148; *Mity* 147, 148

Tannhäuser 64, 67
Tarasti, Eero 2, 6–7,
Tartini, Giuseppe 185
Tchaikovsky, Pyotr 47, 71, 194
Tebelak, John-Michael 95
Ten Easy Pieces for Piano 142
Thatcher, David S. 156
Thayer, Alexander 41
Theory of Harmony (*Harmonielehrer*) 167, 168, 183
Thus Spoke Zarathustra (*Also Sprach Zarathustra*) 3, 15, 17, 20, 69, 78, 87, 92, 99, 101, 107, 109, 111, 112, 121, 123, 129, 130, 138, 155, 189, 190, 193, 194, 195
Tieck, Ludwig 64
Tippett, Michael 133–134; *A Midsummer Marriage* 133–134
The Titfield Thunderbolt (dir. Charles Crighton, 1953) 154
Tod und Verklärung 196
"Der traurige Mönch" 14
Tristan und Isolde 1, 15, 18, 28–29, 32, 34, 36, 51, 52, 64, 77, 83, 124–125, 131, 151, 152, 153, 161, 162, 163
The Triumph of Death 17, 18
Triumphlied 33, 46
The Turn of the Screw 137
Turner, Joseph Mallord William 135
Twilight of the Idols 11, 16, 21
Two Romanian Dances 145
2001: A Space Odyssey (dir. Stanley Kubrick) 79, 116, **126**, 127, 184

Untimely Meditations 29–30, 45, 59

Der Vampyr 26
Varèse, Edgard 168–170; *Arcana* 168–170
Vaughan Williams, Ralph 4, 129
Vechten, Carl Van **173**
Verdi, Giuseppe 68
Verklärte Nacht 51
Verlaine, Paul 157
Veronese, Paolo 19

A Village Romeo and Juliet (dir. Peter Weigel, 1992) 124, 126, 127
Vinci, Leonardo da 18, 19
Violin Concerto 142
Violin Sonata 129
Visconti, Luchino 25, 101, 103, 131, 134, 135, 180, **180**

Waack, Carl 9
Wagner, Adolf 64
Wagner, Cosima 15, 16, 17, 23, 24, 26, 27, 31, 32, 33, 34, 39, 40, 54, 66, 71, 93
Wagner, Richard 1, **2**, 3, 4, 5, 6, 7, 8, 9–10, 11, 12, 15, 18, 19, 20, 22–40, 41–56, 58–63, **52**, 66–74, 76, 77, 80, 81, 83, 87, 91, 93, 94, 96, 99, 104–105, 108, 109, 111, 112, 122, 124, 125, 128, 131–132, 133, 139, 142, 152, 153, 155, 156, 157, 158, 161, 162, 165, 166, 167, 172, 173, 174, 176, 177, 181, 182, 187; "The Artwork of the Future" 162; "Beethoven" 25, 42, 43, 48, 161, 174; "An End in Paris" 9; *Der fliegende Holländer* 19; *Götterdämmerung* 2, 9, 19, 38, 62, 99, 125, 172, 174; *Lohengrin* 9, 17, 19, 67, 77, 125, 142; *Die Meistersinger von Nürnberg* 15, 18, 22, 23, 32, 34, 58, 70, 73, 80, 82, 83, 162; *Opera and Drama* 23; *Parsifal* 12, 19, 44, 51–52, 54, 55–56, **57**, 60–61, 63–65, 67, 78, 82, 105, 124, 153, 163, 164, 177; "A Pilgrimage to Beethoven" 9; "Religion and Art" 67, 111; *Das Rheingold* 1, **2**, 80, 88; "The Ride of the Valkyries" 60, 165, 166; *Rienzi* 172; *Der Ring des Nibelungen* 2, 8, 18, 19, 30, 38, 54, 62, 66, 67, 68, 73, 106, 108, 154, 174, 182; "Shall We Hope?" 12; *Siegfried* 22, 34; *Siegfried Idyll* 15, 22, 24–25, 31, 59, 153; *Tannhäuser* 64, 67; *Tristan und Isolde* 1, 15, 18, 28–29, 32, 34, 36, 51, 52, 64, 77, 83, 124–125, 131, 151, 152, 153, 161, 162, 163; *Die Walküre* 70, **72**
Wagner, Siegfried 31–32
Wagner, Winifred 31
"A Walk to the Paradise Garden" 124, 127
Die Walküre 70, **72**
Walton, Sir William 196
Weber, Carl Maria von 180; *Der Freischütz* 180
Weigel, Peter 127
Weil, Cynthia 193
Weiner, Marc A. 62
Weissmann, Adolf 78
Wesendonck, Otto 55
Wheatley, Dennis 114–115
Wightman, Alistair 150
Wild, Hans **136**
Wilde, Oscar 11
Wilhelm, Kurt 87
Wilhelm II, Kaiser 32
William Tell 8
Williams, John 196

Williams, W.D. 160
Wilson, A.N. 3, 121
Wilson, Colin 112, 128
Wise, Robert 88–89
Witsen, Willem *157*
Wodehouse, P.G. 3, 121
Wolf, Hugo 14, 156–157
Wolf, Leonard 62
Wood, Charles 38
Woolf, Virginia 19
The World as Will and Representation 5, 17

Wyndham, John 174; *The Midwich Cuckoos* 174

Yeats, W.B. 135
Young Apollo 130, 135

Ziegler, Márta 142–143
Zoll, Paul 156
Zuckmayer, Carl 85
Zweig, Stefan 81, 89

www.ingramcontent.com/pod-product-compliance
Lightning Source LLC
Chambersburg PA
CBHW032051300426
44116CB00007B/690